Las Vegas

Deke Castleman
Photography by Michael Yamashita and
Kerrick James

COMPASS AMERICAN GUIDES
An Imprint of Fodor's Travel Publications, Inc.

Las Vegas

Copyright © 1997 Fodor's Travel Publications, Inc.
Maps Copyright © 1997 Fodor's Travel Publications, Inc.
Fifth Edition

LIBRARY OF CONGRESS CATALOGING-IN-PUBLICATION DATA
Castleman, Deke, 1952-
    Las Vegas/Deke Castleman; photography by Michael Yamashita—5th ed.
        p. cm. — (Compass American guides)
    Includes bibliographical references and index.
    ISBN 0-679-00015-1
    1. Las Vegas (Nev.)—Guidebooks. I. Title. II. Series: Compass American guides (Series)
F849.L35C37 1997   97-13082
917.93'1350433—dc21   CIP

Contributing Editors: Julia Dillon, Barry Parr, Peter Zimmerman
Managing Editor: Kit Duane
Designers: Christopher Burt, David Hurst, Julia Dillon
Map Design: schematic maps by Alex Alford/Colourfield, Swannanoa, NC;
              other maps by Eureka Cartography, Berkeley, CA

Compass American Guides, 5332 College Ave., Suite 201, Oakland, CA 94618
Production House: Twin Age, Ltd., Hong Kong   Printed in China
10 9 8 7 6 5 4 3 2 1

Fifth Edition
First published in 1991 by Compass American Guides

Cover: Fremont Street under its canopy of lightbulbs.
Previous pages: The Las Vegas Strip. (both photos by Kerrick James)

PHOTOGRAPHY CREDITS
Unless otherwise stated below, all photography is by **Michael Yamashita**. The picture on page 208 is by **Michael Freeman**. Photo on pages 210-11 is by **Richard Lee Kaylin**. The photos on the front cover, and pages 2-3, 27, 31 (bottom), 45 (bottom), 48-49, 53, 66, 74 (top), 75, 95, 112 (top), 114-15, 122-23, 131-32, 134, 153, 191, 215, 229, and 242 (top and bottom) are by **Kerrick James**.

Archival photos on pages 21, 29, 35, 64, 80, 83, 87, 91, 173, and 204 courtesy of the James Dickinson Library Special Collections, UNLV. Photos on pages 52, 61, 73, 92, and 107 courtesy of the Las Vegas News Bureau. Thanks to Lesley Bonnet for meticulous indexing.

This book is dedicated to Benny Siegel, Davie Berman, Gus Greenbaum, Moe Dalitz, and all the Jewish gamblers who helped build Las Vegas in the 1940s and '50s.

ACKNOWLEDGMENTS

FIRST AND FOREMOST, I'D LIKE TO THANK Anthony Curtis. I knew a few things about Las Vegas and gambling before I met and started working with him; since then, my knowledge of and perspective on this stimulating and bewildering city have grown exponentially higher and deeper. Helping Anthony to write and edit the *Las Vegas Advisor* has been a once-in-a-lifetime opportunity.

I'm also indebted to all the other experts, pros, colleagues, and friends, who've directly or indirectly guided me along the way: Max Rubin, Jeff Compton, Stanford Wong, Peter Griffin, Bethany Coffey, Bobby Rihel, Bob Sehlinger, Merla McCormick, Howard Schwartz, Erik Joseph, Blair Rodman, Bob Dancer, Phyllis Snyder, Russ Hamilton, John Grochowski, David Moore, Carolyn Graham, Adam Platt, Phil Pikelny, Julie Osborne, Stu Alpern, Bob Fuss, Ken Crain, Ken Evans, Dennis McBride, Kathy War, Sue Jarvis, Rachel Greiner, Susan Berman, Len Cipkins, David P. Tarino, Bruce Brown, Hal Rothman, and Mike Krein.

A tip of the hat to the Compass crew—to Kit Duane, who traveled all the way to Alaska just to chat with me; to Chris Burt, who owes me a phone call; and to Julia Dillon, whose decision to become an editor rather than a showgirl is Las Vegas's loss and my gain.

As always, thanks go to the photographers: Mike "It's a Hard Life" Yamashita, who way-back-when set a standard for Las Vegas travel photography, and Kerrick James, who more than lived up to it.

CONTENTS

INTRODUCTION

HOW DO YOU TURN A BROAD VALLEY IN ONE OF THE HOTTEST, driest, and most unlivable terrains on the continent into a cool, moist oasis that's accessible, hospitable, and profitable?

That was the question facing a handful of gamblers who stood, in different eras and various places, and surveyed a small, green valley surrounded by a godforsaken patch of desert and foresaw, somehow, a booming metropolis. Their collective answer, over the years, was first to reach the oasis with transcontinental railroad track and establish a service stop. Later, to erect a monster dam on a nearby mighty river to provide unlimited power and water. Next, to build dozens of skyscraping pleasure palaces, with opulent rooms, bountiful food, free drinks, round-the-clock entertainment, and legal casino gambling, and to illuminate it with a spotlight so bright that it could be seen from everywhere in the world. Then, to lay down long highways and wide landing strips to handle the hordes drawn to its rare diversions.

Railroad magnates, water czars, and never-say-die boosters kept the settlement on life support in the early surly days. The young Bureau of Reclamation dammed the river and blessed the town. Casino pioneers from southern California set up tables and shop, into which racketeers from all over the country moved with money, management, and muscle. Sign engineers dressed the town in neon and theatrical producers undressed the showgirls. Government regulators got rid of the mob and paved the way for today's corporate control.

A mere 90 years of history have created a city that ranks as the biggest boomtown this country has even seen (and the first 40 years don't really even count). The place now attracts more than 30 million visitors annually, who have one thing in mind: letting loose. Doing it, they leave behind nearly 15 billion dollars. Gambling, sex, free booze, cheap meals, show-going, cruising, lounging—the pastimes are legendary and legion, the choices enough to stagger even the most fast-lane hedonist or been-there done-that cynic.

The average out-of-towner, however, stays only three nights. How is that person to understand this place, to put the experience into perspective, to get even a glimpse of the big picture?

A good guide.

DESERT ROOTS
FROM THE PRECAMBRIAN TO THE PAIUTE

HALF A BILLION YEARS AGO (OR SO), NEVADA RESTED UNDERWATER. At least twice during the mysterious 340-million-year Paleozoic era, violent and titanic episodes of uplift raised the ocean floor, drained the sea, and left towering mesas and alluvial plains. Over the next 160 million years, cataclysmic extinctions, megashears, volcanism, and climatic crises, punctuated by long stoic periods of erosion, continually altered Nevada, several times obliterating its life and land-scape. Seventeen million years ago, today's familiar basins and ranges were created by the colossal jostle of tectonic forces. More than 250 separate ranges have been named in Nevada. Ninety percent of them are oriented northeast-southwest, and on a map they look like a herd of earthworms marching toward Mexico. The southwest-trending cavalcade of ranges, however, jams up at a southeast-trending dead end, at the northern edge of Las Vegas Valley. To geologists, this phe-nomenon is known, apparently without irony, as the Las Vegas Zone of Deforma-tion.

Beginning nearly two million years ago, four great ice ages advanced into and retreated from history. Nevada's Basin and Range Physiographic Province, which had been shuffled by earthquakes, tilted by crustal adjustments, and whittled by erosion, was now alternately drowned and drained and ground down by glaciers. By the end of the last ice age, roughly 12,000 years ago, Las Vegas Valley had finally taken the shape it retains today: relatively long and flat, cutting a diagonal 18 by 26 miles across Clark County near the southern tip of Nevada. Except for the Las Vegas Wash, which drains into Lake Mead to the east, the valley is an enclosed sys-tem, cradled by eight or so mountain ranges. The Spring Mountains to the west are peaked by Mt. Charleston, highest point in the area at 11,918 feet, and valleyed by Red Rock Canyon, petrified red sand dunes standing sentinel in front of limestone cliffs. To the north are the Spotted, Pintwater, Desert, Sheep, and Las Vegas ranges, all pointing southward at the valley like accusing fingers. South of the Vegas Valley are the McCullough Mountains. And to the east are Frenchman's and Sunrise peaks, which form a lumpy backdrop to downtown Las Vegas.

Alluvial fans of stone, gravel, and cobble spread down from these mountains onto the valley floor, beneath which lies a concrete-like lake-bottom hardpan

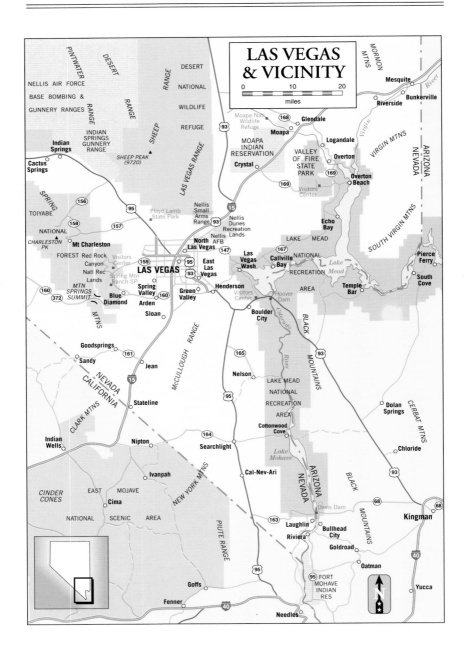

LAS VEGAS & VICINITY

known as caliche—the scourge of construction companies, swimming-pool in-stallers, and gardeners. Underneath the valley is a major system of artesian aquifers. Groundwater has been tapped at levels as shallow as 40 feet and as deep as 1,000 feet. This underground lake is recharged by rain running off the ranges. Before the drastic depletion of the reservoir by the 1930s, artesian pressure forced this water up into the valley, creating what came to be known as "Big Springs," an oasis of tall grasses, mesquite, and cottonwoods, with several short creeks flowing through. The first Spanish explorers who stumbled upon this life-saving lea named it *Las Vegas,* "The Meadows."

■ PALEO-INDIANS

People inhabited Las Vegas Valley as early as 11,000 B.C., at the cold and wet tail end of the Wisconsin Ice Age. These Paleo-Indians lived in shoreline caves and hunted the large Pleistocene mammals—wooly mammoth, bison, mastodon, and caribou—which would disappear from the area within a few thousand years.

Petroglyphs drawn in sandstone by prehistoric Indians about A.D. 500 can be seen at Valley of the Fire State Park.

Several expeditions to Tule Springs, an archaeological and paleontological site in northwestern Las Vegas Valley (now Floyd Lamb State Park), have uncovered prehistoric hearths, fluted arrow and spear points, scrapers, and scarred and charred animal bones.

Human habitation in the valley seems to have varied with the climate. Between 7000 and 3000 B.C., it's believed the area was too arid for settlement. After 2500

LAS VEGAS CLIMATE

Las Vegas is the most flamboyant oasis in the world. It sprawls along the eastern edge of the Mojave Desert, the northern edge of the Sonoran Desert, and the southern edge of the Great Basin Desert. Thus situated on a spot where three deserts merge, it's one of the driest and hottest urban areas in the United States.

Though Las Vegas is now a large city (more than a million people in the metro area), it is still located in the center of some of the most unneighborly terrain imaginable. For at least half the year, the most important miracle of technology that makes the Mojave bearable, let alone livable, is air-conditioning. Don't leave home without it. True, it's a dry heat, but that's also the punchline of a popular local joke about what the devil says to a newcomer who's looking with trepidation at the flames. Even lounging poolside in the summer can be problematic—unless you take off your flesh and sit in your bones.

Wintertime temperatures are mild. Las Vegas's mean annual temperature is a comfortable 66 degrees F, making this resort city a definite year-round destination, with no extended off-season. The quietest weeks in Las Vegas are the first three in December, the last three in January, and the last three in June, in that order.

Las Vegas receives little precipitation and has one of the lowest relative humidities of all metropolitan areas in the country. It's a desert out there, dry as Death Valley sand. However, cyclonic storms in summer are accompanied by cloudbursts that can drop an inch of rain in an hour, rendering the danger of flash flooding real and worrisome. Winds that carry in the summer storm fronts have been known to shift all the dust from the west side of town to the east, and vice versa. But any time of year, the winds can be so strong that a giant 30-foot flag on West Tropicana Avenue stands proudly at a perfect right angle to the pole, you have to hang on tight to the people mover at Caesars Palace so as not to get blown off, and miniature golfing at Scandia Fun Center is hysterical.

B.C., however, the climate changed again to nearly what it is today: cool and damp enough, relatively speaking, to support a newly arrived and evolving Indian society. Known as Archaic or Desert people, these Indians evolved a forager culture, whose members adapted to the use of such high-quality but limited resources as the desert tortoise, bighorn sheep, screwbean mesquite, canyon grape, and cholla fruit. The settlers lived in small groups, scattered from the valleys to the peaks; their numbers grew or shrank according to abundance or scarcity. They built rock shelters, circular stone campsites, and roasting pits, and used the *atlatl* (a primitive but efficient arrow-throwing stick), mortars and pestles, flaked knives, and hammerstones. These Archaic Indians could be considered the behavioral ancestors of the later Paiute people.

■ THE ANASAZI

Whether the Archaic people evolved or were absorbed or evicted is unclear, but around 300 B.C., a new people, the Basketmakers, appeared in the Las Vegas area. Also hunter-foragers, the early Basketmakers were more sophisticated than their predecessors in only one respect. They lived in pit houses: three- to four-foot-deep excavations, with mud floors and walls, brush roofs supported by strong poles, and a central fireplace. By about A.D. 500, the Modified Basketmaker period had arrived, perhaps introduced by Pueblo pioneers migrating to their western frontier. Within two centuries, these Anasazi (Navajo for "Enemy Ancestors") were settled permanently in the fertile river valleys of what is now southeastern Nevada. They cultivated maize, beans, squash, and cotton, wove intricate baskets, fashioned handsome black-and-white pottery, constructed large adobe pit houses, and hunted with bows and arrows.

As their agricultural techniques became more refined and their population increased, the Anasazi entered the peak of their civilization: the Classic Pueblo or Lost City Period (A.D. 850-1000). Living in a sizable urban metropolis known as Pueblo Grande (near today's Overton, 70 miles northeast of Las Vegas), the Anasazi were intricately linked to trading centers throughout the Southwest. These centers in turn were integrated into the politics and economy of Meso-America. For example, Anasazi were present at productive turquoise mines in the

Amargosa Range in what is now eastern California, and near Searchlight, Nevada, 60 miles south of Las Vegas Valley. Anasazi traders traveled to southern and Baja California to barter salt and soft cotton for sea shells and pottery. Trade for woven textiles, parrot feathers, and copper might have been carried on with other Anasazi outposts, such as those at the Grand Canyon and Canyon de Chelly (Arizona), Chaco Canyon (New Mexico), Grand Gulch (southeastern Utah), and possibly Mesa Verde (Colorado). Travelers carried back not only products but new agricultural, technological, religious, and social ideas. Las Vegas Valley and Big Springs made an excellent staging area for excursions west and south. During the population explosion of the Pueblo Grande period, the fertile and watered valley supported an outpost of Lost City Anasazi—the only known prehistoric architecture at Las Vegas.

By the year 1000, Pueblo Grande had become Nevada's first ghost town. The Anasazi packed up and headed out, dispersing throughout the Southwest. They probably returned to the center of their civilization, becoming the ancestors of today's Pueblo Indians.

Why would such a sophisticated and successful civilization abandon a major city? Theories include stress from overpopulation, natural disasters, and encroachment by the Southern Paiute. One eminent archaeologist insists that the swampy river bottomland was a prime breeding ground for malarial mosquitos; after too many deaths, the people simply moved. A recent, provocative explanation holds that the disintegration of this extensive Southwestern society coincides with the collapse of Mexico's vast Toltec Empire. This would have severely disturbed the "global" economic foundation, such as the lucrative turquoise trade between the Pueblo Grande and Chaco Canyon Anasazi. Deprived of primary links, and suffering urban and ecological stresses, the Anasazi confederacy unraveled.

■ LAS VEGAS BAND OF THE SOUTHERN PAIUTE

For the next 700 years, the territory in southern Nevada abandoned by the Anasazi was occupied by the nomadic Paiute. These Indians called themselves *Tudinu*, "Desert People," and spoke a Shoshonean variety of the Uto-Aztecan language, which indicates that they probably arrived from the northeast. The Paiute had some contact with the Anasazi—the newcomers learned a few horticultural skills, and the property owners fortified their dwellings with walls and gates. But the Paiute seem to have been peaceful; there's no evidence of confrontations between the immigrants and emigrants.

The homeland of the Las Vegas band centered on the Big Springs of Las Vegas Valley, from which a creek flowed through lush grassland and thickets of mesquite. But the edges of their territory stretched from the Colorado River (at 450 feet elevation) to the upper slopes of Mt. Charleston (over 11,000 feet). Thus the hunter-forager Tudinu were blessed with ecological variety. The Paiutes established base camps of semi-permanent wickiup shelters (conical brush and pole structures), cultivated squash and corn at the springs and creeks, and traveled seasonally to

The rugged Mojave Desert on the road to Laughlin.

hunt and harvest wild foods. Their diet consisted of whatever game was available: snakes, lizards, rodents, rabbits, desert tortoises, birds, deer, and bighorn sheep. In addition, they collected pine nuts, screw beans, agave, cholla fruit, grasses, berries, and Indian spinach to supplement their crops, stockpiling supplies for the short but lean winters. They ground seeds, pine nuts, and white mesquite beans into flour, which they formed into little cakes and baked over hot stones.

By nature, the Paiutes were independent and free-spirited. They roamed on foot in small, flexible family units. They had no chiefs, only heads of families. No formal structures linked the families, though annual spring and fall game drives and pine-nut harvests united villages for several days. At these times, the members of the Las Vegas band might number a hundred. Courtships were conducted and marriage ceremonies peformed at these festivals. The Paiute practiced a form of polygamy, in which a man took his wife's unmarried or widowed sister. The tradition is generally attributed to the need for survival . . . But who knows what other reasons there might've been?

SOME PAIUTE VOCABULARY

ankle:	*towinwichachang*
basket:	*yoo-ahts*
crazy:	*numpicant*
cactus:	*o'si*
desert:	*yuavi*
rattlesnake:	*toxo'avi*
raven:	*tap'puts*
sin:	*sangwav*
spirit:	*moxoam*
star:	*tava*
sun:	*tava*
sun in sky:	*tava puts*
virgin:	*cach-kumai it mama'its*
white man:	*marukats*

Las Vegas Paiutes in dance dress on July 4, 1889.

■ EUROPEAN CONTACT

The Paiutes' first contact with Europeans occurred in 1776. Around the same time that General Howe's 32,000 British troops were forcing General Washington's 19,000 irregulars into retreat from Brooklyn, New York, two Franciscan friars were establishing both ends of the Old Spanish Trail. On exploring and surveying trips into the northern hinterlands of Spain's colony of Mexico, Father Silvestre Escalante blazed the eastern end of the trail from Santa Fe, New Mexico, to the southwestern corner of Utah. From the west end, Father Francisco Garces traveled toward him through California and Arizona. Garces encountered Southern Nevada Paiute, who by his own account treated him hospitably. But it was another 50 years before further Paiute-European interaction.

Before Mexico gained its independence from Spain in 1822, the Spanish government had enforced strict laws against trespassing. After independence, the first wave of Eastern fur trappers and mountain men penetrated the previously unknown Southwest. In 1826–27, famed trader and explorer Jedediah Smith became the first American explorer to travel through what is now southern and central

Nevada, and he too made contact with Paiutes. Three years later, Antonio Armijo, a Mexican trader, set out from Santa Fe on the Old Spanish Trail. An experienced scout in Armijo's party, Rafael Rivera, discovered a shortcut along the route by way of Las Vegas's Big Springs, thereby making him the first non-Indian to set foot on the land that would become Las Vegas—and at the same time putting the handwriting on the wall for the Southern Nevada Paiute.

After 1830, warring Utes from the northeast used the Las Vegas cutoff of the Old Spanish Trail blazed by Armijo to raid the peaceful Paiute, kidnapping children and women for the slave markets of New Mexico and California. In addition, Spanish and American trading caravans began camping at Las Vegas's Big Springs and creeks: their grazing stock destroyed the precious grasses; their guns killed the limited game. At first the Indians carefully avoided the interlopers, but as natural resources were depleted, some resorted to sneak thievery, stealing horses and cattle to butcher for food. That was when traders and travelers began shooting at the Paiute themselves.

In his excellent and moving *The Las Vegas Paiutes—A Short History,* John Allen writes, "Whites invaded the area, pushed the original occupants to the side, disregarded their rights and interests, neglected their needs, and even ignored their existence. Whites preserved only a fragment of Paiute history, often distorted by insensitivity and a lack of understanding." Within 25 years of initial contact, the Las Vegas Paiute band's spirit was broken, self-reliance was shattered, and dependence had become a new way of life.

In 1844, surveyor and cartographer John C. Frémont noted the Las Vegas Paiutes' sunflower and pumpkin patches by the Big Springs, and watched them fish lizards out of holes. Frémont considered them "humanity in its lowest form and most elementary state." He couldn't understand how they could live with no possessions, no houses, and hardly any clothes. Frémont also noted that they stole everything and ate anything. "Diggers" became their derogatory name.

In 1848, the Las Vegas Paiute initially ran "like wild deer" from trader and traveler Orville Pratt, but he eventually managed to buy beans and corn from them. By 1851, the portion of the Old Spanish Trail from central Utah to Los Angeles had been so tamed and improved by Mormon-guided wagon trains that it became known as the Mormon Trail. This was all part of Mormon president Brigham Young's master plan to establish the great State of Deseret, with boundaries he hoped would eventually enclose the Southwest from the Rockies to the Pacific.

DESERT SURVIVAL TIPS

Southern Nevada's Mojave Desert is not to be taken lightly. From Las Vegas, even nearby day-trips and short hikes in the desert can, unless proper precautions are taken, turn into dangerous situations. Before heading into the Mojave, a few simple preparations might spell the difference between a routine and a life-threatening experience.

First, make certain that your trusty steed has had the best care. Fuel and fluids should be full. Carry at least a gallon of water for the car (some antifreeze is also good to have), along with spare belts and hoses, spare tire and jack, tool kit, flashlight and flares, and shovel. Baling wire and super-glue often come in handy. Don't forget a rag or two. And a well-stocked first-aid kit is essential.

If the car gets hot or overheats, stop until it cools off. Never open the radiator if the engine is steaming. After a while, squeeze the top radiator hose to check the pressure; if it's loose, it's safe to remove the radiator cap. Never pour water into a hot radiator. You could crack your block. If you start to smell rubber, your tires are overheating, which makes them highly susceptible to blowouts. Stop, in the shade if possible, to let them cool.

If you're exploring the backcountry, it's not a bad idea to inform a friend, park ranger, or even highway patrol office where you're going and when you'll be back. (Don't forget to check in upon returning.) Carry double the amount of water you ordinarily would on such an outing, plus an extra five-gallon containerful. If your vehicle gets stuck in the sand, don't panic! Just take it easy and seriously. Let some air out of the tires for traction. If you can't get moving again, stay with the vehicle until after the sun has gone down, then try to dig it out.

Wear dark glasses. Cover up to avoid burning. Drink regularly, but not to excess. Minimize conversation. If outside help is required, send the strongest member of the party to the main road, but only after the sun is down. Most desert deaths occur from dehydration by walking too long in the sun.

Your life expectancy—in extreme heat, resting, in the shade—will be: three days with no water, four days with one gallon of water, five days with two-and-a-half gallons, one week with five gallons. Try not to verify these statistics.

Toward this end, he sent missionaries to colonize Las Vegas Valley, and to convert and civilize the Paiute.

The colony was plagued by problems from the start. A vast desert surrounded the Meadows; the summer heat and winter wind were unbearable; millable timber had to be hauled a great distance; and Las Vegas's isolation sapped what little morale existed among the new settlers. Still, with proverbial Mormon diligence, the missionaries dug irrigation ditches, cultivated farms, befriended a few Paiute, and erected a fort. The mission might have succeeded, but the colonists' discovery of lead nearby prompted Brigham Young to dispatch a party of miners to Las Vegas. Already-meager rations were soon stretched to the limit by the miners' demands. As was often the case in early Nevada settlements, deep-seated tensions between miners and Mormons erupted into bitter disputes—even at Las Vegas, where the miners were Mormons. Their disagreements, compounded by the myriad deprivations and challenges, finally caused the mission, with Young's permission, to disband in 1858—leaving the second ghost town in Nevada.

Less than a year later, discovery of the Comstock Lode up north at Virginia City triggered the first backwash of miners and migrants from the gold fields of California. The Mormon lead mine, known as Potosi, was re-prospected and further developed, attracting hundreds of fortune seekers. Enterprising growers started gardens in Las Vegas Valley and sold produce to the miners. Prospectors fanned out from Potosi and discovered gold on the west bank of the Colorado River at Eldorado Canyon. Among these gold miners was Octavius Decatur (O. D.) Gass who, in 1865, settled near the Big Springs in Las Vegas Valley, building a ranch house and shop inside the decaying Mormon stockade. The Gass family irrigated 640 acres and raised produce, grain, and cattle. By the mid-1870s, Gass had bought up or taken most of the homesteaded land in the valley and held the rights to most of the water.

Still, only a handful of whites lived in Las Vegas at that time. Violence by and against the Paiute occasionally flared. In 1860, three white travelers were killed by Indians, later thought to be encroaching Utes; a punitive expedition led by Major James H. Carleton resulted in the deaths of five Paiute. The Gass family experienced many scares—soldiers were stationed around their ranch from 1867 to 1869. By the 1870s, the Southeast Nevada Indian Agency had been established, and President Ulysses S. Grant had granted nearly 4,000 acres near the Moapa and Virgin rivers, not far from Las Vegas, for a Southern Paiute reservation. Two years later he reduced this to 1,000 acres. But it proved difficult to confine even a small portion of Nevada's early settlers: as nomads, the Paiute were unaccustomed to living in a large, restrictive society governed by a central authority.

Even so, the Las Vegas Paiute fared slightly better than some of their neighbors. Many found work at the mines or on the ranches. The men harvested grain, hauled wood, cut hay, and ran cattle. The women cooked, cleaned, and laundered. The Gass ranch was taken over by Archibald Stewart in 1881. After he was murdered in 1884, his wife Helen Stewart continued to operate the prosperous spread. An enlightened and capable pioneer, Mrs. Stewart also championed the Paiute cause.

■ TWENTIETH-CENTURY PAIUTE

Throughout the last years of the nineteenth century, Las Vegas remained isolated enough for the Paiute to retain a modicum of their tradition, but the arrival of the San Pedro, Los Angeles and Salt Lake Railroad in 1905 ushered in decades of hardship for the Indians. As the white population exploded, the Paiute population quickly declined, primarily through disease and despair. In 1912, Helen Stewart deeded 10 acres of what remained of her Las Vegas Ranch as a colony for the Paiute, in the desolate desert north of town. The U.S. government paid her $500 for the land, but upon her insistence, the Indian Affairs bureaucrats drew up the title in the name of the Paiute band. The colony was surveyed in 1919, but it remained impoverished. Tourists in the 1920s created a market for Paiute baskets— but at wildly exploitive prices. Family heirlooms, or new creations that took a year to make, sold for only five or ten dollars. Paiute children were sent away to boarding school, first at Fort Mojave, Arizona, and then to the Stewart Indian School in Carson City, Nevada.

Improvements were planned for the Las Vegas Indian Colony in the early 1930s, but never implemented. By the late 1940s, the colony had been completely enclosed by the growing city. In the late 1950s, local officials tried to sell the land out from under the Indians, but Helen Stewart's prescient gift of title to the Paiute prevented it. The colony finally received water and sewer services in 1962.

In recent years, the Las Vegas Paiute, like most of the tribes in Nevada, have depended on the sale of cigarettes and crafts for most of its revenues. The tribe buys cigarettes at wholesale prices that include federal taxes, but instead of passing on the high local taxes on tobacco products, the Indians charge a smaller tribal tax, which is reinvested in the tribal organization. (The cheap smokes, along with pottery, jewelry, paintings, and baskets, are for sale at the Las Vegas Paiute Commercial Plaza, 1225 North Main Street, between Washington and Owens.) But the tribe is now developing sources of revenue other than cigarette sales.

A master-planned community, **Snow Mountain,** on 3,700 acres north of the city along US 95, is in its initial phases. The smoke shop is in place, as is **Nu-Wav Kaiv,** the first of four golf courses. Snow Mountain will also encompass residential units, schools, parks, a tribal museum, ceremonial grounds, a cemetery, a factory outlet mall, and a hotel-casino.

(above) The only tree endemic to the Mojave is the Joshua; palms have been either planted or imported. (opposite) Despite its desert setting, Las Vegas boasts one of the world's greatest concentrations of golf courses—more than two dozen in the metropolitan area. (photo by Kerrick James)

UNNATURAL HISTORY
BOOM TOWN, DOOM TOWN, ZOOM TOWN

RARELY HAVE UNLIKELIER CIRCUMSTANCES led to the growth and greatness of a city. From its spontaneous generation as a railroad boomtown and its subsequent struggle for survival in a remote and parched land to its salvation by Hoover Dam, World War II, and legalized casino gambling, Las Vegas seemed always possessed of some evolving equation for success.

And rarely has an unlikelier cast of characters shared such an unflappable faith in such a remote place. From Helen Stewart's patient anticipation of the railroad to Charles "Pop" Squires's tireless campaigning for the dam, from Bugsy Siegel's grand vision of the glamour of vice to Howard Hughes's master plan for the ultimate Southwestern megalopolis, countless believers have invested their imaginations, fortunes, and even their lives in favor of Las Vegas's unique destiny. Today, the sum of all the events, people, and progress has made Las Vegas the undisputed themed-hotel, gambling, entertainment, convention, neon, and cash capital of the known universe.

■ HELEN STEWART

Las Vegas Valley's first "boom" was the shooting of Archibald Stewart. At age 18, Stewart made his way from Scotland to the California gold fields, and by the time he turned 30, he owned a sizable freighting company. Taciturn and miserly, Stewart relocated to Pioche, Nevada, 156 miles north of Las Vegas, during its fleeting heyday as a silver-mining center. There, Stewart's ore hauling expanded into lumber milling, which eventually financed cattle ranching. Even after *borrasca* (final decline of the mines) in 1874, Stewart remained prosperous enough, at 45, to own a house in Pioche and a large ranch just north. A few years later, O. D. Gass, perennially out of cash, secured a $5,000 loan from Stewart, using his 800-acre Las Vegas Ranch and 400 head of cattle as collateral. It's an insight into Stewart's character, and Gass's desperation, that they agreed on a 30 percent interest rate, due in one year. When the year was up, Gass couldn't pay, so they rescheduled the loan for another nine months. When the grace period expired, Gass again couldn't pay, and Stewart foreclosed. The 800 acres and 400 cattle became his.

The only other ranch in the Big Springs area, just two miles north, was owned by Conrad Kiel, a close friend of Gass. Thus, when Stewart took possession of the Gass ranch and moved next door, the blood already ran bad between Kiel and him. In July 1884, Stewart and a ranch hand named Schuyler Henry got into a fight. Carrie Miller Townley, in the *Nevada Historical Society Quarterly* (Winter 1973), says that Schuyler Henry "badgered" Mrs. Helen Stewart and "spread rumors about her conduct during her husband's absences." Nothing more sensational than that has been written concerning this incident. But, given the Las Vegas tradition, literary and otherwise, of extravagance, one might imagine the following scenario. Stewart, 48, had admonished Henry, 33, about the manner in which the latter looked at the former's wife Helen, 29. Yet despite Stewart's warnings, one hot evening while Stewart was away on business, the frustrated ranch hand propositioned Helen, who might or might not have held him off with a gun. Whichever way it went, Henry later bragged that his advances had been encouraged and accepted. When Stewart heard of the incident, he went after Henry at the Kiel Ranch to defend his wife's honor. Since Stewart emerged on the dead side, divine justice might absolve Henry of idle bragging. Human justice certainly did: the grand jury ruled that Henry acted in self-defense.

Helen Stewart (left) sharing the fine points of her Paiute basket collections with a friend.

(above) Downtown before and after the giant awning encompassed four blocks of casinos. (bottom photo by Kerrick James) Vegas Vic (opposite) takes a drag.

SIGN LANGUAGE

In 1898, British chemist Sir William Ramsey took some air, liquefied it, boiled it, and fractionally distilled it into its separate components. In the process, he discovered monoatomic, or inert, gases: helium, argon, krypton, xenon. And neon. Of the various atmospheric gases, it was discovered that neon best permitted the ready passage of an electric current. In 1910, a French inventor, Georges Claude, attached an electrode to a glass tube full of neon gas—*et voilà!* A jewel-like, bright-red shimmering glow materialized. An exciting new form of illumination had been invented.

Neon (and the different colors its neighbor gases produced) immediately captivated Parisian sign-makers. In 1923, a visiting automobile dealer from Los Angeles ordered a custom neon sign that spelled out "Packard" in bright blue letters with orange edging. Installed on Wilshire Boulevard, it caused a nationwide sensation. Six years later, a forward-looking lighting businessman from Ogden, Utah, Thomas Young, emplaced a neon sign in the window of the Oasis Club on Fremont Street, thus establishing the inseparability of neon, Las Vegas, and the Young Electric Sign Company.

The 1940s and 1950s became the Golden Age of Neon in America. Thanks to its decorative and advertising values, neon invaded Las Vegas with a vengeance. Its artistry benefited enormously by the famous local tradition of one-upmanship, inspired by the fierce competition between the major hotel-casinos. The old Boulder Club downtown featured YESCO's first major neon creation in Las Vegas: a free-standing 40-foot sign with vertical letters, topping a bright marquee. Almost immediately, the Frontier Club and Sal Sagev Hotel followed suit. The Pioneer Club then introduced the elaborate Vegas Vic, which has become the city's most enduring image. But the Golden Nugget took the early prize with a 100-foot-high, blindingly bright sign that remained downtown's centerpiece for nearly 50 years.

When Bugsy Siegel opened his fabulous Flamingo in 1946, he abandoned the frontier motif in favor of two 80-foot neon highball glasses fizzing with pink champagne, which framed the nondescript boxes of the lowrise motor inn. This set the standard for the Las Vegas Strip, and helped introduce a new commercial vernacular along suburban "strips" across the country. The western-style false-front architecture of Fremont Street yielded to the modern false fronts of the desert highway: high, wide, and bright signs making visible dark, recessed, and one-story buildings. Remove the signs, and the hotels would disappear. The quintessential example was embodied by the Stardust, which opened in 1958. The huge colorless casino building supported the largest sign, at the time, in the world: more than 200 feet long and

(opposite) Signs of another time at YESCO's graveyard.

nearly 30 feet high, with a gleaming Earth turning in a welter of planets, comets, and flaring meteors.

For the next 30 years, competition along the Strip was as intense as the neon itself, effected by a number of commercial artists, set designers, and animators attracted by Las Vegas's *laissez-faire* sign policies. The Frontier installed the tallest sign in the world in 1966, at 184 feet. Then the Sahara built one 36 feet taller. Today, the Las Vegas Hilton sign is supposedly the tallest in the world at 262 feet.

Neon does not burn out. Undisturbed, a sign can last 30 years or more. Wind and rain, birds, short circuits, and vandalism, however, keep large sign-company spotter

(continues)

and repair crews busy year round. But neon's popularity across the rest of the country has diminished since the 1960s. In Las Vegas, the new electronic billboards, or message marquees, have supplanted static neon with increased brightness, versatility, and animated effects; Caesars' 32,000-bulb readerboard was installed in 1984 for a cool million, and now most of the big joints have message marquees. Also in the mid-1980s, the famous Golden Nugget sign downtown was replaced by an elegant marble-and-brass façade. The designers of the new megaresorts seem to consider neon the "old Las Vegas," and employ little if any neon around the exterior. Likewise, avant-garde artists, who've rediscovered the gas, seem to be trying to separate the art form from the gaudy glow of Las Vegas.

Nevertheless, the Strip remains the undisputed brightest stretch of road in the world. Maybe neon could be neon without Las Vegas, but Las Vegas could never be Las Vegas without neon.

Helen Stewart, 10 years married with four kids, and three months pregnant with the fifth, buried her husband and ran the ranch. She took time off only to give birth to a son, Archibald. Her parents moved to Las Vegas, and she hired a Scot, James Megariggle, to tutor her brood. Helen and her father speculated in real estate along the predicted right-of-way of the rumored Salt Lake–Los Angeles railroad. She established a comfortable campground for travelers and miners, with water, good grub, and shade. She befriended the Paiutes and had a collection of their finest baskets. Finally, in 1902, at 47, she'd amassed 1,800 acres to sell to William Clark's San Pedro, Los Angeles and Salt Lake Railroad for $55,000. Helen Stewart then married her longtime foreman, Frank Stewart (no relation to Archibald), and reigned as the first lady of Las Vegas till her death in 1926.

That she married a second Stewart, 20 years after the death of the first, retained water rights to her family cemetery, deeded 10 acres of land to the few remaining Las Vegas Paiute, and was buried next to her original husband could confirm that she did indeed point that gun at Schuyler Henry.

■ THE COMPANY TOWN

It took 35 years and a total of six different railroad companies to complete the track that connected Salt Lake City to Los Angeles, built along the old Mormon Trail. Thanks to its strategic location and plentiful water, in 1902 Las Vegas was designated by William Clark's San Pedro, Los Angeles and Salt Lake Railroad a division point for crew changes, a service stop for through trains, and an eventual site for repair shops.

In 1903, Helen Stewart hired J. T. McWilliams to survey her property for sale to the railroad. McWilliams discovered and immediately claimed 80 untitled acres just west of the big ranch. He platted a town site and began selling lots to a steadfast group of true Las Vegas "sooners." A year later, in fall 1904, the railroad track was laid across Las Vegas Valley. In January 1905, the track working its way from Los Angeles met up with the track coming from Salt Lake City, and the golden spike was driven into a tie near Jean, Nevada, 23 miles south of the Las Vegas townsite—in a brief, stiff, one-cheer ceremony. Thus the American Southwest, the

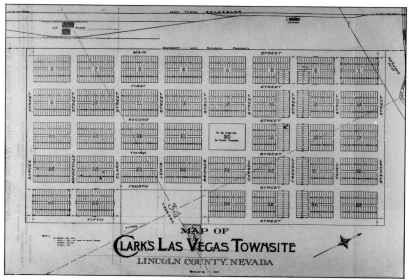

Map of the San Pedro, Los Angeles and Salt Lake Railroad's town site, oriented to the tracks. Each of the 40 blocks was 300 by 400 feet, with 32 lots for sale.

last vast frontier of the continental United States, was finally conquered by the great iron-horse "civilizer," the transcontinental railroad.

By the time the first train had traveled the length of the track, McWilliams's Las Vegas town site, better known as Ragtown, boasted 1,500 residents, brickyards,

---

LAS VEGAS GLOSSARY

action—sum total of all wagers made

bankroll—amount of money an individual or a casino has to gamble with

basic strategy—computer-generated strategy for blackjack based on the best odds for player's hand against dealer's up card

black chip—$100 casino chip

book—among many meanings, the room where sports and race wagers are made

boxcars—rolling a 12 in craps

boxman—craps dealer who supervises the game

cage—main casino cashier

card counting—the ability to track cards already played at blackjack and to base play on the variable odds of the remaining deck or decks

carpet joint—casino catering to high rollers

checks—casino chips

comp—freebie; free rooms, meals, drinks, shows, golf, airfare; also see *RFB*

compulsive gambler—a gambler who will gamble on anything and everything, anywhere, any time, has no control over the urge to gamble, and will not stop until all the money, credit, assets, and hope are gone

crossroader—casino cheat

degenerate gambler—a gambler who will play until his or her bankroll is gone—but can stop then

drop—total cash traded for chips at the gaming tables

folding money—greenbacks

george—a gambler who tokes or places bets for the dealer

green chip—a $25 casino chip

grind—low roller

grind joint—casino that caters to low rollers; also known as *sawdust joint*

hard count—counting the change from slot machines

(previous pages) The volcano explodes regularly outside the Mirage, if the wind cooperates.

weekly newspapers, a bank, an ice plant, a tent hotel, and mercantiles. But its existence was brief. In April 1905, with the start of regular through service, the San Pedro, Los Angeles and Salt Lake Railroad organized the subsidiary Las Vegas Land and Water Company, platted its own town site, bulldozed all the desert

---

high roller—any gambler able and willing to spend $5,000 or more in a weekend at Las Vegas; there are an estimated 35,000 bona fide high rollers (almost all of them men) in the world

hold—house profit from all the wagers; what the casino wins

house advantage—mathematical winning edge that the casino gives itself by manipulating the rules of the games to ensure profitability; also known as the *percentage, P.C., vigorish, vig*

juice—power; influence; knowing the right people

junket—group of high rollers, usually flown in on a plane chartered by the casino, and accorded full RFB

ladderman—baccarat supervisor

Las Vegas total—typical Las Vegas experience of room, food, gambling, show, and commercial sex

low roller—typical tourist making $1 and $2 bets; aka *grinds, suckers, tinhorns*

Marryin' Sam—wedding-chapel minister

percentage (or *P.C.*)—house advantage, measured in percentage points

pit—casino employee area behind the table games

plunger—gambler who chases his losses; also known as *screamer* or *pigeon*

points—percentage of ownership in a casino

The Pencil—having the juice to write comps

RFB—means room, food, and beverage: a full comp

sawdust joint—casino catering to grinds

shnorrer—Yiddish for compulsive borrower

soft count—counting the folding money

stickman—crap dealer who handles the dice

stiff—winning gambler who doesn't toke the dealer

toke—gratuity; tip

turkey—gambler who's unpleasant to the dealer

vigorish (or *vig*)—house advantage; comes from the 5-percent commission on all wagers charged by the original bank-craps operators, which brought in money with "vigor." Gamblers added a syllable of jargon to get "vigorish."

scrub from the 40-block area, and scheduled the auctioning of lots for May 15. Each block, a regulation 300 by 400 feet, consisted of 32 lots, each 25 by 140 feet, fronted by an 80-foot-wide street and split by a 20-foot-wide alley. Block 20 was reserved as a public square; the sale of liquor was assigned to blocks 16 and 17. The railroad advertised heavily in newspapers on both coasts, and transported speculators and investors to Las Vegas from Los Angeles ($16) and Salt Lake City ($20)—fares to be deducted from the deposit on a lot.

The auction was conducted at the corner of what would soon be Fremont and Main, site of today's Plaza Hotel. In the heat of the moment, choice corner lots listed at $150 to $750 sold for up to $1,750; well-located inside lots sold for double their listed value. The literal heat became so oppressive that the auction concluded at 3 P.M., after 175 lots had earned the railroad $80,000. Ragtown locals grumbled about the railroad tactics of encouraging out-of-town speculators to bid up the prices. In his classic history, *Las Vegas—As it Began, As it Grew,* author Stan Paher quotes an observer who commented, "The auction was a nice clever scheme—the simplest way of giving everybody a fair shake (down)." In response to complaints, the following day's auction was canceled and the remaining lots were sold for fixed prices within the listed range. In all, more than 700 lots were purchased, netting the company $265,000, an almost 500-percent profit over what they paid Helen Stewart for the whole property three years earlier. And Las Vegas was on the map—one of the last railroad boomtowns on one of the last major lines across the United States.

The initial excitement lasted all of a month and a half. The early euphoria gave way to the dismal demands of domesticating a desert. Service policies of the railroad as implemented by Walter Bracken, the imperious manager of the Las Vegas Land and Water Company, were conservative and bureaucratic. Flash floods tore up track and interrupted service. And the usual fires, conflicts, and growing pains of a new company town dampened local optimism. Even so, frame houses replaced tent shelters and soon Las Vegas boasted hotels, saloons, restaurants, warehouses, mercantiles, a school, and a two-story bank. Las Vegas Land and Water lived up to its pledge to grade and oil city streets, construct curbs, and lay water mains, pipes, and hydrants—but only within the boundaries of the railroad's own town site. Although a dozen eight-foot-deep wells had been drilled around old Ragtown west of the tracks, lack of access to company water sealed its fate: most of it burned to the ground in September 1905. It was then that the after-hours revelry was transplanted to Block 16.

Bounded by First, Second, Ogden, and Stewart streets, this infamous block served as Wild West Central, surrounded by the buttoned-down company town. The Double O, Red Onion, Arcade, and others served 10-cent shots, featured faro, roulette, and poker, and sported cribs out back for customers with the urge. Bibulous burros begged for beer from bearded bartenders, while bow-tied ivory ticklers pounded out ragtime tunes on honky-tonk uprights. The Arizona Club became the Queen of Block 16, with its expensive glass front and $20,000 mahogany bar; a few years later a second story was added for the convenience of its ladies of the night and their gentlemen.

Other than Block 16, Las Vegas was run strictly for the convenience of the Company. Distribution of water to the town site, for example, was considered of secondary importance to railroad operations, and requests for water outside the railroad's official town were consistently refused. Similarly, other railroad policies, handed down from Los Angeles and Salt Lake City, discouraged land speculation and subdivision of the surrounding desert. Still, Las Vegas slowly expanded in area and population in its first ten years. Charles "Pop" Squires, publisher of the *Las Vegas Age* newspaper and indefatigable town booster, together with Walter Bracken founded the Vegas Artesian Water Syndicate, which "mined" water around the valley. The first deep well was drilled in July 1907 to a depth of 301 feet; by 1911, 100 artesian wells had been tapped. William Clark's new Las Vegas and Tonopah Railroad reached the mining boomtown of Beatty (115 miles northwest of Las Vegas) in late 1906, furthering Las Vegas's ambitions as a crossroads. To further its ambitions as an administrative seat, in 1909 supporters of slicing a new county off vast Lincoln County emerged victorious from a hotly contested election, and immediately pushed a bill through the state assembly. Clark County, named after the railroad magnate, became official in July 1909. When Las Vegas incorporated two years later, the town counted a population of 1,500 residents.

■ Slow but Steady

The locomotive repair shops opened for business in 1911, creating 175 new jobs and stimulating the development of additional residential subdivisions outside the original town site. The population doubled, growing to 3,000 between 1911 and 1913—two years marked by growing prosperity and progress. A milestone was reached in 1915, when round-the-clock electricity was finally supplied to residents.

But the 10-year crescendo of the first boom had climaxed, and Las Vegas went into a slow but steady slide. In 1917, the Las Vegas and Tonopah Railroad suspended operations; hundreds of workers were laid off and left. By 1920, the population had dropped to 2,300. An elderly William Clark sold his interest in the renamed Salt Lake and Los Angeles Railroad to Union Pacific in 1921. If the old management in Los Angeles had run Las Vegas like a company store, the new management in New York City barely knew Las Vegas existed. Its employees, immediately disgruntled, joined a nationwide strike of 400,000 railroad workers in 1922. Locally, some violence erupted between strikers and strikebreakers. When the strike was settled, Union Pacific punitively closed the Las Vegas repair shops, eliminating hundreds more jobs and residents.

Though many urban improvements had been implemented in the town's first 15 years, in the early 1920s Las Vegas was at its lowest and most isolated moment. Long-distance telephone service was still nonexistent. Telegraph messages had to be sent along the railroad's private wires and public communications always took a back seat to company transmissions. Even so, decisions and instructions from corporate headquarters, often concerning urgent situations faced by Las Vegas Land and Water such as large leaks in water mains, frequently took weeks to be made and dispatched. To travel to the state's capital at Carson City or its urban center at Reno, one had to ride the train via Los Angeles and San Francisco, or Salt Lake City. A primitive auto road followed the old Las Vegas and Tonopah rail bed, but it was better suited for a desert safari than a joyride.

The key to Las Vegas's resurrection? It flowed just 25 miles away. By 1924, the Bureau of Reclamation had narrowed potential sites for a dam on the Colorado River to two locations east of Las Vegas: Black and Boulder canyons. Anticipation alone began to fuel a noticeable spurt in growth. During the latter half of the 1920s, laws were passed, interstate details negotiated, and money allocated for "Boulder" Dam—named for the Boulder Canyon Project Act, even though the site chosen turned out to be Black Canyon. (The dam was eventually named to honor Herbert Hoover, Secretary of Commerce at the time.) And so Las Vegas began to revitalize in earnest. By the end of the decade, the town had long-distance phone service, a federal highway from Salt Lake City to Los Angeles, regularly scheduled airmail and air-passenger services, over 5,000 residents, and one of the world's most colossal engineering projects about to get underway just over the next rise.

■ THE BEST TOWN BY A DAM SITE

In the early 1930s, as the nation's banks were falling like dominoes, the dam was rising block by block. Meanwhile, state lawmakers in Carson City passed a typically Nevada version—front-running, nonconformist, and permissive—of the New Deal. Wide-open gambling was legalized in 1931, and the residency requirement to be eligible for a divorce was reduced to a scandalous six weeks. Combined with unimpeded bootlegging, legal prostitution, championship boxing matches, and no-wait marriages, Nevada became the only state in the union to spurn the moral backlash that followed the Roaring Twenties. Vice-starved visitors and hopeful dam workers flooded southern Nevada, thereby transforming Las Vegas from a dusty railroad stopover into a bright spot on the gloomy horizon of the Great Depression—first step on the yellow brick road to becoming the ultimate Oz.

The dam, when completed, was 720 feet tall, 660 feet thick at the base, and nearly a quarter mile long at the crest—the sum total of more than three million cubic yards of concrete. At its peak, the dam employed 5,000 workers, with a monthly payroll of half a million dollars. More than 50 miles of new railroad track connected Las Vegas to the damsite; Las Vegas's railhead warehouses and freight yards were expanded to handle the innumerable tons of building supplies transferred from the mainline. Almost overnight, Las Vegas's permanent population increased by 50 percent to 7,500, with transients and visitors further swelling the ranks. The local infrastructure underwent continuous improvement. Hotel and housing construction boomed. Congress appropriated millions of New Deal dollars for a new post office, federal building, and general relief. Business prospered. Urbanization accelerated.

(top) Looking up at the Las Vegas Hilton; (bottom) Looking down at Hoover Dam.

(top) The Big Six migrated from the carnival to the casino after Nevada legalized gambling in 1931. (bottom) World's largest gold nugget on display at the Golden Nugget. (bottom photo by Kerrick James)

"Dateline Las Vegas" became a staple of newsreel and newsprint, and tens of thousands of tourists arrived, many by automobile, to enjoy the spectacle of dam construction and experience the Wild West boomtown nearby. Saloons, gambling dens, and hotels enjoyed a steady flow of visitors. Downtown, the venerable Northern Club, the neon-lit Silver Club, and the low-roller Tango Club—all located along Fremont Street between First and Third—received the town's first gambling licenses. To escape the restrictive policies of the conservative officials of incorporated Las Vegas, Tony Cornero, a gambler from southern California, built the posh $31,000 Meadows Club just beyond the city limits on the road to Boulder City. Las Vegas's first "luxury" hotel, the Apache, opened downtown. Five thousand Shriners from southern California inaugurated Las Vegas, in 1935, as a convention town.

Also from southern California on the heels of Tony Cornero, Las Vegas received its first wave of outside illegal gambling operators. Fletcher Brown, elected mayor of Los Angeles in 1938, immediately began to fulfill his campaign promises

EXACTLY AS IT REMAINS TODAY

*L*as Vegas is seat of Clark County and distributing center for a very large but thinly populated mining and ranching country. It is also developing into one of the chief travel and recreation centers of the Southwest. In part this new role is a matter of accident, the result of a key position in an area with widely varying natural attractions plus the man-made wonder, Boulder Dam. A sound and far-sighted public policy, however, has taken advantage of national interest in the dam to make the city and the area around it attractive enough to bring visitors back repeatedly. Public buildings and houses are under construction all over town. The rows of catalpas and poplars planted during the early days are being protected and lengthened. Relatively little empahsis is placed on the gambling clubs and divorce facilities—though they are attractions to many visitors—and much effort is being made to build up cultural attractions. No cheap and easily parodied slogans have been adopted to publicize the city, no attempt has been made to introduce pseudo-romantic architectural themes, or to give artificial glamour and gaiety. Las Vegas is itself—natural and therefore very appealing to people with a wide variety of interests.

—Nevada—A Guide to the Silver State, 1940

by enforcing the city's previously ignored vice laws and closing its brothels and casinos. (It has also been suggested that Benjamin "Bugsy" Siegel, dispatched in the late 1930s by East Coast Syndicate bosses to "organize" the California underworld, provided additional incentive for the freelance gamblers to flee Los Angeles.) Guy McAfee for one, commander of the L.A. vice squad and an operator of gambling parlors, quickly moved to Las Vegas and purchased the Pair-o-Dice Club, three miles south of city limits on the Los Angeles Highway. Sam Boyd, a bingo mogul in L.A. and Honolulu, started with a roulette concession at the Eldorado Club. Tudor Scherer and partners opened the Pioneer Club. With their experience and expertise, these L.A. operators immediately gained respectability within the budding legal casino business, and helped improve not only its management, but its image as well.

An expected exodus of dam builders lightened Las Vegas's load in the late 1930s. Even so, the water situation deteriorated. The Las Vegas Land and Water Company remained reluctant to extend itself to service the edges of town. An upgraded delivery system—new mains, better sewers, and increased pressure—was desperately needed and slow in coming. To make matters worse, what had seemed like an inexhaustible supply of artesian water was running dry. And this was *before* the population boom of the war years. (This particular Las Vegas water crisis wasn't alleviated till 1948, when Lake Mead water was tapped and piped to town for the first time.)

The imminence of World War II fueled the renewal of federal spending in southern Nevada. In 1940, with the population at 8,500, city officials teamed up with the Civil Aeronautics Agency and the Army Air Corps to develop a million-acre training facility for pilots and gunners. Over the next five years, the Las Vegas Aerial Gunnery School trained tens of thousands of military personnel; during that time the facility expanded to three million acres.

In 1942, a monster metal-processing plant, Basic Magnesium, Inc., was constructed halfway between Las Vegas and Boulder City—large enough to eventually process over 100 million tons of magnesium, vital to the war effort for flares, bomb housings, and airplane components. At its peak in 1944, BMI employed 10,000 factory workers, many of whom lived nearby in housing projects at the new town site of Henderson.

Now, thanks to Hoover Dam, the gunnery school, and Basic Magnesium, the Las Vegas area clearly had the power to accommodate large-scale industry, the influence to attract massive infusions of federal capital, and the magic to lure hundreds of thousands of vacationers with a year's savings in their pockets.

All it needed was a good hotel.

■ THE FOUNDING OF THE STRIP

Guy McAfee, the Los Angeles cop and gambler who owned the Pair-o-Dice Club (later renamed Club 91), drove the few miles between his roadhouse and downtown Las Vegas so often that he began referring to it as "the Strip," after the beloved Sunset Strip in his hometown. Though there's no record of any meeting, it seems likely that McAfee would've had a chat with another southern Californian, Thomas Hull. A number of other civic leaders certainly did, convincing Hull, who owned a chain of El Rancho motor inns, to open a franchise in Las Vegas. The grand opening for El Rancho Vegas was held on April 3, 1941. The 65-room bungalow-style motor inn, on the corner of Highway 91 (now the Strip) and San Francisco Avenue (now Sahara), came complete with casino, steakhouse, showroom, shops, swimming pool, palm trees, and lawns. Just beyond the city line, Hull's El Rancho Vegas attracted the traffic coming in from southern California, as well as locals escaping the claustrophobia of Fremont Street. Business boomed from the beginning, and Hull quickly expanded the hotel to 125 rooms. Management difficulties compelled Hull to sell the hotel, which changed hands a few times before it was destroyed by fire in 1960. The site, across the Strip from the Sahara Hotel, remains a vacant lot to this day. The El Rancho Vegas experience, however, initiated a number of trends, all of which remain in place well over 50 years later: a hurricane of subsequent construction and competition, the desirability of building outside the city limits along Highway 91, and a revolving door of managers and owners.

Eugene Moehring, a resident historian in Las Vegas, has written that the El Rancho, in one bold and brilliant stroke, revolutionized Las Vegas development. By building in an unincorporated area of Clark County, Hull avoided the higher

(previous pages) A sunset view of the Strip includes the MGM Grand, Excalibur, and New York–New York. (photo by Kerrick James)

city taxes on property and gambling revenues, as well as the control of powerful city casino operators. Less stringent building codes reduced the cost of construction and the wide-open desert permitted ease of accessibility and plentiful parking for motorists, unavailable in congested downtown. In fact, this "motel" triggered the transition from a town organized around and dependent on the railroad to one better served by cars and trucks. Hull's bold move coincided with an overall suburbanization of America in the 1940s, and specifically with Los Angeles's spreading lowrise sprawl. Indeed, by the grand opening of the El Rancho Vegas in April 1941, Las Vegas was a mere seven hours from Los Angeles by car.

Only a month after the El Rancho opened, two southern California real estate dealers financed construction of the El Cortez Hotel on Fremont and Sixth Street; it took nine months and nearly $160,000 to complete downtown's first resort hotel. By then, R. E. Griffith, a movie-theater magnate, was already building the Strip's second casino-motel, the Last Frontier, a mile south of the El Rancho on property purchased from Guy McAfee. Griffith's architect nephew, William Moore, designed the motel such that, as with its predecessor on the Strip, the casino, showroom, restaurants, and lounges were contained in the main building, while the 107-room motel stretched behind it. But the Last Frontier inaugurated a tradition of one-upmanship that has not changed over the course of nearly six decades and half as many major hotels. In *Playtown U.S.A.,* Best and Hillyer described it thus: "Its lobby was a rustic, big-beamed conglomeration of mounted buffalo heads, of huge sandstone fireplaces, of Pony Express lanterns hanging from old wagon wheels. Its sluicing parlor was a replica of an old forty-niner saloon, with Texas cattle horns mounted on panel walls, a mahogany bar with bullet holes in it, and leather bar stools in the shape of saddles. Its casino was plushly pioneerish with a ceiling of pony hide and ornately papered walls hung with paintings of nudes done in gold-rush gaudiness. A dip of the flag for the self-described Early West in Modern Splendor."

Eugene Moehring picks up the theme. "In addition, the hotel provided guests with horseback and stagecoach rides and pack trips. To reinforce the frontier ambience, Moore later added the Last Frontier Village, a small town site filled with 900 tons of Robert 'Doby Doc' Caudill's Western artifacts. The collection was extensive, consisting not only of wagons, antique firearms, bar stools, barbers' chairs, and the like, but also big items, including a Chinese joss house, full-size mining trains, and actual jails from Nevada's smaller mining camps." Without a doubt, the Last Frontier was Las Vegas's first tourist-attraction themed hotel.

Downtown, meanwhile, felt the competition from the new Strip acutely. Guy McAfee expanded his operations by purchasing the Frontier Club, then acquiring enough property along Fremont between Second and Third to open the Golden Nugget, at that time the largest casino in Las Vegas. The Golden Nugget set a standard for extravagance that obliged the reconditioning of many Fremont Street sawdust joints. Tony Cornero, whose Meadows Club on Boulder Highway had failed 10 years earlier, returned from L.A. to open the Rex Club. Wilbur Clark, a gambler from San Diego, set up shop with the Monte Carlo Club. Benny Binion, a well-known Texas gambler, arrived, invested in the Las Vegas Club, then bought the Western Club. By the end of the war, Fremont Street was already one of the most glittering stretches of downtown in the entire country.

The war years had fueled the growth of Las Vegas to an unprecedented degree. By the time the Last Frontier had settled into a profitable routine, classes of 4,000 aerial gunners were arriving and departing Las Vegas every six weeks. Basic Magnesium was shipping five million pounds of magnesium ingots to airplane and

Downtown Las Vegas was a neon canyon by the early 1950s; the Golden Nugget boasted the largest casino and sign. Thanks to the Fremont Street Experience light show (opposite), Fremont Street glitters more than ever. (photo by Kerrick James)

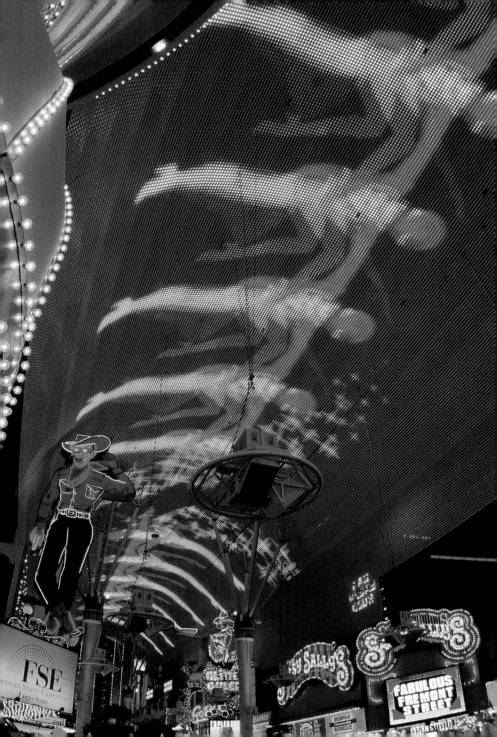

ordnance factories in Los Angeles every day. Subdivisions were mushrooming to accommodate an exploding Las Vegas population, which doubled between 1940 and 1943, surpassing 35,000. The War Department in 1942 pressured Las Vegas to finally shut down Block 16. And casino owners emerged as the civilian power elite, the early 1940s' Las Vegas Establishment.

■ GANGSTER ANGST

Las Vegas and Benjamin Siegel, better known (though only behind his back) as "Bugsy," were born in the same year, 1905—Las Vegas in southern Nevada and Benny in Brooklyn, New York. In 1923, before he was 20 years old, Siegel had already committed every heinous crime in the book: assault, burglary, bookmaking, bootlegging, extortion, hijacking, murder, mayhem, narcotics, numbers, rape, white slavery. In the late 1930s, his boyhood buddy and mob partner Meyer Lansky sent Benny to Los Angeles to consolidate the disparate elements of the California mob, where he quickly eliminated the competition (including Guy McAfee, who beat a hasty retreat to Las Vegas), bankrolled offshore gambling ships (including the *Rex,* run by Tony Cornero), established a smuggling ring for Mexican narcotics, and grabbed control of the bookmakers' national wire. At the same time he hobnobbed with the nabobs of Hollywood, befriending movie stars such as Cary Grant and Clark Gable, seducing starlets and countesses, and initiating his love affair from hell with Virginia Hill, ultimate "Mistress of the Mob." As Carl Sifakis writes in *Mafia Encyclopedia,* "Just because Siegel was a bit of a psychopath doesn't mean he wasn't a charmer."

In the early 1940s, Bugsy muscled in on the Las Vegas racebook wires, and soon he had his grubby paws in several counting rooms of the old-time Las Vegas gambling halls. But with his new Hollywood sensibilities, he envisioned a resort hotel straight out of Xanadu (or maybe Miami)—the highest-class casino for the highest-class clientele. Over the next several years, Siegel managed to raise a million dollars for his Flamingo Hotel (named after the "lucky" birds that lived at a pond inside the Hialeah Racetrack in Florida, in which he had a part interest). Construction began in 1946.

Bugsy hired the Del Webb Company of Phoenix to put up the Flamingo. But building materials were scarce after the war, and Siegel's extravagance was limitless,

SEEING VEGAS IN THE FUTURE

*I*t didn't start with Vegas. Rather, the concept that culminated in "Vegas" got drawn toward a place where some very strange and not dissimilar stuff has been happening for a very long time. The stuff that is "Vegas" is coming up out of the ground out here. I'm very serious. In other words, Las Vegas as it is presently constituted may not be a gross ecological travesty; Vegas may be what the place wants. This is, as they say in Vegas, the "juice," the "action," that this environment itself likes. It's been drawing strangeness to itself for thousands of millenia.

This is how strong I think that draw really is: 400 years before Vegas happened, Spanish conquistadors kept trying to find it. They were sure that somewhere to the north and west, across the great deserts, would be a city of gold and light, incredible riches, eternal youth, exquisite pleasures—an intoxicating city of riches and dreams. Expedition after expedition failed to find it, yet they were sure. They just felt it out there. Many of them staked everything on the certainty that a city very like Las Vegas already existed. And they would never know how right they were—right that there was such a city, right that it lay in the great western desert. They were just wrong about when.

The place itself was generating Vegas-vibe, and they felt it and were called by it, but the place would need 400 more years to generate an actual Las Vegas.

—Michael Ventura, "Las Vegas: The Odds on Anything," *Letters at 3 A.M.: Reports on Endarkenment,* 1993

matched only by his greed; he dispatched Virginia Hill to Switzerland on occasion to deposit cash skimmed from construction costs. Overruns, reluctantly financed by his old pal Lansky, finally reached a healthy (or unhealthy, as it turned out) five million bucks, and the project began to exact a heavy toll on Siegel's already questionable nerves, not to mention his silent partners' notorious impatience. Legend has it that at a meeting of the bosses in Havana on Christmas Day 1946, a vote was taken. If the Flamingo was a success, Siegel would be reprieved, and given a chance to pay back the huge loan. If it failed . . . *muerta.* (However, in *Little Man,* the biography of Meyer Lansky, author Robert Macy reports that it might have been Siegel's Las Vegas partners who ordered him hit. Apparently, they feared that the fate of legal gambling in Nevada was too fragile to survive Bugsy's notoriety.)

The hotel opened the next day. Movie stars attended, headliners performed, but

Palms and flamingos entered the Nevada neon scene by way of Los Angeles and Miami.

the half-finished hotel, miles out of town, on a rainy and cold day after Christmas, flopped. Worse, the casino suffered heavy losses, which the bosses suspected to be further skim. In a prophetic and now famous statement, Bugsy reassured a nervous Del Webb, "We only kill each other." In early January 1947, the Flamingo closed. It reopened in March, and started showing a profit in May, but Siegel's fate had been sealed. In Virginia Hill's Beverly Hills mansion in June, Benny Siegel was hit. Before his body was cold, Phoenix boss gambler Gus Greenbaum had already taken over the Flamingo.

So began 40 years of the Italian-Jewish crime-syndicate's presence in Las Vegas. And 10 years of the biggest hotel-building boom that the country had ever seen. It also triggered an increasing uneasiness among state officials over the condition of the casino industry; they quickly moved to assume regulatory responsibilities from the counties, which had overseen the casinos since gambling was legalized in 1931. In 1945, they authorized the Nevada Tax Commission to collect one percent of gross gambling revenues over $3,000, and to have a hand in approving licenses for operators. After two years of tax collecting and a better idea of revenues, the state increased the tax to two percent. And in 1949, with Las Vegas gaining a reputation as a haven for the underworld and its money, Tax Commission agents were deputized and given broad powers to investigate license applicants.

■ TWO BOMBS DROP ON SOUTHERN NEVADA

To complicate matters, for the first time Las Vegas began to feel a new type of heat. Federal.

In November 1950, the Committee to Investigate Organized Crime, led by Tennessee Senator Estes Kefauver, came to town. Questioned were Wilbur Clark and Moe Dalitz of the Desert Inn, Bugsy's advance man Moe Sedway, Nevada Tax Commissioner William Moore (of the Last Frontier), Lieutenant Governor Clifford Jones, and others. In two days of hearings, many existing Las Vegas trends were revealed and clarified: there was indeed a connection between the casino industry and the national crime syndicate; gangsters from California, New York, Cleveland, and Chicago were running the big hotels and gambling dens, having been licensed by county and state officials who shrugged off their convictions for gambling offenses in other states; millions in mob money was already invested and millions more was redistributed without the nuisance of accounting paperwork; and the out-of-state operators were quickly gaining a measure of respectability as bona fide Nevada businessmen.

The Kefauver Commission revealed beyond any shadow of a doubt that Las Vegas had completed its transition from a railroad company town to a gambling company town. The biggest gamblers were in charge. On the twentieth anniversary of legalized gambling in 1951, the questionable histories of the people waist deep in gambling revenues became public. After Kefauver departed for Los Angeles, the spotlight turned to the Tax Commission, the state's licensing board. Best and Hillyer write that, "The tax commissioners were businessmen of unassailable reputation chosen from the fields of real estate, mining, ranching, and other un-sullied-by-gambling endeavors—in other words, the least likely to know about muscle men. Their traffic with underworld characters had been, up to the Bugsy Siegel affair, negligible, and newspapermen who attended license-application meetings thereafter reported that commission members would frequently ask such unsophisticated questions as 'Who is this Frank Costello?' and 'What does the witness mean when he refers to snake eyes?' These ingenuous gentlemen were suddenly called upon to control an almost uncontrollable situation."

The Kefauver hearings triggered two additional unexpected (though typical) events. First, it created a media hysteria that flooded the rackets divisions of police departments around the country with authorization and funding to wipe out the illegal gambling operations within their jurisdictions. This, of course, engendered the mass migration to Las Vegas of expert casino owners, managers, and workers, all sticking a thumb into the perfectly legal, largely profitable, and barely policed pie.

Black money from the top dons of the Syndicate and their fronts and pawns poured in from the underworld power centers of New York, Chicago, and Havana. Illegal casino operators, with their bankrolls, dealers, enforcers, and tricks, made a beeline for the promised land from the big-time games of Boston, Miami, New Orleans, St. Louis, Cleveland, Dallas, Phoenix, and Los Angeles. Hustlers, scam artists, small-time hoods, prostitutes, thieves, degenerate and compulsive gamblers, boomtowners, tradesmen, and tourists flooded the place. But just as men considered criminals throughout the country turned into legitimate business-men in Nevada, the respectable tourists seemed to turn into naughty boys and girls.

But who could resist the impropriety? Certainly not the legions of gamblers, dreamers of jackpots, hoping beyond hope to be struck by the lightning bolt of sudden and eternal fortune. Besides, this was true glamour: rubbing elbows and shooting craps with mobsters, movie stars, and millionaires. The publicity was priceless, even if it was of an infamous sort. The Chamber of Commerce, of course, did its bit to focus on the "good" aspects of the town, with its "Howdy Pardner," "Fun in the Sun," and "Come As You Are" ad campaigns. And the Desert Sea (later Las Vegas) News Bureau was established to keep the national media supplied with uncritical and non-sensational local PR.

The second bomb to hit Las Vegas was, in fact, The Bomb. Two months after Kefauver blew through town, the Atomic Energy Commission conducted its first above-ground nuclear test explosion in the vast uninhabited reaches of the old gunnery range, which now encompassed the Nellis Air Force Base and the Nuclear Test Site. For the next 10 years, nearly a bomb a month was detonated above ground a mere 70 miles northwest of Las Vegas. For most blasts, the AEC erected realistic "Doom Town" sets to measure destruction, and thousands of soldiers were posted within a tight radius to be purposefully exposed to the tests. Hundreds of reporters and photographers who covered the tests began to be referred to as "Men of Extinction." Moe Dalitz and Wilbur Clark planned the opening of the Desert Inn to coincide with a detonation; the former garnered more coverage than the latter. Locals worried which way the wind blew and seemed to contract a strange "atom fever"—marketing everything from atomburgers to cheesecake frames of a mushroom-cloud bathing-suit-clad Miss Atomic Blast. But mostly, Las Vegans reveled in the AEC and military payrolls, massive attention from the media, notoriety approaching cosmic dimensions, and the neon-thermonuclear aspects of the whole extravaganza.

■ "I Just Met a Man Who Isn't Building a Hotel"—Joe E. Lewis

In 1948, the Thunderbird Hotel was built, and in 1950 the Desert Inn. Two years later, the Sahara and the Sands opened. Then the Showboat, afloat out on Boulder Highway. Within three years, the Riviera, Dunes, Royal Nevada, Moulin Rouge, New Frontier, Hacienda, Fremont, and Mint held grand openings. By 1958, the $7-million Stardust and $10-million Tropicana had joined the ranks. Since conventional sources were stingy with the capital necessary to build casinos and resorts, mobsters from all over the country financed construction, and installed their own front men, managers, and workers. Lansky and his New York gang controlled the Flamingo and had an interest in the Thunderbird, Sands, and others. Cleveland's Moe Dalitz controlled the Desert Inn, with Wilbur Clark out front. Chicago's Sam Giancanna and Tony Accardo were connected to the Riviera and Stardust casinos. New England's Raymond Patriarcha was suspected of being behind the Dunes. When don Frank Costello was shot in an attempted assassination in New York, a slip of paper found by detectives in his pocket contained the exact number of the Tropicana's first-month profits; the connection was quickly traced to Phil Kastel, of the New Orleans mob. Clearly, Las Vegas had been declared "open territory" by the Mafia, meaning that any family with the inclination could operate there, without fear of territorial reprisals.

The Las Vegas mushrooming around the casinos was becoming the ultimate American suburb. Highway 91, the new Las Vegas Strip, with its restaurants, bars, motels, and service stations, all highlighted by neon, emerged as the prototype for main drags across the country. Row-house subdivisions occupied by casino workers' families surrounded the Strip with an aura of normalcy. Operators, dealers, even hoods traveled a new road toward respectability, while tender-footed tourists, starry-eyed girls, and boomtowners headed for moral compromise. Las Vegas became a microcosm of the innocence and optimism (though without, perhaps, the thin veneer of Victorian propriety) of America in the 1950s.

However, the foundation of the place was shaky as ever. By 1955 the town was spectacularly overbuilt, and an epidemic of hotel-casino failures, mergers, buyouts, buy-backs, shuffling owners, and musical-chair managers kept the two state investigators for the Tax Commission fairly busy. That year the state finally created the Gaming Control Board, separate from the Tax Commission, specifically for licensing and policing duties. In one of its first actions, the new board suspended the gambling license of the Thunderbird Hotel, after discovering that Jake Lansky, Meyer's brother, held a hidden interest. Even so, by 1959, when the legislature tightened its grip on the gambling industry with the formation of the policy-making State Gaming Commission, the 10 major Strip hotels were veritable fiscal monoliths. Hundreds of constantly changing names and faces held points in the operations. In addition, the regulators faced a mosaic of corporations: some owned the casinos and others ran the casinos, some owned and others operated the hotels, some held the real estate and others held the holding companies. To add to the complexities, the state found itself trying to walk a tightrope between regulating casino operations and lubricating them, since gambling taxes provided a major share of its own revenues.

So this was the situation in Las Vegas as the '60s rolled around. The big casino bosses had been entrenched for 15 years. The local heat (the sheriff and county commissioners) conscientiously protected the action and got its cut. The state heat

Vegas Vic waiting for Vegas Vickie on Fremont Street in the mid-1950s.

(young regulatory apparatus) was lukewarm at best, safeguarding its own cut and holding its own against only the most notorious "undesirables." The federal heat was just beginning to refuel in Washington, D.C., as the new Attorney General, Robert F. Kennedy, planned to pick up where Estes Kefauver left off. But it was the national media that put Las Vegas into the pressure cooker. Crime reporters, investigative journalists, magazine staff writers, scholarly essayists, and pulp novelists all descended on this Wild West set of a tough town that refused, as late as the 1960s, to be tamed. Their collective characterization of Las Vegas has come to be called the Diatribe. Books such as *The Great Las Vegas Fraud, Las Vegas—City of Sin, Las Vegas—Playtown U.S.A.,* and *Las Vegas—City Without Clocks* combined a wide-eyed view of the glittery surface with a peek at its slimy underbelly. Diatribe journalism culminated with *Green Felt Jungle,* a savage indictment of the corrupt, immoral, mob-controlled, whore-ridden, crime-infested den of iniquity that was Las Vegas. Though highly sensational, this book was lively and authoritative, and it became a veritable desk reference for many exposé writers to come.

■ STALEMATE

Regardless of the titillating power plays among the casino owners, politicians, tax collectors, law enforcers, and whistle-blowers, everybody else was partying. Las Vegas sucked up gamblers, tourists, migrators, movie stars, soldiers, prostitutes, petty crooks, musicians, preachers, and artists like a vacuum cleaner. Between 1955 and 1960, the city's population mushroomed from 45,000 to 65,000, with another 20,000 people living in Henderson and Boulder City. A dozen major hotels on the Strip, and several downtown, accounted for nearly 10,000 rooms, along with all the pools, shops, restaurants, and chuckwagon buffets. A score of showrooms and lounges featured topless floor shows, Hollywood's and television's biggest stars, and up-and-coming acts. In the casinos in 1963, 11 million visitors lost a record $375 million, up from $50 million in 1953. Juice flowed as freely as champagne: a lowly pit boss could comp rooms, food, tickets, and hookers. The Rat Pack—Frank Sinatra, Milton Berle, Sammy Davis, Jr., Joey Bishop, Don Rickles, Henny Youngman, Jerry Lewis—appeared everywhere nightly, all earning $25,000 a week, and during the day filmed *Oceans 11,* a prototype celluloid

"Great Las Vegas Heist." Thirty-thousand weddings and 10,000 divorces were performed yearly. A convention center and meeting facility opened in 1959, providing potential visitors with a reason other than gambling to come to Las Vegas. Atom bombs went off like clockwork up the road.

No new hotels were built between 1958 (Stardust) and 1966 (Aladdin). This allowed the Gaming Commission to consolidate and pontificate, and the Control Board to investigate and repudiate. They tightened licensing procedures and took stricter account of revenue reporting. Tax collections spiraled. State investigators even circulated the infamous "black book" of absolute undesirables, whose very presence could cost a casino its gaming license. Journalists continued asking nosy questions and publishing unflattering answers. Just as Las Vegas had a somewhat naughty image in the public consciousness, the image of the casino industry throughout conventional financial institutions remained anathema. Publicly traded corporations were ineligible for licensing since each stockholder in a casino had to be approved individually and personally. On the other hand, the industry's high profitability continued to attract non-mainstream capital—the Teamster Union's Central States Pension Fund, for example, with its ties to the Chicago-Midwest syndicate. Teamster money, which had been dribbling into Las Vegas since the mid-1950s, arrived in a big way in 1963, financing major expansions of the Desert Inn, Dunes, and Stardust, and the opening of the $25 million Caesars Palace.

By then, Las Vegas found itself the main battleground in the intensifying federal war on organized crime. Robert Kennedy embarked on a personal crusade to rid Las Vegas of the underworld that he strongly believed controlled it. A planned full-scale invasion by 65 Justice Department agents was barely headed off at the pass by Nevada's Governor Grant Sawyer. But the FBI moved in wholesale—wiretapping, bugging, photographing, and harassing. The IRS was simultaneously dispatched to investigate suspected large-scale cash-skimming operations. The Department of Labor, the Bureau of Narcotics, and several task forces all came calling. The Diatribe reached a feverish pitch. In 1963, just as the Nuclear Test Ban Treaty forced the explosions underground, so federal heat sent the questionable investors deeper under cover. Even legitimate owners were besieged. The situation stagnated in a tense stalemate.

◼ HOWARD ROBARD HUGHES

Enter Howard Hughes, at midnight, incognito, from an ambulance, through the back door of the Desert Inn, trailing a truckload of Kleenex and a retinue of Mormon advisors. Like Las Vegas and Bugsy Siegel, Howard Hughes was born in 1905. At age 21, he inherited the multi-million-dollar Hughes Tool Company and made a beeline for Los Angeles, where he launched an eclectic career as film producer, airplane designer, pioneer pilot, airline mogul, and sex investor—"probably no other person in history invested as much money in his sex life as did Howard Hughes," according to *The Intimate Sex Lives of Important People*. In 1965 he sold TWA for a half billion dollars, cash, giving him a larger bankroll than anyone else in the world, and he felt like spending some. Hughes's attraction to Las Vegas dated back to the early 1950s and I suppose he decided to see how much the whole city might cost to buy.

The story of his official entry into the casino scene is pure Las Vegas, and combines all the divergent elements of the Hughes myth. Apparently, Howard wore out his welcome at the Desert Inn; he and his non-gambling assistants occupied all the high-roller suites on the ninth floor. But he'd grown so "comfortable" (with armed guards stationed at the entrances, an air-purifying system working round the clock, blackout draperies, and a special phone system), that he wasn't in the mood to be evicted. So in March 1967, he paid DI owner Moe Dalitz, by now 68 years old and sweating under the unrelenting federal spotlight, $13.2 million for the hotel.

Rare photo of Howard Hughes in all his sartorial splendor, probably taken at the Los Angeles County Courthouse in the mid-1950s.

Hughes didn't move again for over three years. But he moved his cash in a big way, embarking on the most robust buying spree Nevada had ever seen. When the dust settled, Hughes owned the DI, the Sands, Castaways, and Frontier, and was ready to buy the Stardust when anti-trust laws were invoked. That sale failed, but he did later buy the Silver Slipper, the Landmark, and large lots on the Strip and around the city, the North Las Vegas Airport, the Alamo Airways facility next to McCarran Airport, a TV station, a small airline, casinos in Reno, and mining property around Nevada. And he unveiled, in a personal statement that broke 15 years of official silence, the master plan for his city: to turn it into a space-age airport that would accommodate the giant supersonic (SST) jets of the future. In all he dropped $300 million.

And suddenly, according to conventional chronology, Las Vegas was swept clean of its entire undesirable element by the huge broom of corporate respectability. Although Hughes ultimately contributed nothing to the Las Vegas skyline or industrial sector, the presence alone of the billionaire master financier added an enormous degree of long-needed legitimacy to the city's tarnished image. And though his ex-FBI, ex-IRS, and MBA managers managed to alienate high-rollers and entertainers and send his hotels into a major decline, Hughes's investments stimulated an unprecedented speculation boom. The Aladdin, Caesars Palace, Four Queens, Circus Circus, Landmark, and the International all joined the ranks of Las Vegas joints by 1970. In addition, the Fremont, Mint, Riviera, Sands, Sahara, and others all expanded with more hotel rooms and larger casinos.

In the final analysis, the Hughes era was a rousing success for everyone but Hughes himself. In 1970, he divorced his wife, Jean Peters, lost a $150-million lawsuit to TWA, and fled Las Vegas the way he came: on a stretcher. Yet the special dispensations Hughes received from the state casino regulators paved the way for the Nevada Corporate Gaming Acts of 1967 and 1969, which allowed publicly traded corporations to acquire gambling licenses without the need for every stockholder to be individually licensed. MGM, Hilton, and Holiday Inn quickly secured financing from legitimate sources to build their own hotels. Best of all for Las Vegas, the Diatribe ended, and the mob story was relegated to yesterday's news.

■ "MOB ON THE RUN"

Organized crime might have passed out of the media spotlight, but some original connections continued to play themselves out. In 1973, for example, past owners

of the Flamingo pleaded guilty to a hidden interest by Meyer Lansky from 1960 to 1967. In 1976, the audi. division of the Gaming Control Board uncovered a major operation that was skimming a full 20 percent of slot revenues at the Stardust. Along with the Fremont, Marina, and Hacienda hotels, the Stardust had been purchased by Allen Glick of Argent Corporation with nearly $70 million in loans from the Teamsters Pension Fund arranged by Allen Dorfman, long known to maintain connections to the Chicago mob. This group of hotels made Glick, a thirty-something whiz-kid lawyer from Los Angeles, the second biggest owner in town, behind Hughes's Summa Corporation. His partner, Frank "Lefty" Rosenthal, was accepted and admired by Las Vegans as an influential and charitable civic leader, who hosted his own weekly TV talk show and was honored as Las Vegas Man of the Year in 1975. When the dust settled from the skimming revelations, however, the Stardust slot manager disappeared. Glick and Rosenthal, found to be front men for the Midwest crime syndicate, lost their hotels. A Las Vegas detective, newspaper manager, and insurance executive were implicated in the skim. Suspicions even reached the governor, Robert List, and the four-term senator, Howard Cannon, costing them both their jobs in the next election.

According to Las Vegas crime reporter Ned Day, in a 1987 two-hour special report for Las Vegas Channel 8 Eyewitness News, the Argent scandal coincided with the Organized Crime Treaty of 1977, in which the New York–East Coast families assumed control of the new gambling cash cow, Atlantic City. In return, the Chicago–Midwest families were guaranteed control of Las Vegas.

Meanwhile, in 1979, four men were convicted in Detroit of concealing hidden mob ownership in the Aladdin Hotel, which had been funded with $37 million of Teamsters' money. Also in 1979, casino and hotel executives of the Tropicana were recorded meeting with Nick Civella, reputed Kansas City don, who also turned out to be connected to St. Louis attorney Morris Shenker, part owner of the Dunes Hotel, from which Tony "The Ant" Spilotro, cold-blooded enforcer for the Chicago interests in Las Vegas, had recently been banned. By 1983, Allen Dorfman, the Pension Fund fixer, had been assassinated, the Stardust's Frank Rosenthal barely escaped with his life (his Cadillac exploded), and Allen Glick, along with Carl Thomas and Joe Agosto of the Tropicana, had turned state's evidence. Their testimonies helped convict the capos of the Chicago, Kansas City, and Milwaukee

Depending upon your perspective, the Strip can be very surreal. (photo by Kerrick James)

organizations—leaving them, in the words of Ned Day, "monsters without heads." Subsequently, Tony Spilotro made a bid to fill the void left by the dons' imprisonment; he and his brother Michael were later found buried in a cornfield in Indiana. Ned Day concluded that for the first time since Benny Siegel muscled into town more than 40 years earlier, Las Vegas was finally free of mob involvement. Or was it? Ned Day himself, in his early 40s, disappeared in Hawaii in 1988.

T-MEN IN LAS VEGAS

*I*n the spring of 1955, U.S. Treasury agents walked into the Horseshoe Club and asked to see owner Joe W. Brown, a Texas multimillionaire, and his right-hand man Robert "Doby Doc" Caudill, former Texas gambler and collector of Western Americana. This is not a moment especially savored by casino owners, but the T-men weren't up to anything more sinister than enforcing an obscure federal statute that forbids the reproduction of paper currency.

The Horseshoe has on display in its casino one million dollars, one hundred $10,000 bills in actual currency. The hundred $10,000 bills are pasted in rows of twenty length-wise and five across on heavy paper and framed in two layers of plate glass in the shape of a horseshoe. It's what Las Vegas calls its "most authentic" display and costs a small fortune in lost interest. But it is a customer attraction beyond the dreams of a promotional genius and is goggled at by thousands of tourists every day, all of whom then drop a dollar or two in the slots, and is by far the most popular backdrop in Las Vegas for snapshots to send the folks back home who have never seen a $10,000 bill, much less a hundred of them.

The T-men didn't mind the display, no matter how lurid it may have seemed to them. What they minded was the photographs. They confiscated 150,000 souvenir post cards of the display from the club, and combed the town for prints and negatives of all photographs ever taken. Misters Brown and Caudill weren't exactly amused, but they weren't unamused, either. They foresaw a lifetime's work for the government agents. Some 8,000 photographs had been taken in front of the million dollars and mailed all over the country; souvenir post cards had gone out by the hundreds of thousands; the display had been photographed in scores of newsreels and had appeared in several television shows including Ed Murrow's "See It Now" program. "I never did see a T-man's job," said Doby Doc. "Now I really don't."

—Katherine Best and Katherine Hillyer, *Las Vegas: Playtown, U.S.A.,* 1955

■ VIVA VEGAS!

As the feds were cleaning out the last (known) mobster interests in Las Vegas, the corporate sanitization begun by Howard Hughes had rendered the city's image, in a word, kosher. But not without its own costs. The 1930s innocence, the 1940s Wild West period, the 1950s freewheeling days, the 1960s saber-rattling, and the 1970s consolidation all metamorphosed into the 1980s bottom line which remains to this day. (The transformation of Las Vegas into a corporate volume industry is lamented by many who feel the city has lost its soul.) The bottom line, however, did hit bottom in the late 1970s and early 1980s. The early days of Atlantic City as the East Coast's casino center, along with the deep recession of the early Reagan years, considerably reduced visitor volume and gambling revenues. The terrible fire at the MGM Grand (now Bally's) left 84 dead and nearly 700 injured; the Grand closed from November 1980 to July 1981. A fire at the Las Vegas Hilton in February 1981 took another eight lives. But the recovery of the economy in the mid-1980s, along with Atlantic City's stabilization (and gradual decline), triggered what has become Las Vegas's biggest boom yet.

Check it out. The Las Vegas annual visitor count has now topped 30 million each year. Tourists (and locals) lose more than six billion dollars inside the casinos and spend another six billion on travel expenses. Two million visitors attend conventions. Roughly 204,000 get married. Another 40,000 people—over 1,000 a week—relocate to Las Vegas. The population has swelled to 1.2 million in the metropolitan area, making Las Vegas the fastest growing city in the country and by far the largest city in the country to have been founded in the twentieth century. The population is increasing so rapidly, in fact, that Las Vegas is the only city in the country which needs an updated Yellow Pages every six months.

Las Vegas today claims more than 100,000 hotel rooms, more than any other city in the world by a mile. At least 25,000 new rooms in 15 new joints have been announced and are slated to be built before the turn of the millennium. But even that won't be enough to handle the up to 40 million yearly visitors projected for Las Vegas in the year 2000. And it's not just hotel rooms that are happening around here. With casinos now proliferating around the country, Las Vegas is going to ever-greater lengths to maintain its status as the Ganges of gambling. There's no end in sight to the development of themed attractions, amusement parks, high-tech entertainment, and unabashed spectacle. Eight years after the Mirage got the ball rolling, Las Vegas is still on its biggest and fastest roll ever, though all it's really doing is trying to keep pace with the fulfillment of its own destiny.

CITYSCAPE

A TALE OF SEVENTY HOTELS

TRAVELERS ALONG THE OLD MORMON TRAIL paused at well-watered, shady, and bountiful Las Vegas Ranch while the Gass family tended it (1865-1883), and the tradition continued throughout Helen Stewart's stewardship (1883-1904). Rough lodging was available at J. T. McWilliams's original Las Vegas townsite (1904-1905) in a large tent, euphemistically signposted Ladd's Hotel, where two strangers were assigned one double bed for eight hours at a cost of a dollar apiece —but only after both had passed a body-bug test.

As the Las Vegas Land and Water Company auction neared in spring 1905, a long tent-cabin was constructed a block north of the auction site to accommodate investors. The Hotel Las Vegas boasted 30 rooms with canvas walls, a modern kitchen and dining room, cold beer and a large stock of cigars, and an interior temperature of 120 degrees. After the auction, two blocks from there at Fremont and Main, one of the first downtown establishments to receive water service from the company was Miller's Hotel.

Prominent Las Vegans began hankering for a major hotel as early as 1911, when Charles "Pop" Squires, the original Las Vegas booster, wrote, "An up-to-date, not too expensive, winter resort hotel in Las Vegas will prove a bonanza, without a doubt." In the mid-1920s, the Chamber of Commerce, promoting the town's "healthful climate, year-round sunshine, and lure of the desert," predicted that Las Vegas could become "an international attraction, if we can only get a hotel built to accommodate wealthy travelers."

But it wasn't until the early 1930s, with Hoover Dam under construction and wide-open gambling legalized, that Las Vegas experienced the first of its many and ongoing tourist-hotel building booms. The Nevada Hotel, which replaced the early Miller's Hotel, added a third story. Across the street, the venerable Las Vegas Club opened. The MacDonald Hotel on North Fifth added 16 rooms. Hotel Virginia was built on South Main. The Miller-turned-Nevada turned into the Sal Sagev (Las Vegas spelled backwards). But Las Vegas's first luxury hotel, the Apache, finally opened in March 1932, at the corner of Fremont and Second (where the Horseshoe now stands), complete with elegant furnishings, a large banquet room, and the town's first elevator and air-conditioned lobby.

(previous pages) Caesars' famous fountains front the pink portico and soft-blue neon building border.

Still, throughout the 1930s, downtown Las Vegas retained its Western frontier flavor. The newly legalized casinos remained saloons and sawdust joints where railroaders, miners, construction workers, and gamblers drank cheap whiskey and played faro and poker. Outside of town, the Kiel Ranch, renamed Boulderado, became a dude ranch in the Reno tradition, where wealthy guests waited out the six-week residency requirement for divorce. And the first two truly luxurious resort hotels built on what is now the Strip were the hacienda-style El Rancho Vegas and Last Frontier.

■ THE FABULOUS FLAMINGO

None of this Wild West theme-park hokum for Benjamin "Bugsy" Siegel. Bugsy had a dream. He would become the greatest guardian of public gambling and private prostitution in the country. His hotel would provide the best resort facilities in the world. His casino would be the most luxurious and offer the finest service. His employees, down to the lowliest janitor, would wear tuxedos. His guests would be famous, glamorous, rich. He spent $6 million to bedeck his dream palace and pop out the eyes of his mobster financiers, movie-star friends, competition

The original Flamingo Hotel, muscled into place on Highway 91 in the desert far south of town by Benjamin "The Bug" Siegel.

(top) Tutankhamen's mask is projected onto fine mist at Luxor, while the world's most powerful spotlight shines from the hotel pyramid (photo by Kerrick James). (bottom) The gilded arches brand the night sky.

Between the lightbulb awning and the neon signage of casinos such as Binion's Horseshoe, Fremont Street downtown is a four-block-long arcade of color and light. (photo by Kerrick James)

present and future, and attract battalions of citizens who'd come to play the games and live to tell the tale. And the best part? The whole thing was legit! Bugsy didn't even have to buy off, scare off, or run from the cops. It was poifect.

The Flamingo transcended any mere tourist attraction. Las Vegans took the long drive out Highway 91, 12 miles round trip, just to stare. The incomparable Tom Wolfe, in *The Kandy-Kolored Tangerine-Flake Streamline Baby*, explains, "Siegel put up a hotel-casino such as Las Vegas had never seen—all Miami Modern. Such shapes! Boomerang Modern supports, Palette Curvilinear bars, Hot Shoppe Cantilever roofs, and a scalloped swimming pool. Such colors! All the new electrochemical pastels of the Florida littoral: tangerine, broiling magenta, livid pink, incarnadine, fuchsia, demure, Congo ruby, methyl green, viridian, aquamarine, phenosafranine, incandescent orange, scarlet-fever purple, cyanic blue, tesselated bronze, hospital-fruit-basket orange. And such signs! Two cylinders rose at either end of the Flamingo—eight stories high and covered from top to bottom with neon rings in the shape of bubbles that fizzed eight stories up into the desert sky all night long like an illuminated whisky-soda tumbler filled to the brim with pink champagne."

Wolfe makes the point that throughout the history of art, the aristocracy had been solely responsible for style—for the simple reason that aristocrats alone had the time and money to cultivate it. World War II, however, changed all that forever. "The war created money. It made massive infusions of money into every level of society. Suddenly, classes of people whose lives had been practically invisible had the money to build monuments to their own styles. Las Vegas was created after the war, with war money, by gangsters."

But all that—the shapes, colors, signs—was just the exterior, the false front, designed to grab your eye as you cruised by at 30 miles an hour. Inside, you were presented with another false front: the promise. Of the indulgence. In the three oldest, most primal, irresistible, and taboo pastimes of human nature: intoxication, gambling, and sex. All this electric glamour in the desert, all this style, seduction, and cushioned comfort—all to debar the barrier to your bankroll. And then! From the backstage special-effects control booth appeared the wizard, controlling Oz, wielding the Percentage. The Edge That Must Be Obeyed. A legal game, an honest game, but by no means a fair game. All designed to pass the cash over to the custodial side of the pit. Never to return. It *was* perfect.

Except that Bugsy, like most empire builders and some lifestyle creators, either suffered from delusions of immortality or clearly recognized the imminence of his own fall. Whichever, along the way he forgot to cover his ass. He literally gave his life to the vision, but not before initiating the Golden Age of Las Vegas.

In early January 1947, 14 days after it opened, the Flamingo financially flopped. By June, the Flamingo was being managed by Gus Greenbaum, boss gambler from Phoenix, and Davie Berman, boss gambler from Minneapolis. Both had arrived a few years earlier in Bugsy's wake, helped him run the El Cortez downtown, then after his death fronted the Flamingo for hidden owner Meyer Lansky. In 1955, after Greenbaum and Berman moved over to the Riviera, the hotel was sold to Thomas Hull, who'd built the El Rancho Vegas, and Al Parvin, who was to buy and sell a number of hotels over the next 20 years. In 1960, the Flamingo was again sold, to a large group of investors headed by Miami hotel magnates Morris Lansburgh and Sam Cohen. Lansky received a hefty "finder's fee" for both sales. It was later determined that he'd held an interest all the way up to 1967. That year, entrepreneur Kirk Kerkorian bought the Flamingo for $13 million during the Hughes whirlwind to use as a "hotel school" for the core staff of the huge International that Kerkorian was then planning. He immediately sank another $2.5 million into improvements: the casino and theater were expanded, and the champagne towers were torn down.

Hilton Corporation bought the Flamingo in 1970, becoming the first major hotel chain to enter the Nevada market. Hilton embarked on a colossal expansion program that added 500-room towers in 1977, 1980, 1982, and 1986; a 728-room tower in 1990; and a 908-room tower in 1993. The grand total of 3,575 rooms makes the Flamingo the fifth largest hotel in town. The 1990 expansion required tearing up the 45-year-old rose garden planted by Bugsy himself. The 1993 expansion required tearing down the original bungalows from the 1940s so that the pool area could be expanded to cover 15 acres. Also demolished was the Oregon Building, where Bugsy Siegel himself had a suite on the fourth floor. It was replaced with a 440-unit Hilton timeshare tower.

Today, the Flamingo is the highest-class bona fide resort on the Strip—no gimmicks, no spectacles, just pure vacation. The pool area is the finest in Las Vegas; the series of pools is connected by water slides (the tot pool has a tiny slide of its own). The Flamingo, in a rare demonstration of nostalgia, erected a little brick shrine to Bugsy, with a plaque commemorating his life, a bas relief of his face, and even a garden full of the man's treasured roses. *Flamingo Hilton, 3555 Las Vegas Boulevard South; (702) 733-3111/(800) 732-2111.*

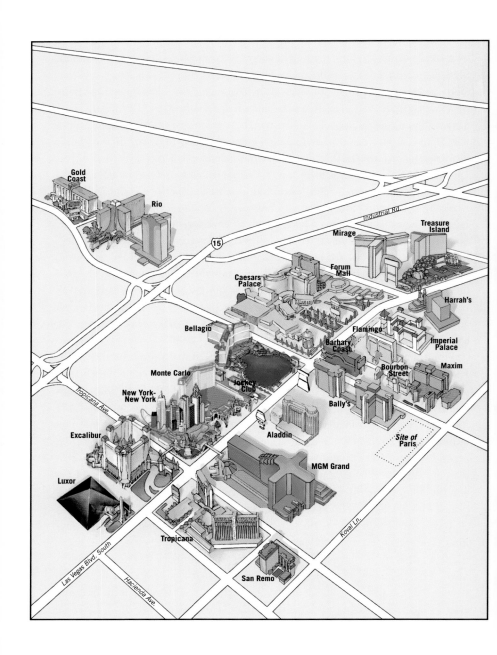

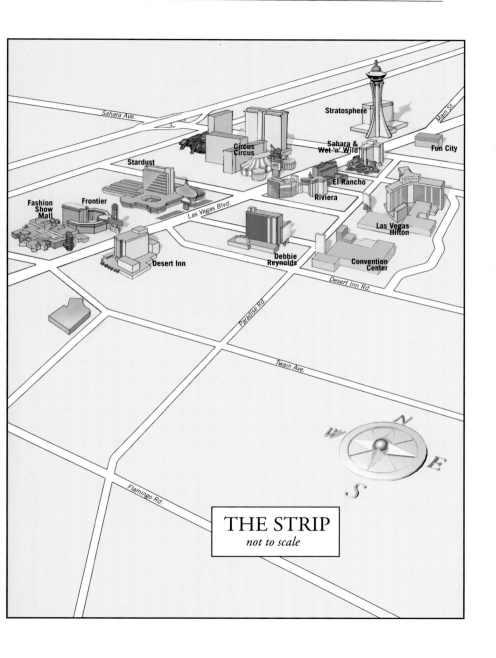

THE STRIP

not to scale

EL CORTEZ HOTEL

The El Cortez Hotel opened in November 1941, and occupied half a city block a little beyond congested downtown on Fremont Street between Sixth and Seventh, just outside Clark's original Las Vegas town site. It boasted 71 rooms and eight two-bedroom suites, cost $160,000 to build, and sported a Wild West resort motif to compete head to head with the new El Rancho Vegas out on Highway 91. In 1945, the El Cortez was bought by Benny Siegel, with Davie and Chickie Berman, Gus Greenbaum, and Willie Alderman. But when they all moved over to the Flamingo in 1947, the downtown resort was sold to a group of 19 investors, which included such luminaries as J. Kell Houssels, Bill Moore, Sam Boyd, and Joe Kelley. By 1954, attrition had reduced the group to Houssels and Kelley; they sold it back to Marion Hicks, who'd built the place, in 1961. Jackie Gaughan acquired the property in 1982, and he owns it today.

A $12-million, 14-story, 200-room tower was added in 1983 at the corner of Sixth and Ogden, giving the El Cortez a whole city block. Fortunately, part of the old hotel, at the southeast corner of Fremont and Sixth, has been left undisturbed all these decades, and remains today exactly as it appears in this historical black-and-white photograph from the early 1950s, even then unchanged from the day it opened in 1941. Thus this small wing of the El Cortez is by far the oldest original casino in Las Vegas—and therefore in the country.

■ THE THUNDERBIRD

Next came the $3 million Thunderbird, named for a mythological Navajo creature. Built in 1948 by Marion Hicks (a local contractor who also constructed the El Cortez) and Clifford Jones (then lieutenant governor of Nevada—at age 35), the Thunderbird catered to local families with great food and an informal setting. Since Lt. Governor Jones had the juice, the Thunderbird also became the hangout of many prominent politicians. But the Gaming Control Board exercised its new authority on the hotel in 1955, when a sting operation conducted by local newspapermen uncovered a loan to the owners by Jake Lansky, Meyer's brother. Its license was revoked, and though it was later restored by the courts, the Thunderbird's aura faded.

Del Webb purchased the hotel in 1964 for $10 million. Eight years later, Caesars World bought it for $13 million, but Caesars' managers quickly realized they didn't want it, and turned it over to E. Thomas Parry of Valley Bank for $9 million. He sold it to the Dunes' Major Riddle in 1977, who changed its name to Silverbird. Riddle sold it in 1981 to Ed Torres, a longtime Las Vegas hotel manager, who changed its name to El Rancho, after the original hotel on the Strip, which once stood across the street. The hotel closed in 1992. Torres sold it for $25 million to a group of investors who've tried to reopen it as Countryland U.S.A., but haven't managed to pull it off yet.

■ THE DESERT INN

In 1950, the $4.5 million Desert Inn opened. Possibly no other Las Vegas hotel has generated more ink than the DI— about Wilbur Clark on the bright side, and about Moe Dalitz on the shady side. Clark started out in Southern California as a bartender, luggage handler, and crap dealer, and later owned a string of taverns. After selling out in California, he set up in Las Vegas in the late 1930s, and speculated in casino points. In 1946, he sold his share in the El Rancho Vegas for $1.5 million, and began construction of his dream hotel, Wilbur Clark's Desert Inn, modeled after its posh Palm Springs namesake. Like Bugsy, he immediately ran out of money, and work ground to a halt. A full three years later, in 1949, Clark finally obtained $3 million from the boss gambler of Cleveland, Morris Dalitz, and his three partners, who retained an equivalent 75 percent ownership in the Desert

All that glitters.

Inn. Immediately, Clark reverted to front-man status, and he initially played his role as media manipulator with gusto and a touch of brilliance. He fondly displayed a veritable Strip-sized billboard of articles, clips, and ads about the hotel and himself, and was even proclaimed Ambassador of Las Vegas, the ultimate shill. But Dalitz held all the juice.

Moe Dalitz was 50 when he moved to Las Vegas to run the DI. He'd grown up on the streets of Detroit and was already a big-time bootlegger, having run booze between Canada and Cleveland—by age 25. He branched out into racketeering and eventually operated a string of illegal casinos from Cleveland to Kentucky. He also had extensive interests in legitimate business and industry: steel, real estate, race tracks, and his family laundry operation in Detroit (which is how he came to know Jimmy Hoffa). In *Green Felt Jungle,* Dalitz is described as having "the big fix in half a dozen city halls, organizational ability which he used for corruption, and legitimate enterprises which simplified the fix—stock deals and percentages are the modern ways to pay off graft." This is supported by Carl Sifakis in *Mafia Encyclopedia:* Dalitz was expert at "the deft use of the bribe rather than the bullet," and so great an organizational genius that Meyer Lansky "derived inspiration from him."

In *Gambler's Money,* Wallace Turner delves deeply into the skills and qualities that eventually earned Dalitz the most juice of all the gangster bosses in Las Vegas. These young illegal gamblers learned many unusual and useful lessons. They learned, for instance, how to conduct business without the benefit of binding contracts or legal recourse. They developed their own code of trust in a world where a man's word was his deed: enemies and possible betrayers were cultivated and respected but never trusted, while a solid reputation for honoring the pledged word among allies held the highest value. They considered their fellow men as suckers to be plucked, dishonest authorities to be bribed, thieves to be caught, usurpers to be foiled. They

Moe Dalitz, the ultimate Las Vegas survivor, looking dapper and happy at age 82.

learned the mechanics of the games: how to analyze percentages, how to spot cheaters, how to cheat the players without being spotted. They learned the psychology of the compulsive gambler and perfected the means of taking *all* his money. They were well versed in all the tricks that the underworld used to protect its illegal investments. "They could soon learn the tricks the legitimate world had devised to protect its investments through courts, contracts, and franchises," Turner concludes.

Gus Greenbaum, Davie Berman, and Moe Dalitz absorbed Bugsy's vision and proceeded to make it work. They mustered all their knowledge and experience to accent the old tricks and invent new ones. They continually identified and exploited the weaknesses, gaping loopholes, and naiveté of the state's regulatory apparatus. They celebrated their own styles—perfecting the seduction and worshipping the great god Percentage. They made enviable profits look easy. And best of all, they became respected elders of the local community—influential, charitable, religious. Ultimately, they opened the door for a veritable flood of gamblers from around the country to invest their hot cash in legalized gambling and personal legitimacy. They built the Strip, fine-tuned the casinos, and laid the foundation for modern Las Vegas.

Dalitz (and Clark) also inaugurated a number of other trends. For opening night, timed to coincide with an atomic test blast, they spent $13,000 to fly in a hundred high rollers. They opened the first resort golf course and sponsored the Tournament of Champions (1953). They hired a famous sheriff, Don Borax, to be Chief of Security.

In 1963, the DI added its first nine-story tower. In 1964, Wilbur Clark finally sold his minority interest in the DI to Dalitz (Clark died of a heart attack a year later). In March 1967, Dalitz sold the "whole schmear" to Howard Hughes for $13.2 million. Though licenses often took months to process, Hughes's application was approved post haste—no fingerprints, photographs, interview, or investigations were required. The 14-story Augusta Tower was built in 1978 and shortly thereafter the seven-story Wimbledon Tower, fronting the golf course, was added. Kirk Kerkorian bought the DI (along with the Sands) from Summa Corporation in February 1988 for $161 million, then resold it for $160 million cash to ITT Sheraton in 1993. Immediately, ITT spent $50 million renovating the hotel rooms and golf course, and two years later, embarked on a $150 million expansion (the first in nearly 20 years), adding two new buildings with mini-suites, suites, and penthouses, and completely remodeling the casino. Still, the DI remains one of the smallest major hotels on the Strip, catering to a select upscale clientele. *Desert Inn, 3145 Las Vegas Boulevard South; (702) 733-4444/(800) 634-6906.*

■ THE HORSESHOE

Meanwhile, downtown, Benny Binion opened his Horseshoe Club in August 1951. Binion was born in 1904 in Pilot Grove, Texas. Like Moe Dalitz, Binion started out as a rough kid on the rough streets, then became the boss bootlegger of Dallas before he was 25, and the boss gambler before he was 30. Reid and Demaris quote "a retired Dallas police captain who had been active during the gang wars of the Binion era," whose story included a litany of bloodletting and gore that would make a Sam Peckinpah movie look like Mary Poppins, and that was before Binion's alleged gangland feud with Herbert "The Cat" Noble, the body count of which would make an Arnold Schwarzenegger movie look like Disney. (It's all there in *Green Felt Jungle* for anyone who's interested.)

On the other hand, in an interview with Binion recorded in 1973 for the University of Nevada's Oral History Project, he claims, "The Texas Rangers, the FBI, and the whole works know that I didn't have nothin' to do with the Noble killin'. It would've took me a half hour to kill Noble if I'd wanted to kill him. There's no way in the world I'd harm anybody for any amount of money. But if anybody goes to talkin' about doin' me or my family any bodily harm, I'm very capable for easily takin' care of 'em in a most artistic way."

Binion fled the Texas heat in 1946 for downtown Las Vegas, where he quickly bought into and sold out of two downtown casinos. He then purchased the old Apache Hotel and the Eldorado Casino next door, and rebuilt the properties into the Horseshoe, which opened in the same month that Herb Noble was finally laid to rest. Binion paid some dues by serving four years at Leavenworth in the mid-1950s for that old workhorse, federal income tax evasion. Before he went away, he had to "sell" the Horseshoe to Joe Brown, a multimillionaire friend who, in Benny's words, "held it together" in a "kind of a deal" until he regained his freedom and "bought back" the hotel. In 1988, the Binion family acquired the famous Mint Hotel next door to the Horseshoe, giving the joint its own city block.

Above all, Benny Binion was a survivor—of the Dallas gang wars of the 1930s, the Las Vegas cutthroat competition of the 1940s, the federal confinement of the 1950s. He didn't only survive, he prospered. And ultimately, Benny reached a status not unlike Dalitz's: beloved elder statesman. Binion died in early 1990 at the age of 85. His oldest son, Jack, now runs the Horseshoe, known far and wide as the quintessential old-time gambling hall. You can make the largest bets in the world here. You can watch the World Series of Poker every April to May, where the first prize is a million bucks. You can eat a complete late-night steak dinner for $4. And you can have your picture taken in front of a hundred rare $10,000 bills—best souvenir in town, and it's free. *Binion's Horseshoe, 128 Fremont Street; (702) 382-1600/(800) 237-6537.*

■ THE SAHARA

In December 1952, the $5.5 million Sahara Hotel opened across the Strip from the El Rancho Vegas, replacing the popular Club Bingo (which is well remembered after more than 40 years). Milton Prell, a Los Angeles jewelry mogul, lined up a grubstake from Portland boss gamblers, Desert Inn owners, Sam Boyd (a clever

Frank Sinatra's Las Vegas reign began in 1952, when he was sold nine points in the Sands Hotel. He and other members of the Rat Pack gathered there for the next 15 years.

Benny Binion posing in front of his cool mil.

West Coast bingo operator who'd worked his way up through a decade of Las Vegas ranks to be a juiceman), and Del Webb, whose construction company built the Flamingo, and then the Sahara in return for 20 points in the property. The hotel's sign was 100 feet tall, free-standing, with a letter design that hasn't changed in almost a half-century. The Sahara added an African style to the desert theme of the Las Vegas Strip, with big plaster camels out front, and the Caravan coffeeshop, Casbah Lounge, and Congo Showroom inside. (Clydie the camel remains, and the original names haven't changed.)

In *Playtown, U.S.A.,* Best and Hillyer described the Sahara, the fifth hotel on the Strip. "Its casino was larger than anybody else's— up to that time. Its swimming pool was the biggest in Las Vegas —so far. Its theater-restaurant had greater seating capacity than any other in town—as of that date. Its stage was the most spacious on the Strip—right then." Two weeks later the Sands opened, prompting the authors to add, "Periodically, Las Vegas sits back, takes a deep breath, and asks itself: When will the saturation point in all this prosperity come? When will the one-too-many swank caravansary go up on the Strip? When will all these millions of tourists stop streaming into town?" They were writing in 1954.

The Sahara's owners built the Mint Hotel downtown in 1956. Del Webb purchased controlling interest in both properties in 1961. In 1964, the Sahara's entertainment director, Stan Irwin, booked the Beatles for two shows at the Convention Center. Performing for 8,500 Las Vegans at $4 a ticket, the shows have been called "Las Vegas's biggest entertainment event of all time." A 14-story, 200-room tower was added to the Sahara in 1966, less than a year after the Mint Hotel downtown rose to 26 stories, tallest building in Nevada, with its skydeck pool. In 1968, a 24-story, 400-room tower was added to the Sahara.

Paul Lowden bought the Sahara from Del Webb in 1982 for $50 million. He'd started out in Las Vegas as a musician in 1965. He was promoted to music director first at the Flamingo, and then at the Hacienda in which he purchased points. Lowden wound up owning the Hacienda in 1977 (after the Allen Glick scandal), and parlayed it into the Sahara. He installed a third tower (26 stories, 575 rooms) and a convention center in 1988, and put up a 600-room tower in 1990. Lowden then opened the 200-room Santa Fe north of town on US 95.

Lowden sold the Sahara in 1995 to William Bennett, former CEO and chairman of Circus Circus, for $150 million. Bennett has since embarked on a costly expansion: he is adding a new hotel tower and parking garage, and doubling the size of the casino. *Sahara, 2535 Las Vegas Boulevard South, (702) 737-2111/(800) 634-6666.*

■ THE SANDS

When the Sands opened in December 1952, two weeks after the Sahara, nearly three million visitors were passing through Las Vegas annually. The hotel's original 200 rooms, contained by five two-story Bermuda-modern buildings named after race tracks and set in a semi-circle around the pool, provided accommodation even more luxurious than the Flamingo next door, and remained filled, continuously, for the rest of the decade.

In a shrewd maneuver, Frank Sinatra and Dean Martin were sold nine points each in the Sands, to provide incentive for the superstars to perform there, in the famous Copa Room. Their friends Milton Berle, Sammy Davis Jr., Danny Thomas, Lena Horne, and others hung out at the Sands; together, these Hollywood glitterati came to be called the Clan, and later the Rat Pack. The Sands' $40,000 steam room was famous for 15 years as a gathering place of the Clan and its functionaries.

In July 1967, Howard Hughes purchased the Sands; Hughes's company owned it for 21 years, till it was sold to Kirk Kerkorian. Kerkorian turned around and sold the Sands in 1989 to Sheldon Adelson of the Interface Group, the world's

HOTEL-ROOM ART

*M*artin Lowitz, a jolly German-born art collector and one-time Latin scholar, sells some 20,000 original pictures a year that he has mass-produced for him by a string of assembly-line artists who are able with fair aim to imitate their peers at the rate of a dozen a day. Anyone wanting 50 Vermeers, 25 Roualts, a dozen Eakinses, may have same at prices as low as $17.50 each, with frame.

The Lowitz operation is strictly a cut-rate, noncreative performance that has caused art connoisseurs to recoil as though stabbed with a poisoned paintbrush. But his boys' pictures are bright and effective and, on the whole, much appreciated by the inhabitants of hotel bedrooms who have been whimpering in silence through the years at the seemingly limitless sight of mordant ducks and dying swans. Strip hotels have bought thousands of Lowitz originals.

In 1947, Martin Lowitz sold 83 of these originals to Marion Hicks, who was then building his Thunderbird Hotel. The Thunderbird opened in September 1948, and two days later it was discovered that three paintings had disappeared from a room. Mr. Hicks wasn't particularly disturbed. "Wait," he said to the distraught housekeeper. "The guest who was in that room plays roulette in our casino. Besides, he has a reservation to return."

The Thunderbird evidently had made the absconder feel so at home that he now wanted home to seem more like the Thunderbird. He returned shortly, stayed one night, played roulette and departed next morning laden with oversized luggage. Mr. Hicks again was not only unperturbed, he was pleased. His casino books showed that the visitor had lost $6,000 his first visit and $8,000 his second. The pictures he had stolen cost less than $200. In a happy haze of appreciation of art, Mr. Hicks wired Mr. Lowitz an order for 200 more paintings.

—Best and Hillyer, *Las Vegas: Playtown, U.S.A.,* 1955

leader in trade conferences and exhibitions. Adelson built a million-square-foot convention center at the rear of the historic property, which helps host the gargantuan Comdex computer trade show that invades Las Vegas every November. Adelson founded and owned Comdex till selling it to a Japanese computer conglomerate in 1995 for $800 million.

In November 1996, Adelson imploded the Sands to make room for the Venetian, a massive resort and casino with a Venice theme.

■ THE SHOWBOAT

The $2 million, 200-room Showboat opened in 1954 under the ownership of William Moore of the Last Frontier, and J. Kell Housells, a longtime downtown juiceman. Moe Dalitz and the DI gang managed the casino. The Showboat was quite an anomaly—a Mississippi riverboat, complete with paddlewheel and smokestacks, out in the boondocks of Boulder Highway just down from the venerable Green Shack restaurant. The day before the grand opening, an enormous storm dumped torrential rains, which almost washed the Boat away! But the hotel floated along in the Las Vegas current, steering around snags, pausing in port for repairs, but rarely foundering, all under the able captainship of Joe Kelley, appropriately a one-time Southern California offshore gambling-boat manager.

In 1959, Kelley built bowling lanes at the hotel and sponsored tournaments, which attracted low rollers from around the country; the Show Boat Invitational, inaugurated in 1959, is the longest-running tournament on the Professional Bowlers Association Tour. He also introduced the 49-cent breakfast, which brought the locals running. And later, he was first to hook all his slot machines up to a computer to keep track of earnings. The Boat expanded in 1963, got a facelift in 1968, added nine stories and 250 rooms in 1973, and expanded again in 1975. It was completely redecorated (with a Southern plantation theme) in 1995; the bingo hall is the fanciest, airiest, and most comfortable in town. Today, only a small vestige of the Showboat facade (and some original rooms around the pool) remain, but the bowling alley, large bingo parlor, and low rollers keep it steaming full speed ahead. *Showboat, 2800 East Fremont Street, (702) 385-9123/(800) 826-2800.*

■ THE RIVIERA

The Riviera, in April 1955 the seventh hotel to open on the Strip, provided a major departure from the distinctively dry styles of the Desert Inn, Sahara, and Sands. Built by Miami hotelmen and reminiscent of the princely palaces along the Mediterranean, the T-shaped Riv rose nine stories from the desert floor, and cost nearly $10 million—about $4 million more than the investors were able to pay. The New Frontier, Dunes, Royal Nevada, and Mint opened right on the Riv's heels, and Liberace was paid an unheard-of $50,000 a week to headline; within three months, the hotel was bankrupt.

From left: Benny Gottstein, Moe Sedway, and Gus Greenbaum.

The Chicago mob immediately moved in and came away with the pie, then blackmailed Gus Greenbaum of Phoenix out of retirement and into running it. Reluctantly taking over the unchecked casino, Greenbaum, along with his cronies Davie Berman and Willie Alderman, managed to strong-arm the operation into submission and began to turn a profit—for Chicago don Tony Accardo's "front seat in the counting room." But Gus again couldn't stay away from his old bad habits—the gambling, drugs, and showgirls. He owed a million dollars in markers to Chicago loan sharks. And his old bosses at the Flamingo were irritated that he'd gone to work for the competition, taking with him all the Flamingo's secrets. (On a visit home to Phoenix for Thanksgiving in 1958, Gus and his wife Bess had their throats slashed in a hit ordered from on high.)

The Riviera, which has had one of the most upwardly mobile histories—with an occasional crash—was taken over by a group including local millionaire Jerome Mack and Broadway producer David Merrick. In 1967, they added a $10 million, 11-story wing during the great expansion race of the late 1960s, then sold the hotel, in 1973, to Meshulam Riklis of Boston's American International Travel

(above) The Riviera—almost continually under construction since it opened.

Services, one of the largest travel companies in the world. Riklis built a $20 million, 12-story tower in 1975, added 200 more rooms ($6 million) in 1977, paid Dolly Parton a jaw-dropping $350,000 a week in 1981, and was bankrupt within two years, first in a series of major hotel failures in the ruinous recession of 1983-84.

The Riviera recovered by 1985, and in 1988, a $28-million, 24-story tower was completed. In April 1990, a major addition expanded the casino to 125,000 square feet, one of the largest in the world. Today, the Riv is known best for its entertainment: four showrooms with an extravaganza ("Splash II"), female impersonators ("La Cage"), dirty dancin' ("Crazy Girls"), and comedy (The Comedy Club). *Riviera, 2901 Las Vegas Boulevard South, (702) 385-9123/(800) 634-6753.*

■ THE FRONTIER

If ever the transformation of a hotel symbolized the transformation of Las Vegas— in time and space—it was on the day, April 4, in the critical year, 1955, that the Last Frontier rode off into the sunset and the New Frontier dropped whole from high orbit to take its place. The old hotel, which opened in 1942, had been sold in

1951 to Bernie Katleman and Jake Kozloff, who also owned the El Rancho Vegas. By 1955, the Last Frontier, second hotel to be built on the Strip and 13 years old, was one of 10 competing properties, and long due for a complete modernization. Luckily, Best and Hillyer were there to describe it. "The Frontier, New, had a lobby of black and white Italian marble, and a casino carpeted in French lilac weaving so deep that sparks flew when the mauve-tinted slot machines were touched. Some said even the sparks were mauve. Chandeliers in the shape of men from outer space, flying saucers and spinning planets hung from raspberry glacé and daphne-pink ceilings. Walls of diadem violet and Ruby Lake magenta displayed three-dimensional amethyst murals depicting the twelve signs of the zodiac. The cocktail lounge was named Cloud 9, the dining room was called Planet, and the theater was known as Venus. On this particular afternoon, the doors closed on the dear old homespun grandeur of the Last and opened, a few hundred feet up the corridors, on the Out-of-this-World-ly phantasmagoria of the New."

Immediately after the renovation, Kozloff and Katleman sold the hotel to a group of L.A. investors, which leased it to other operators, who ran it into the ground. The casino closed and stayed that way throughout most of 1957, until it was leased to Warren Bayley, who owned the Hacienda. He ran the New Frontier profitably until his death in 1964, at which time his rights reverted to the estate executors. The casino again closed; a year later the entire old New Frontier was razed to raise the new Frontier. Just before it opened in July 1967, Howard Hughes bought it—all 650 rooms, along with the million-dollar sign, 200 feet tall, at that time the largest in the world. In 1982, Hughes's Summa Corporation expanded the casino to the tune of $7 million.

Summa sold the hotel in 1988 to the Elardi family. The new owners immediately added a 15-story, 396-room tower and instituted union-busting tactics, causing the powerful Culinary Union local to call a strike. The strikers were immediately replaced, picketers took up their vigil on the Strip sidewalk, and the situation has dragged on ever since. The Elardis have consistently lost in court, yet still the strike continues. As I write, it's five and a half years and counting. The Frontier is popular with people in their twenties and early thirties. The crowds are generally hip young Gen-Xers who appreciate the mini-suites, the good pool area, the good cheap food, the friendly dealers and floormen, and the full-pay video poker machines (and who don't care much about crossing a picket line). *Frontier, 3120 Las Vegas Boulevard South, (702) 794-8200/(800) 634-6966.*

■ THE FREMONT

Next came the $6 million, 155-room Fremont Hotel. Ed Levinson, a partner in the Sands, and Louis Lurie, a San Francisco investor, got together and built the first Strip-type carpet joint and highrise in downtown: its 15 stories made it the tallest building in Nevada when it opened in May 1956. The Fremont used all the Strip tricks—tony casino, gourmet restaurants, and a showroom with big-name entertainers (including a teenage Wayne Newton, who had to be escorted through the casino to the stage). At the same time, it addressed downtown sensibilities by incorporating a large parking garage, a local television studio, the telephone company, and Las Vegas Press Club business offices.

The Fremont had three unusual characteristics: it sparkled in the sun, thanks to quartz aggregate chips in the outer walls; it employed a cantilevered design in which the rooms were staggered, instead of on top of each other, for support, saving millions in construction costs; and it had an above-ground swimming pool. The hotel expanded in 1963, using nearly $5 million in Teamsters Pension Fund loans. The Parvin-Dohrman group bought the Fremont in 1966, which led to wunderkind-turned-bad-boy Allen Glick's ownership in 1973. Glick gave the Fremont its famous face-lift, adding the block-long neon marquee for $750,000. After Glick, the Fremont changed hands several times, until the Boyd Group added the hotel to its holdings in 1985.

Today, the Fremont is known as a solid downtown joint with older rooms, typical action, and good food, especially at the Second Street Grill, where the creative California cuisine has an Asian accent, and at the seafood buffet, which takes place three nights a week. *Fremont, 200 Fremont Street, (702) 385-3232/(800) 634-6182.*

■ THE HACIENDA

The $6 million, 266-room Hacienda Hotel, at the far southern end of the Strip across from McCarran Airport, opened in June 1956. Like the El Rancho Vegas, the Hacienda was one of a chain of California lowrise motor hotels. Like the Showboat, the Hacienda was located just far enough off the beaten track to pursue its own course, along the rocky road of hotel competition, for 40 years. Over the

(opposite) The "pirate ship" Hispaniola at Treasure Island resort. (photo by Kerrick James)

years, it expanded twice; it was a 1,000-room joint when Circus Circus bought it in 1995.

Circus ran the Hacienda for a year and a half, then knocked it down on New Year's Day, 1997. The giant hotel company, which owns a Miracle Mile on the west side of the Strip from Tropicana to Russell, plans to build a 3,600-room megaresort called Paradise, with a South Seas' theme. A 400-room non-casino multi-starred Four Seasons Hotel will also occupy the old Hacienda site; construction is expected to be completed in early 1999.

■ THE TROPICANA

Here it was, a full 25 years since wide-open gambling was legalized in Nevada, and more than 10 years since the Nevada Tax Commission had been granted policy and procedure powers over the casino industry. Fifteen major resorts amounted to a total investment in Las Vegas of more than $100 million, and already accounted for more than half of the entire state's gaming revenues. Yet, the state Gaming Control Board had been in existence a mere two years. Mob money, and the jungle law of gamblers and hoods, ruled the day. Nowhere was this more evident than in the situation of the last two hotels to be built on the Strip in the Grifty Fifties: the Tropicana and the Stardust.

The Trop was the brainchild of "Dandy" Phil Kastel, who'd spent 25 years managing the entire Louisiana gambling scene for Frank Costello, a boss of bosses in New York, partners with Meyer Lansky and Lucky Luciano. Kastel enlisted Ben Jaffe, of the Miami Fontainebleau Hotel, to invest and front for him in the Tropicana. Jaffe, who held an interest in the recently completed Riviera, hired the same Miami construction company to build the Trop. On opening night in April 1957, Jaffe had infused more than $7 million, plus another $7 million of other investors' capital (to Kastel's $300,000); licensing had been held up for a year, until Kastel's name was dropped from the application.

The $15 million, 300-room, Y-shaped Tropicana Hotel quickly earned the nickname, "Tiffany of the Strip." Designed as the ultimate resort hotel, like the Riviera, the Trop oozed elegance in a Havana Modern style. Its 60-foot tulip-shaped fountain in the center of a 110-foot-diameter pool stood as a landmark at the south end of the Strip for 20 years. The mahogany-paneled casino was tastefully

(opposite) The famous 4,000-square-foot leaded stained-glass dome ceiling at the Tropicana.

screened from the lobby by ornamental horticulture, and "Peacock Alleys" from the front desk to the rooms actually bypassed the gaming tables. The Celebrity Gourmet Room was enclosed by a 150-foot curved glass wall, highlighted by colorful dancing fountains and massive Czech chandeliers.

The genteel calm, however, was shattered a month later, when Frank Costello was wounded in an attempted hit in New York and detectives found a slip of paper in his pocket with a tidy sum of figures, which turned out to be the gross profits from the Trop's first three and a half weeks of operation. Out went Kastel as *persona non grata* and in came J. Kell Houssels, a powerful downtown juiceman. Houssels had earned his stake at a blackjack table in Ely, Nevada, in the 1920s. He then moved to Las Vegas just after gambling was legalized and spent 25 years as an owner of the Las Vegas Club, El Cortez, and Showboat before taking on the Trop. He managed the hotel for 10 years, adding 300 rooms, an 18-hole golf course and country club across Tropicana Avenue, and the famous Parisian floor show "Folies Bergere."

The Trop changed hands several times in the 1970s, until heiress Mitzi Stauffer Briggs bought it. She expanded the theater, brought back the "Folies," and built the $25-million, 600-room Tiffany (now Paradise) Tower, which finally doubled the size of the hotel (removing the landmark fountain in the process). However, organized-crime trouble returned a year later, when a conversation among entertainment director Joe Agosto, casino executive Carl Thomas, and Kansas City don Nick Civella was recorded, in which the three discussed duping Briggs and skimming casino cash. (Later, Thomas and Agosto turned state's evidence; their testimony helped convict many Midwestern capos, which finally broke the grip of the Chicago mob on Las Vegas.)

Ramada acquired the Trop in 1979, and immediately redesigned the casino in art nouveau style, adding the breathtaking $1 million, 4,000-square-foot leaded-glass dome and 28-color carpeting. They built a stunning five-acre water park and the 22-story, 806-room Island Tower. Today, the Tropicana is somewhat overshadowed in the glitz department by its neighbors at the intersection of Tropicana Avenue and the Strip, all built since 1990. It calls itself the "Island of Las Vegas" and it is: an island of '50s history, low-rise motel rooms, and original sin. *Tropicana, 3801 Las Vegas Boulevard South, (702) 739-2222/(800) 468-9494.*

■ THE STARDUST

Eighth, last, and largest hotel to go up on the Strip in the 1950s, the Stardust also possesses perhaps the most outrageous and scandal-scarred history of them all. It all began in the feverish mind of Tony Cornero as a Bugsy Siegel–style vision: to build the biggest resort hotel in the world. Cornero had already survived an incredibly checkered career as a bootlegger, hijacker, rum-runner, freelance spy, gambling-boat and freighter operator, smuggler, and legitimate Las Vegas businessman. In 1955, he launched his hotel company with $10,000 cash and two million shares of privately printed "stock" that he neglected to mention to the Securities and Exchange Commission. He personally sold his stock to speculators and gamblers, mostly in L.A., and bought 36 acres of land right next door to the Royal Nevada (which opened and closed in 1955). He drew up grandiose blueprints and arranged for contractors, labor, and building supplies. The Stardust began to rise from the desert in that boom-and-bust spring of 1955 across the Strip from the Desert Inn.

But by this time, Cornero was so notorious for his unusual business practices that the governor of Nevada himself, Charles Russell, intervened to prevent him from receiving a gaming license. The SEC, too, began insisting that he subscribe to standard stock-registration procedures. As these and other pressures mounted,

The Stardust in the late 1950s, after swallowing whole the Royal Nevada next door.

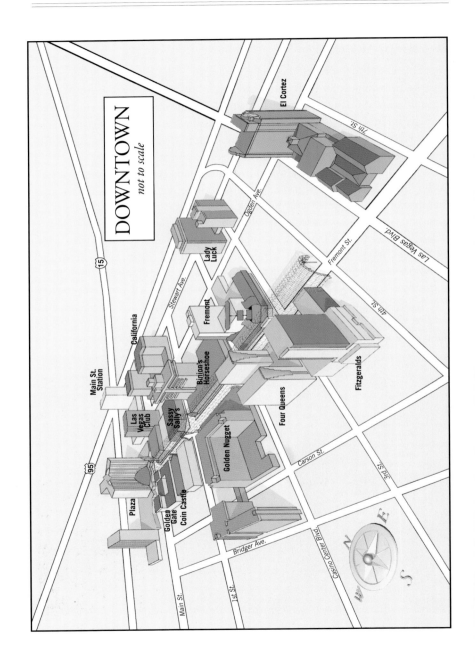

DOWNTOWN
not to scale

Tony Cornero, like Bugsy, began to unravel. By summer 1955, 3,000 investors had contributed $6 million—some of which was quickly dropping into the lock boxes behind the Desert Inn crap tables. The DI's Moe Dalitz and his Cleveland boys, too, were holding a grudge against Cornero, for building his monstrosity directly across from them. Ironically, Cornero suffered a massive coronary the night of July 31, 1955, shooting dice at the DI! But even death didn't end his troubles.

SEC auditors pieced together the financial puzzle of Stardust, Inc., and found $4 million owed to contractors and suppliers, and no cash in the till. The hotel was half finished. The investors were all finished. To the rescue rode John "Jake the Barber" Factor, cosmetics magnate Max Factor's brother and, according to *Green Felt Jungle,* an L.A. realtor, self-proclaimed philanthropist, stock-swindler par excellence, and crony of Al Capone. Factor promised to pay off the 3,000 investors at 34 cents on the dollar, wrote checks for more than $4 million to cover construction debts, and poured another $6 million into completing the behemoth.

When it finally opened in July 1958, the Stardust claimed 1,032 hotel rooms (largest in the world), a 16,500-square-foot casino (largest in Nevada), 105-foot swimming pool and 20,000-square-foot casino (both largest in Nevada), and a landmark electric sign (largest in the world). The sprawling Stardust also boasted "Horseman's Park," a rodeo arena with stables and bleachers, the first casino dealer school, and the "Lido de Paris" appearing in the town's largest dinner theater on one of the biggest and most high-tech stages in the world. Donn Arden, the Desert Inn's entertainment director, was hired to import the famous French nude floor show, which necessitated McCarran Airport to set up a special customs facility to process the performers, wardrobes, and equipment. The show opened the same day as the hotel, and played there for 33 years; more than 25 million people saw "Lido" at the Stardust.

Factor was widely believed to be a front for the Chicago organization, bossed by the notorious Tony Accardo. Moe Dalitz's group leased and operated the gigantic casino for 10 years, then sold it to Parvin-Dohrmann Corporation, which also had a bad rep with the SEC for stock manipulation. In 1968, when Howard Hughes cast his wanton gaze toward the Stardust, he already owned five casinos, and the Stardust's sale to Hughes was enjoined by the Justice Department as monopolistic. That same year, Ad Art of L.A. installed the brilliant Stardust sign: 188 feet high, with each letter between 18 and 22 feet tall and the name nearly 100 feet across; 286 multicolored stars; and 27 different lighting sequences. When the "Lido" closed in early 1991, the sign was redone. The venerable Stardust lettering was replaced with boring, boxy typography. Even with the changes, the Stardust sign continues to be to the Strip what Vegas Vic is to downtown: one of Las Vegas's most enduring and representative images.

Allen Glick's Argent Corp. purchased the Stardust in 1974 from Recrion, an offspring of Parvin-Dohrmann, as part of a four-hotel deal using $70 million in Teamsters Pension Fund loans arranged by fixer Allen Dorfman. Glick, a Vietnam vet, graduated from Ohio State and went on to law school, and was a member of the Pennsylvania and California bars. He was all of 34 years old when he fronted the Recrion-Argent deal, which made him the second largest casino owner in Las Vegas. But a massive skimming operation on his properties was uncovered by the audit division of the Gaming Control Board. This revealed the Chicago-Midwest underworld's continuing interest in Argent's hotels, and insured that Glick's "era" in Las Vegas was short-lived. His license was suspended in 1979, and he later turned state's evidence to avoid prosecution.

The Stardust (and Fremont) were soon sold to Al Sachs of Trans-Sterling Corporation. Sachs had managed the Sundance Hotel (now Fitzgeralds) downtown, which was owned by Moe Dalitz. But the Stardust's troubles still were not over. In 1983, another raid exposed a phony fill-slip skim scheme perpetrated by four executives. Finally, in 1985, the Stardust was sold to the highly reputable Boyd Corporation, where it remains, along with Sam's Town on Boulder Highway, the Fremont, California, and Main Street Station downtown, and the Eldorado and Joker's Wild in Henderson. Through the years, the Stardust has expanded twice: in 1965, it added a 9-story, 176-room tower; and in 1992, a 32-story, 1,500-room addition gave the hotel a respectable 2,300 rooms. Today, the Stardust is known for its gorgeous race and sports book (complete with a "Handicappers Library"), popular low-limit poker room, and sizzling extravaganza, "Enter the Night." *Stardust, 3000 Las Vegas Boulevard South, (702) 732-6111/(800) 634-6757.*

■ THE ALADDIN

The Aladdin started out as the Tally-Ho in 1963, a large motel that billed itself as the first non-gaming resort on the Strip. It was an idea whose time had not yet arrived, and it folded after eight months. When it reopened in 1964, it was called the King's Crown, which lasted six months. Finally, Milton Prell, the congenial L.A. investor who sold the Sahara to Del Webb a few years before, bought the property for $16 million in the fall of 1965. He added a casino, 500-seat show-room, lounge, and gourmet restaurant, and completely refurbished the rooms. Prell succeeded in completing the new Aladdin in a miraculous three months, in order to open on New Year's Day 1966. Aladdin's Magic Lamp—15 stories high, 40,000 lightbulbs, $750,000—fronted the new Strip resort. Elvis and Priscilla were married in Prell's private suite in 1967.

Prell suffered a stroke not long after the famous wedding, and the glamour times of the Aladdin started to fade. It was bought in 1968 by the Parvin-Dohrmann group, which also owned the Stardust and Fremont. Continuing to decline, the Aladdin was sold to St. Louis investors in 1972 for a fire-sale $5 million. In 1974, the Aladdin was investigated by both state and federal regulators for its alleged role as an "R&R center for the underworld." And although a major expansion in 1976 added the 10,000-seat Theatre for the Performing Arts and a 20-story highrise, two years later hotel executives were convicted of conspiring to allow hidden interests to profit from the property. In March 1979, the Gaming Control Board closed the Aladdin.

A year later, Wayne Newton and Ed Torres reopened it; the partnership failed, and Newton sold out quickly. Further legal and financial troubles plagued the hotel, which finally went bankrupt in 1984. In October 1985, Ginja Yasudi bought the Aladdin for $51.5 million in cash, but he went bankrupt in 1989. A court-appointed receiver held the place together with super glue and baling wire until 1995, when a local real estate magnate, Jack Sommer, bought the Aladdin for $80 million.

In May 1996, Sommer announced ambitious plans to expand the aging hotel, which will add 1,500 rooms, a 250-room timeshare tower, a mall, as well as a new 400-room hotel-casino, at a total cost of $600 million. The project is expected to be completed in early 1999—if the financing can be lined up, of course. *Aladdin, 3667 Las Vegas Boulevard South, (702) 736-0111/(800) 634-3424.*

■ CAESARS PALACE

Of all the hotels in the world, Las Vegas's Caesars Palace is one of—if not *the*—most famous. And rightly so. Simply put, the fact that Caesars has so much to recommend it as an international tourist attraction and destination might explain why Steve Wynn felt he had to spend $650 million to put a hotel next door.

You can wander for 30 minutes from one end of the $100 million Forum Shops at Caesars, one of the most exclusive malls in the country, to the far end of the casino at the spiral staircase up to Palace Court, one of the most expensive restaurants in town. A 20-foot statue of Caesar, hailing a cab, fronts the driveway to the main entrance. Beyond, 18 fountains spew 35-foot-high columns of water, and 50-foot-tall Italian cypresses guard the long approach to the front doors. A four-faced and eight-armed Brahma rests nearby, a replica of one of Thailand's most popular shrines. The original was cast in 1958 to ward off bad luck after various disasters had befallen the Erawan Hotel in Bangkok during construction. Las Vegas's four-ton Brahma—cast in bronze, plated in gold—was presented as a gift to Caesars Palace in 1984 by a Thai tycoon to promote good fortune and prosperity for the hotel and its guests.

Two people movers, one at the north end of the property near the Mirage, the other at the south end near the corner of the Strip and Flamingo Avenue, propel you to your every fantasy. Stroll past Cleopatra's Barge dance lounge, and a replica of Michelangelo's *David:* 18 feet high, 9 tons, 10 months to carve, and uncircumcised—one of the greatest artistic misrepresentations in history! Make it a point to peak into the Bacchanal, Empress Court, Palace Court, and Primavera restaurants, and check out the Garden of the Gods pool area, modeled after the Pompeii baths with 8,000 inlaid tiles imported from Carrara, Italy.

Conventional history gives the credit for Caesars Palace to Jay Sarno, hotel builder and owner of the Cabana Motor Inn chain (though Ed Reid, in his book, *Grim Reapers,* a sort of sequel to *Green Felt Jungle,* reports it a little differently). The $25-million hotel received Teamsters Pension Fund financing and opened in August 1966, with 680 rooms in a crescent-shaped, 14-story tower, as well as the Bacchanal restaurant and the 1,200-seat Circus Maximus Showroom. In September 1969, the hotel was bought by Lum's Corporation, which owned a chain of 440 restaurants around the country. In 1970 the 14-story, 222-room Centurion Tower was added, along with Cleo's Barge and the Ah'so Japanese restaurant. An expansion in 1974 incorporated the 16-story, 361-room, $16-million Roman Tower, and another in 1979 added the 600-room, $47-million Olympic Tower. Behind the big two-story windows of the Olympic Tower are 10 two-story, two- to four-bedroom suites, complete with sunken tub, round beds, and giant wet bar, as enjoyed by Tom Cruise and Dustin Hoffman in *Rainman.*

Another $20 million expansion in 1985 opened the NASAesque race and sports book, with 21 video screens. A large parking structure was also built in the rear. The Forum Shops complex opened in 1992. It features a sky that changes from dawn to dusk every hour or so, the Festival Fountain of animatronic Roman statues (shows on the hour), restaurants including Spago (the best place to eat in Vegas), and more stores with Italian names than anywhere else this side of New Jersey.

In 1995, ITT Corporation, which also owns the Desert Inn, bought Caesars World, Inc., for $1.7 billion; included in the deal were Caesars Palaces in Lake Tahoe and Atlantic City. Since then, ITT has invested another billion dollars in expanding and upgrading the 32-year-old joint at center Strip: another 1,800-room tower (for a total of 3,700 rooms), three new parking garages, a near doubling of the size of the Forum Shops, a full renovation of the pool area, a completely remodeled facade, and numerous other smaller changes. The whole job is expected to be completed in 1998.

One final note: the hotel's name was the object of one of the great all-time editorial decisions over the use of an apostrophe. After critical consideration and long deliberation, the possessive apostrophe in "Caesar's" was purged because, instead of implying that the hotel belonged to a single Caesar, Jay Sarno wanted to suggest that every guest in his hotel is a Caesar, and should feel like a Roman emperor. *Caesars Palace, 3570 Las Vegas Boulevard South, (702) 731-7110/(800) 634-6661.*

■ CIRCUS CIRCUS

The success of Caesars apparently went to Jay Sarno's head. In 1968, two years after his Palace coup, Sarno opened Circus Circus across from the Riviera. Unlike the Tally-Ho, the hotel without a casino that became the Aladdin, Circus Circus was a casino without a hotel. It did have elephants, acrobats, clowns, trapeze and high-wire performers, popcorn and peanuts—and an admissions charge. No lie. Unless you had a local ID, you had to pay to get in to gamble. What's more, it was targeted toward high rollers. Needless to say, Circus Circus struggled for several years. And though Sarno did manage to build a 15-story, 400-room tower in 1972, in 1974 he sold out to William Bennett, an Arizona furniture mogul and Del Webb casino executive. Bennett's arrival triggered Circus's meteoric rise to the top of Las Vegas's profitable properties.

One year after Bennett took charge, a 15-story, 395-room tower was added. In

1979, Circus acquired Slots-A-Fun next door and added its 421-space RV park in back. In 1980 it added five three-story motel buildings and a year later acquired the Silver City across the Strip. In 1983, Bennett took the company public. Three years later the 29-story Skyrise Tower was added. Along the way, Circus evolved into the best managed and most profitable casino corporation in the country and parlayed its profits into eight additional properties in Nevada: Excalibur, Luxor, Slots-A-Fun, and Silver City in Las Vegas; Circus Circus and Silver Legacy in Reno; and Colorado Belle and Edgewater in Laughlin. Currently, Circus Circus Enterprises is building Paradise, a 3,600-room megaresort on the site of the old Hacienda.

Today, Las Vegas's Circus Circus runs at nearly 100 percent occupancy year-round, and over 100 percent during high seasons (by reselling rooms cancelled past refund time). It has been called the K-mart of casinos. It features low table limits, nearly 3,000 slot machines, the cheapest buffets in town (which explains why four million buffet meals are served here every year, making it the busiest restaurant in the world), and a midway for the kids, with every ball-rolling, hoop-ringing, clown-drenching, camel-chasing, milkcan-drowning, and rubber-chicken-propelling carnie come-on known to man. Circus acts are presented continually throughout the day and evening on the midway.

Grand Slam Canyon, a five-acre amusement park inside the big pink dome behind Circus Circus, opened in August 1993. It features the world's largest indoor roller coaster, a flume ride, some kiddie attractions, and an arcade. In early 1997, another 1,000-room tower was added onto Circus Circus, giving it nearly 3,800 rooms and making it the fourth largest hotel in Las Vegas (and therefore the fifth largest hotel in the world). In addition to the tower, a new hotel lobby, retail area, and two restaurants were opened. *Circus Circus, 2880 Las Vegas Boulevard South, (702) 734-0410/(800) 634-3450.*

■ THE INTERNATIONAL/LAS VEGAS HILTON

Kirk Kerkorian was born in 1917 in California's San Joaquin Valley, the fourth of four children of an Armenian farmer and landowner. But when Kirk was five years old, his father went broke and moved the family to teeming Los Angeles. Kirk grew up by his wits, selling newspapers, caddying, boxing in amateur matches, and doing a stint in the Civilian Conservation Corps. His first entrepreneurial venture was steam-cleaning engines for used-car dealers. Though the steam-cleaning failed, he succeeded in the used-car market, which revealed the keen talent that would eventually elevate Kerkorian's bankroll to a dozen digits: horse trading. At another job, working for an oil-burner company, a fellow employee who was a private pilot introduced him to what would become his second great skill: flying. Kerkorian quickly earned his private pilot's wings, became a flight instructor in the early 1940s, and then went to work for the British Royal Air Force, ferrying airplanes from their North American manufacturers to England for the war effort.

After the war, he went into business buying and selling military surplus aircraft. In 1947, he bought the Los Angeles Air Service, one of a number of charter flying companies that offered non-scheduled flights around the country for a fraction of the fares charged by the major airlines. It was then he began flying charters to Las Vegas—and behaving like a high roller at the blackjack and crap tables. In *Kirk Kerkorian, An American Success Story,* Dial Torgenson describes the fierce competition and hand-to-mouth existence of the 150 post-war "non-sked" airlines as "part jungle and part comic-strip adventure." Kerkorian's was one of only a few that were successful, thanks to the supplementation of his uncertain income from the air-charter business with his shrewd used-airplane dealings. In 1962, Los Angeles Air Service became the first non-sked to put a jet, a DC-8, into operation. By then, the company had been renamed Trans-International Airlines. In the mid-1960s, Kerkorian sold TIA to

(below) Hughes's Landmark and Kerkorian's International opened during the same weekend in 1969.

Studebaker, and later bought it back at a profit. He then sponsored a public stock offering in the company, which he merged with TransAmerica Corporation. He leveraged that into a majority share of Western Airlines. By then Kerkorian was worth hundreds of millions, and the deals kept coming his way. In one, for example, he bought property on the Las Vegas Strip for less than a million dollars and leased it to Jay Sarno for Caesars Palace. After collecting $4 million in rent in Caesars' first two years, Kerkorian sold it to the owners for another $5 million.

In 1967, he bought 82 acres on Paradise Road, a few blocks east of the Strip, next to the Convention Center, for a new pet project: building the International, largest hotel in Las Vegas. That same year, he also bought the Flamingo, which he used as a "hotel school" to train the International's staff. The sale of the Flamingo to Kerkorian finally eliminated the 20-year, behind-the-scenes involvement of the eastern underworld in the house that Bugsy built.

The International was big news in Las Vegas. It was several hundred rooms larger than the Stardust, which had been the biggest for 12 years. It was designed as a single unit, as opposed to the tacked-on towers and leap-frogging cubes of rooms of the other Strip properties. All $60 million of the construction costs were borne by Kerkorian himself. The hotel opened on July 3, 1969, with Barbra Streisand appearing in the 2,000-seat theater, a packed 30,000-square-foot casino (largest in Las Vegas), a Benihana of Tokyo hibachi restaurant, and a $25 million yearly payroll for 3,000 employees.

Elvis Presley made his great Las Vegas comeback at the International during opening month (and performed there exclusively, logging 837 sold-out shows, until his death in 1977). But Kerkorian quickly left all the hotel ballyhoo behind. As soon as it was up and running, the financier was off on a new venture: buying Metro-Goldwyn-Mayer Studios. But while Kerkorian was distracted by Hollywood, his emerging Las Vegas empire was caught short by unforeseen events. The recession of the early 1970s was gaining steam and Vegas hotels went into a slump. In addition, the SEC disallowed a public stock offering in the International, which would have paid off the hotel's debt in full. Kerkorian was unable (or unwilling) to produce old financial records from the Flamingo, which the feds needed to bolster its skimming case against past owners, particularly Meyer Lansky. Thus deprived of expected revenues, in 1970 Kerkorian was forced to sell part of the International to Hilton for $21.4 million, less than half of what the stock was worth.

(top) The Golden Nugget, downtown's original carpet joint. (bottom) Augustus Caesar hails a cab.

One year later, he received another $31 million for the Flamingo and the rest of the International, which had been renamed the Las Vegas Hilton. Then in 1973, a new 1,500-room wing was added, giving the Hilton more than 3,000 rooms and making it one of the largest hotels in the world. It remained the largest in Las Vegas for 16 years, until the Flamingo Hilton surpassed it, with 3,500 rooms, in March 1990.

Today, the Hilton is known for its Superbook, the first giant race and sports book to open in a casino (in 1985), its nine restaurants, and Andrew Lloyd Webber's "Starlight Express" in the showroom. In the summer of 1997, the Hilton, in partnership with Paramount, opened "Star Trek: The Experience." The 50,000-square-foot attraction consists of a 22-minute experience in which participants assume the roles of "Star Trek" characters, interact with video and virtual on the bridge command center, and are forced to escape in a motion-simulation shuttle. The Experience will also include the Cardassian Restaurant, Starfleet Lounge, a trekkie souvenir shop, and a 20,000-square-foot "Star Trek"–themed casino. *Las Vegas Hilton, 3000 Paradise Road; (702) 732-5111/(800) 732-7117.*

■ BALLY'S

But Kirk Kerkorian wasn't through with Las Vegas. Not by a long shot. As controlling stockholder of MGM Studios, only a year after selling his two hotels he unveiled company plans to build a Las Vegas hotel even larger than the Hilton. The (old) MGM Grand Hotel was named after the 1932 movie of the same name, and designed to spotlight great movie events, personalities, and legends. The property, on the corner of Flamingo Avenue and the Strip, was originally occupied by the Bonanza Hotel, a $2.5-million, 160-room sawdust joint that, facing the Dunes, the Flamingo, and Caesars Palace, lasted surprisingly long—three months. Closed for a year, it was bought, reopened to marginal success, then closed again. Through a series of complicated legal, corporate, real estate, and financial maneuvers involving MGM stock, Kerkorian's personal portfolio, and even some money from the still-ubiquitous Moe Dalitz, MGM Studios acquired the Bonanza and some adjacent property in 1971. They closed the casino, managed the hotel as a training facility, and began construction in June 1972 on the mammoth, L-shaped, 2,100-room, 26-story, 4,500-employee, $120-million Grand Hotel. Eighteen months later, in December 1973, it opened—with the world's largest casino, a 2,200-seat jai alai fronton, and the third largest shopping mall in the state.

BLACKJACK UNDER THE BIG TOP

*T*he Circus Circus is what the whole hep world would be doing on Saturday night if the Nazis had won the war. This is the Sixth Reich. The ground floor is full of gambling tables, like all the other casinos . . . but the place is about four stories high, in the style of a circus tent, and all manner of strange County Fair/Polish Carnival madness is going on up in this space. Right above the gambling tables the Forty Flying Carazito Brothers are doing a high-wire trapeze act, along with four muzzled Wolverines and the Six Nymphet Sisters from San Diego. . . . So you're down on the main floor playing blackjack, and the stakes are getting high, when suddenly you chance to look up, and there, right smack above your head is a half-naked fourteen-year-old girl being chased through the air by a snarling wolverine, which is suddenly locked in a death battle with two silver-painted Polacks who come swinging down from opposite balconies and meet in mid-air on the wolverine's neck. Both Polacks seize the animal as they fall straight down toward the crap tables—but they bounce off the net; they separate and spring back up toward the roof in three different directions, and just as they're about to fall again they are grabbed out of the air by three Korean Kittens and trapezed off to one of the balconies.

This madness goes on and on, but nobody seems to notice.

—Hunter S. Thompson, *Fear and Loathing in Las Vegas,* 1971

To finance hotel construction, Kerkorian's MGM Board of Directors divested itself of almost all the studio's production facilities and employees, to the vociferous objections of some stockholders. But once again, Kerkorian's gamble paid off: in 1974, MGM earned a record $29 million in profits, $22 million of which were from the Grand.

In September 1980, the Grand added a second, 800-room wing, at the south end of its parking lot. On November 21, 1980, the worst disaster ever to strike a Las Vegas hotel occurred at the Grand, when fire erupted in one of the kitchens. Before it was brought under control, the whole main wing had been engulfed by flames or smoke. Seven hundred people were injured. Eighty-four died. Refurbished, the Grand opened again nine months later, in July 1981.

In 1985, Bally Corporation bought the hotel for $550 million, $110 million of which was earmarked for settling the unresolved lawsuits from the fire. Today,

At New York–New York (top), Lady Liberty welcomes the huddled masses—to her casino. (photo by Kerrick James) A centurion stands guard at Caesars Palace. (bottom)

Bally's is still big, the tenth largest hotel in Las Vegas. It has great food in all its restaurants and is especially known for the Sterling Sunday Brunch, best in town. It also features a newly renovated mall on the lower level and a monorail that connects it to the MGM Grand, a mile south.

But Kerkorian wasn't through with Las Vegas. Not by a long shot. In 1988, he bought the Sands and the Desert Inn, then sold both a few years later, doubling his money. In 1990, he bought and quickly closed the Marina Hotel, which is now incorporated into the 5,005-room MGM Grand (see "MGM Grand," page 125).

In late 1996, Hilton Hotels, with its new management team, absorbed Bally's Corp. in a friendly takeover for roughly $3 billion. Both Bally's hotel-casinos (in Las Vegas and Atlantic City) have retained their names for brand identification and loyalty, though the revenues go directly to Hilton's bottom line, which is threatening to surpass both Circus Circus's and ITT's as the largest in the casino industry. *Bally's, 3645 Las Vegas Boulevard South; (702) 739-4111/(800) 634-3434.*

■ AND THE HOTELS JUST KEPT ON COMING

In 1970, the Royal Las Vegas (now the Royal) opened on Convention Center Drive near the corner of the Strip with 238 rooms, same as it has today. A year later, Sam Boyd built downtown's largest (at that time) hotel, the $20-million, 500-room, 22-story Union Plaza, at 1 Main Street—site of the 1905 railroad auction where modern Las Vegas was born. Appropriately, the back of the building overlooks the Union Pacific yards, while the front stares right down the throat of Glitter Gulch. The Union Plaza opened the first race and sports book in a Las Vegas casino in 1975. A 26-story, 526-room tower was added to the Union Plaza in June 1983. Jackie Gaughan, longtime downtown owner, bought the hotel in 1990 and changed the name, appropriately enough, to the **Plaza**. *Plaza, 1 Main Street, (702) 386-2110/(800) 634-6575.*

In 1972, Holiday Inn came to town, in the form of the 1,000-room Holiday Hotel, next door to the Flamingo. A 35-story, 734-room tower was completed in December 1989, making it the largest Holiday Inn in the world. In 1990, a major facelift transformed the Holiday into a 450-foot-long Mississippi riverboat. Its 80-foot-diameter paddlewheel, 85-foot-tall stacks, and gangways, crow's nest, and pilot room earned the hotel the nickname, "Ship on the Strip," one of several

(following pages) The Luxor is a sort of ancient palace of the future. (photo by Kerrick James)

riverboat casinos floating in a sea of Nevada sand. The Holiday's name changed in 1992 to **Harrah's**; Harrah's is owned by Promus Corporation, which owns the most casinos in the country. In 1997, Harrah's completed another expansion and renovation, to the tune of $150 million. It's adding a 35-story, 700-room tower and retail and restaurant space; it's expanding the casino; and it's replacing the Ship on the Strip hoopla with a more elegant (read "generic") facade.

In 1975, the **Continental Hotel** opened, on the corner of Flamingo Avenue and Paradise Road. It has expanded once, to its present 400 rooms. In 1996, the Continental was sold to a Las Vegas cataloguer of 1950s nostalgia merchandise; at press time, the new owners were remodeling and expanding the hotel-casino, which they renamed Back to the '50s. *Continental Hotel, 4100 Paradise Road, (702) 737-5555/(800) 634-6641.*

Also in 1975, the Boyd Group opened the $10 million, 12-story, 325-room **California Hotel** downtown on Ogden Street. Like Benny Binion, Jackie Gaughan, Moe Dalitz, and J. Kell Houssels, Sam Boyd was a beloved pioneer of the Las Vegas gambling industry. He started out as a carnie, then worked at bingo clubs in southern California in the 1930s. He dealt cards and craps on the offshore gambling boats, then moved to Hawaii in 1934 as a bingo-parlor operator. In 1940, he relocated to Las Vegas and, starting with bingo parlors downtown, worked his way up to an executive position at the Sahara, and later the Mint. He went on to build the Union Plaza in 1971, and formed the Boyd Group (today Boyd Corporation), chaired by his son Bill, in 1975. The California started out with a So.-Cal. theme—Long Beach Lounge, Balboa Bay Bar, and Santa Barbara Buffeteria—but now attracts a predominantly Hawaiian clientele. *California, 12 East Ogden Avenue; (702) 385-1222/(800) 634-6255.* The Boyd Corp. subsequently opened Sam's Town in 1979, Sam's Town Laughlin (now Gold River) in 1984, acquired the Fremont and Stardust in 1985, and reopened **Main Street Station** across the street from the California in 1996. Sam Boyd passed away in January 1993. *Main Street Station, 200 North Main Street; (702) 387-1896/(800) 465-0711.*

The **Maxim Hotel** opened in 1977 with 400 rooms; another 400 were added in 1980. The Maxim is a popular off-Strip hotel with cheap rooms and continuous promotions. *Maxim, 160 East Flamingo Road; (702) 731-4300/(800) 634-6987.*

Also in 1977, the **Golden Nugget** finally became a hotel. After nearly 30 years as one of downtown's major casinos, the Nugget, under the direction of Steve Wynn, opened an $18 million, 579-room tower. Steve Wynn first visited Las

Vegas in 1952 at the age of 10 with his father, an East Coast bingo operator and compulsive gambler. The younger Wynn graduated from University of Pennsylvania in 1963 a few months after his father's death, and took over the Baltimore bingo parlor. In 1967, he moved to Las Vegas and was quickly taken under wing by E. Parry Thomas, most influential banker in town. Wynn bought and sold Strip real estate and a liquor distributorship, then acquired 100,000 shares of Golden Nugget stock in 1972. Within a year, at the age of 31, he controlled the Golden Nugget. In 1978, he built the Golden Nugget in Atlantic City, which he sold in 1987. Two highrise extensions in the 1980s gave the Las Vegas Nugget nearly 2,000 rooms, largest in downtown, with two full blocks of rooms, plus a quarter-block-long parking structure. Today, Wynn is Las Vegas's top celebrity casino owner, a position he has solidified since opening the monumental Mirage in 1989 and Treasure Island in 1993, with plans to open the billion-dollar Bellagio in 1998. *Golden Nugget, 129 Fremont Street; (702) 385-7111/(800) 634-3454.*

The ranks of Las Vegas hotels were greatly increased in 1979. **Sam's Town** opened out on Boulder Highway with 200 rooms. It didn't expand till 1994, when it burst its seams with a $100 million, 450-room, glass-roofed addition, complete with live trees, rock waterfall, and a laser-and-dancing-waters show featuring an animatronic wolf. The Sam's Town atrium is a Las Vegas must-see attraction. *Sam's Town, 5111 Boulder Highway; (702) 456-7777/(800) 634-6371.*

Also in 1979, the **Barbary Coast** grafted itself onto the famous corner of Flamingo and the Strip, between the Flamingo and Bally's. It opened with a classy casino and 150 rooms; another 50 rooms were added in 1983, when the fourth floor of the parking garage was turned into the first floor of hotel rooms. The Barbary Coast is best known for Michael's, a gourmet restaurant that many consider the best in town and some consider the best in the country. *Barbary Coast, 3595 Las Vegas Boulevard South; (702) 737-7111/(800) 634-6755.*

On the other side of the Flamingo, the Flamingo Capri Hotel became the **Imperial Palace** in 1979. Over the years, the IP has undergone typically major expansions; the latest, a $50 million, 19-story, 547-room tower completed in December 1988, raised the count to 2,700 rooms (twelfth largest hotel in the world), and filled all the available space on the 12-acre site. The IP boasts Las Vegas's only antique car collection, the hottest cocktail uniforms in town, and the venerable "Legends in Concert" superstar impersonator show. *Imperial Palace, 3535 Las Vegas Boulevard South; (702) 731-3311/(800) 634-6441.*

In 1980, the 33-story, 655-room Sundance Hotel opened downtown. It was built by Moe Dalitz, still wheeling and dealing at 84 years young! The hotel was managed by Al Sachs for a few years, and then Jackie Gaughan for another few, until the Gaming Commission finally forced Moe out of the Nevada casino business for good. In late 1986, a group of investors who'd opened Reno's Fitzgeralds Hotel in 1984 assumed the court-appointed supervisorship of the Sundance. They purchased the hotel in November 1987 and changed the name to **Fitzgeralds.** This 400-foot-high hotel was Nevada's highest skyscraper for nearly 15 years, till 1994 when the Stratosphere Tower overtook it on its way to 1,149 feet. *Fitzgeralds, 301 Fremont Street; (702) 388-2400/(800) 274-5825.*

Also in 1980, like the Golden Nugget before it, the **Las Vegas Club** went from a venerable casino dating back to the earliest days of legalized gambling to a downtown hotel, by adding its 224-room tower. In 1996, the Las Vegas Club opened a new 188-room tower and casino addition, complete wiht a bona fide hotel lobby and two new restaurants. The Las Vegas Club boasts the most liberal blackjack rules in the world; hype aside, it does have the most liberal multi-deck blackjack game *in town. Las Vegas Club, 18 Fremont Street, (702) 385-1664/(800) 634-6532.*

The **Lady Luck** also became a hotel, with 112 rooms, in 1983. It had started out as a tiny slot joint in 1964, with 18 machines and a hot-dog stand. The east tower, completed in December 1986, and the west tower in July 1989, have given the Lady a total of 700 rooms. The LL is famous for its free foot-long hot dog and its trio of prime rib meal-deal cuts in the coffeeshop, which have been judged by the *Las Vegas Advisor* as the best of 58 prime rib deals in town. *Lady Luck, 206 North Third Street; (702) 477-3000/(800) 523-9582.*

Also in 1983, the **Four Queens** expanded into a major downtown presence. It opened in 1965, and was named for the owner's four daughters. Eighteen years later, the 18-story, 400-room tower was added. *Four Queens, 202 Fremont Street; (702) 385-4011/(800) 634-6045.*

In 1984, the 500-room **Alexis Park** opened, and this casino-less hotel, near the corner of Harmon and Paradise, seems to be an idea whose time has finally come. The 500 suites range in size from 475 to 1,250 square feet, the smallest a one-bedroom, the largest a two-story, two-bedroom suite with a loft. *375 East Harmon Avenue; (702) 796-3300/(800) 582-2228.*

Also in 1984, the 350-room Royal Americana, on Convention Center Drive next to the Royal Las Vegas, removed a few hundred rooms and became the Paddlewheel, owned by Horn and Hardart, of New York City "automat" coffeeshop fame. The Paddlewheel closed in 1992, and was purchased by Debbie Reynolds and her husband. It's now called **Debbie Reynolds Hollywood Hotel Casino and Movie Museum**. Though the casino closed in 1995 and Debbie sold the troubled hotel to an Arizona timeshare company in 1996, she still appears nightly in her own showroom and her priceless collection of Hollywood movie memorabilia is on display in a stunning museum. *Debbie Reynolds Hollywood Hotel Casino, 305 Convention Center Drive; (702) 734-0711/(800) 633-1777.*

In 1986, Michael Gaughan, son of Las Vegas pioneer Jackie, opened his second "Coast" hotel, the **Gold Coast**, just west of his Barbary Coast on Flamingo across Interstate 15. Starting with 150 rooms, the Gold Coast expanded in late 1987 with another 150 rooms, and again in 1990 with a 10-story, 400-room tower. The Gold Coast has a big bingo parlor, an even bigger bowling alley, great meal deals in the restaurants, and the most popular slot club in town. *Gold Coast, 4000 West Flamingo Road; (702) 367-7111/(800) 331-5334.*

In 1988, the 166-room Shenandoah Hotel, on East Flamingo between the Barbary Coast and the Maxim, was purchased by Hotel Investors of Nevada, Inc., and renamed **Bourbon Street**. Bourbon Street was sold for a bargain-basement $7.8 million to a southern California developer in 1996; at press time, the casino is closed, though the 180 rooms are available for rent. *Bourbon Street, 120 East Flamingo Road; (702) 737-7200/(800) 634-6956.* The Holiday Inn South, across from the Aladdin, was also sold and renamed the Boardwalk; in 1995, the Boardwalk went back into partnership with Holiday Inn. In early 1996, the **Holiday Inn Boardwalk**, taking advantage of all the megaresorts growing up around it, completed an $80 million expansion, which added 400 hotel rooms, a parking garage, a showroom, and a snack bar, and doubled the size of the casino. *Holiday Inn Boardwalk, 3750 Las Vegas Boulevard South; (702) 735-2400/(800) HOLIDAY.* **Arizona Charlie's**, on the west side at Decatur and Charleston, opened with 100 rooms, and has expanded to 268 rooms. *Arizona Charlie's, 740 South Decatur Boulevard; (702) 258-5200/(800) 342-2695.* In July 1989, the 322-room **San Remo Hotel** opened where the Polynesian Hotel had been, next to the Trop on East Tropicana. The San Remo immediately constructed another 400-room tower. *San Remo Hotel, 115 East Tropicana Avenue; (702) 739-9000/(800) 522-7366.*

■ THE MIRAGE

The Mirage picks up four months after the San Remo and 16 years after the (old) MGM Grand (now Bally's) left off. This $650-million, three-wing, 29-story, 3,049-room megaresort was the first Strip hotel to be built from scratch between 1973 and 1989 and officially inaugurated a hotel construction boom conservatively estimated at $12 billion (and counting). All of Las Vegas's roaring history combined perhaps hasn't made a noise louder than the one now underway. But leave it to Las Vegas to kick it off with a Mirage.

Has anybody not heard about the erupting volcano in front of the hotel? This show-stopping spectacle, with just a sidewalk between it and the Strip, takes place atop a 54-foot man-made mountain, for three minutes every half hour after dark, in which steam escapes on cue with a serpentine hiss, flames lick at the night, water in the reflecting pool begins to roil, "lava" magically flows—and pedestrian traffic grinds to a halt. A thousand palm trees shade the scene. Some people even walk inside the casino after the eruption.

The three-million-square-foot building is fronted by an atrium with a 100-foot-high glass dome sheltering a tropical rainforest. A 57-foot-long aquarium backs the front desk: 20,000 gallons of water, seven-inch acrylic walls, $1.2 million. Pygmy sharks warn credit customers against not paying off on markers. So do the white Bengali tigers, co-stars of the eye-popping "Siegfried and Roy" illusion show, displayed in a show-biz habitat on the Caesars' side. The pool area attracts some of the most beautiful swim-suited bodies in town at any given time, and connects to the "Secret Garden," which features a million-gallon saltwater captive dolphin habitat and a few of the elephants and tigers that appear nightly in "Siegfried and Roy." The hotel can accommodate 10,000 guests, including hundreds of high rollers in 260 penthouse suites. Nearly 6,000 employees make the staff larger than most towns in Nevada. And the electricity used could power a city twice the size of Carson City, the state capital.

Amazing what can be done in Las Vegas with $650 million. *Mirage, 3400 Las Vegas Boulevard South; (702) 791-7111/(800) 627-6667.*

■ THE RIO

The Rio could be the quintessential Las Vegas hotel-casino of the 1990s. It opened in January 1990 on Flamingo Avenue about a mile west of the Strip with 400 suites, a sandy beach by the pool, and a neon sign that finally, after eight years, beat out the Stardust for first place in the "Best of Las Vegas" local competition in the *Las Vegas Review-Journal.* The Rio also took first place in cocktail-waitress uniforms (see for yourself). The place took a little while to catch some wind in its sails, but since then it's been full speed ahead with no looking back.

The Rio has been in expansion mode almost continuously since 1993; two more towers have been added for a total of 1,300 suites. The casino has been expanded twice and a showroom opened, the highest-tech theater in town, with video screens that wrap around the room. The buffet is Las Vegas's most colorful, curvaceous, and cacophonous, and boasts 11 "islands" serving every kind of food from french fries to sushi to Mongolian barbecue. The other restaurants are consistently rated among the best in town. And so's the service.

But the Rio isn't resting on its laurels. In February 1997, the Rio completed another expansion, this one to the tune of $200 million. It opened a new 41-story 1,000-suite tower, along with Masquerade Village casino. The new casino is a sort of Forum Shops at Caesars meets Mardi Gras in Brazil. It combines a couple dozen upscale retail stores, five new restaurants (including Las Vegas's only seafood buffet and the Voo Doo Cafe on the 41st floor), and a "Show in the Sky" consisting of a 12-minute extravaganza (free) every two hours between 1 and 11 P.M., featuring parade floats that inch along a 950-foot track suspended from the high ceiling, full of dancers, jugglers, singers, and even casino patrons, all in Mardi Gras costumes and masks. It's a must-see. *Rio Suite, 3700 West Flamingo Road; (702) 252-7777/(800) 888-1808.*

■ EXCALIBUR

This medieval monster was the first of four megaresorts to be built near the corner of Tropicana Avenue and the Strip where the Tropicana Hotel sat in lonely splendor for more than 30 years. Excalibur, since the new MGM Grand opened across the street and since Luxor added 2,000 rooms next door, is now the third largest

hotel in town; turrets, spires, and a 265-foot-tall bell tower front four 1,000-room towers. Downstairs from the casino in the Fantasy Faire are midway games that might have been played in Sherwood Forest, along with Merlin's Magic Motion Machine, Las Vegas's original (and now somewhat primitive) motion simulator. Upstairs from the casino is the Renaissance Village, with four restaurants, including the 1,450-seat buffet (largest in town), and the Court Jester's Stage, where singers, acrobats, magicians, and jugglers entertain. Nightly, two dinner shows in the arena feature banquets where you eat with your hands and pound on the tables to root for your favorite knight. The King Arthur theme includes music, dance, jousting, magic, even fire-eating. There's a pretty big casino here too. *Excalibur, 3850 Las Vegas Boulevard South; (702) 597-7777/(800) 937-7777.*

■ LUXOR

You can't miss this hotel. The sleek bronze pyramid, standing tall and triangular in the midst of squat beige boxes, draws your eye first, and then the rest of you. It's irresistible.

Luxor opened in October 1993, the first of the three megaresorts that constituted the early '90s' Las Vegas boom. It cost Circus Circus $375 million to build and had 2,500 rooms. The exterior encompasses 13 acres of glass in the form of 39,000 windows. Inside is the largest atrium in the world: 29 million square feet of open space. The spotlight that beams through the apex packs a 40-billion-candlepower punch. The elevators, renamed "inclinators," rise at a 39-degree angle. The second floor houses the Attractions Level, with three high-tech theater presentations: two high-impact motion simulators, a large-screen high-rez video, a stunning 3-D segment, and a 70-foot-tall IMAX movie.

The casino is roomy, airy, and round. There are seven restaurants and an ice cream outlet. The bi-level state-of-the-art video arcade has games for all age groups, including a room full of air hockey and a six-car interactive road race. In late 1996 and early 1997, Luxor completed a $250 million expansion. Nearly 2,000 hotel rooms were added in "stepped" towers between the pyramid and the castle next door, making Luxor the second largest hotel in Las Vegas (third in the world) with 4,476 rooms. Also added were a 1,200-seat showroom, resort spa, three new restaurants, and a people mover to Excalibur. Circus Circus is probably done with Luxor for a year or two. *Luxor, 3900 Las Vegas Boulevard South; (702) 262-4000/(800) 288-1000.*

■ TREASURE ISLAND

The TI, built by Mirage Resorts for $450 million and opened in November 1993, is sort of an annex of the Mirage. It's right next door, connected by monorail, and continues the Mirage's luxuriant South Seas theme. Everything here is somewhat scaled down compared to next door—the rooms, the casino, the restaurants—except for the pirate show outside, which blows the volcano right off the same block.

Every night is the Fourth of July at Buccaneer Bay, Treasure Island's venue for a battle royal between pirates and the British Navy (six times nightly every 90 minutes). The HMS *Brittania* sails around the corner of one of the hotel towers to engage the *Hispaniola*. After a little back-and-forth palaver, the opposing factions get down to trading more potent blows, and the pirate-technics will singe your eyebrows.

Inside, the TI maintains the pirate theme—along with the casino amenities that Mirage resorts are famous for: highly trained personnel, generous comps, an excellent slot club (for dollar players), and attention to detail. Treasure Island also boasts in its showroom the must-see Cirque du Soleil, a circus that takes surrealism to new heights. *Treasure Island, 3300 Las Vegas Boulevard South; (702) 894-7111/(800) 944-7444.*

■ MGM GRAND

This place is about as big as a hotel-casino-entertainment complex can get and still run with any efficiency. Opened in December 1993 for a billion dollars, the MGM has 5,005 rooms (largest in the world), 171,000 square feet of casino space (so big that it's divided into three separate themed casinos), a monumental race and sports book, a 16-lane valet staging area, a 15-store mall, a mile-long monorail to Bally's, 93 elevators, a 15,000-seat arena for rock concerts and championship boxing matches, a 1,700-seat theater presenting the $40 million ultimate extravaganza "EFX," restaurants, fast-food court, game arcades, and a 33-acre amusement park on the backlot with seven major rides.

This one will be hard to top. *MGM Grand, 3799 Las Vegas Boulevard South; (702) 891-1111/(800) 929-1111.*

■ FIVE MORE IN EIGHT MONTHS

In December 1994, the 200-room **Fiesta** opened in North Las Vegas at the corner of North Rancho and Lake Mead Boulevard. It was an immediate sensation with the northwest suburbanites, thanks to its excellent video poker, trendy Southwestern and steakhouse restaurants, and cheap margaritas. The Fiesta has since added a drive-up sports-betting window with pneumatic tubes and everything. It also added the Festival Buffet, which goes the Rio's Carnival World one better. Along with a Mongolian barbecue and serving islands dishing out Chinese, Mexican, Cajun, Italian, and American, the Festival has the largest open-pit barbecue around; if it can be grilled, broiled, roasted, or barbecued, you'll find it to eat here. The Fiesta calls itself the "Royal Flush Capital of the World," and is probably the best place in town to play video poker—if you can get a machine! *Fiesta, 2400 Rancho Drive, North Las Vegas; (702) 631-7000/(800) 731-7333.*

In May 1995, the 200-room **Boomtown** opened three miles south of town at the Blue Diamond exit off Interstate 15. It's popular with truckers (big parking lots), RVers (roomiest and classiest RV park in Nevada), locals (good video poker machines and slot club), and even gold panners (there's a trough spiked with flakes where you can practice your panning technique). *Boomtown, 3333 Blue Diamond Highway; (702) 263-7777/(800) 588-7711.*

In August 1995, the 300-room **Boulder Station** opened on Boulder Highway between the Showboat and Sam's Town. Stations Casinos, owners of the highly successful Palace Station on West Sahara, simply had to duplicate the formula at Boulder Station to ensure a success. They did so, but added many nice touches, such as a high-ceilinged pit, fast-food counters outside the excellent restaurants, a big country-western dance hall, and wood and brick floors. Very classy joint. *Boulder Station, 4111 Boulder Highway; (702) 432-7777/(800) 683-7777.*

The world's first **Hard Rock Hotel-Casino** opened on the corner of Harmon Avenue and Paradise Road in March 1995. It's a small casino with a big theme: rock 'n' roll. Music, memorabilia, and custom gambling layouts abound (rock art and Grateful Dead lyrics on the blackjack and crap tables). There's a bank of "Save the Rainforest" slot machines. The staff is young, friendly, and very hip. *Hard Rock Hotel-Casino, 4455 Paradise Road; (702) 693-5000/(800) 473-7625.*

Stations Casinos opened its third locals' casino, the 200-room **Texas Station**, in July 1995 across the street from the Fiesta in North Las Vegas. This is a sprawling casino for such a small hotel and uses the same successful formula as Palace and Boulder Stations. The carpet sports Texas graphics, there's a 200-pound mirror-covered disco armadillo, and attached to the hotel is a 12-screen movie complex with 3,300 seats. Texas Station has a Coke-Pepsi thing going with Fiesta across the street, and the competition is intense in the buffet department. Texas's Market Street Buffet has a Texas chili serving island, cooked-to-order fajitas, and a root-beer-float station, plus Italian, Mexican, traditional American, and freshly wokked Chinese dishes, seafood, barbecue, pizza, and luscious desserts. *Texas Station, 2101 Texas Star Lane, North Las Vegas; (702) 631-1000/(800) 654-8888.*

■ STRATOSPHERE

Stratosphere Hotel, Tower & Casino opened in April 1996 and kicked off the mini casino boom of that year. Located on the site of the old Bob Stupak's Vegas World, Stratosphere Tower is the tallest observation tower in the United States and the ninth tallest building in the world, with the world's two highest thrill rides, 1,500 rooms, a shopping mall, a showroom and lounge, six restaurants and several fast-food outlets, and a 97,000-square-foot casino that boasts some of the best odds in Las Vegas. In March 1996, Stratosphere seemed a sure-fire winner.

At press time a year later, Stratosphere is bankrupt.

It's a long, convoluted, and fascinating story that stretches from Sydney, Australia, to Minneapolis, Minnesota, from the Las Vegas Strip to New York City's Wall Street (and you can read the whole tale in *No Limit—The Rise and Fall of Bob Stupak and Las Vegas' Stratosphere Tower* by John L. Smith; see "RECOMMENDED READING"). But basically, Stratosphere fell victim to its not-so-hot location, boom financing ($210 million worth of junk bonds), and a questionable marketing plan. The casino and hotel are still operating and the view from the tower is outstanding, but the original stock is worthless and the bankruptcy-court judge has to approve most decisions.

Meanwhile, the disappointing initial revenues from the casino prompted Stratosphere bosses to offer a better gamble than at most other casinos in town. You'll see signs all over the joint insisting that the better odds are "certified." Otherwise, high-speed double-decker elevators whisk you up to the top of the observation tower, where the 360-degree view of Las Vegas Valley and environs will take your breath away. The Top of the World restaurant makes a complete 360-degree revolution once every 80 minutes or so. The roller coaster (if it's running) and the Big Shot will take a few years off your life, but it's worth it! *Stratosphere, 2000 Las Vegas Boulevard South; (702) 380-7777/(800) 998-6937.*

■ MONTE CARLO

Next up was this gorgeous $350 million 3,000-room megaresort, built by Circus Circus, which opened in June of 1996. Modeled after the opulent Place du Casino in Monaco, the Las Vegas version of Monte Carlo replicates its fanciful arches, chandeliered domes, ornate fountains, marble floors, gas-lit promenades, and Gothic glass registration area overlooking the lush pool area. And it all took 14 months—from groundbreaking to grand opening—to put together.

Within Monte Carlo are: a beautiful casino that combines European elegance and American informality; five restaurants, a microbrewery, and a fast-food court; Circus Circus's signature high-tech arcade; a big bingo parlor upstairs; a waterpark consisting of adult and children pools, Jacuzzi, and a wave pool and "lazy river" combo; and the Lance Burton Theater, a 1,200-seat showroom featuring world-class illusionist Burton, which is modeled after European opera houses and is one of a kind in Las Vegas. *Monte Carlo, 3770 Las Vegas Boulevard South, (702) 730-7777/ (800) 311-8999.*

■ NEW YORK–NEW YORK

Andy Warhol would have been proud. Putting a Las Vegas spin on the Big Apple has created the single most monumental piece of pop art the world has ever seen. It's a caricature to be sure, a kind of superstar impersonation of New York on a Las Vegas stage, but it's done with style, affection, and incredible attention to detail.

Outside, the mini-skyline recreates a half-size Statue of Liberty and Empire State Building, along with the Chrysler, Seagrams, and CBS buildings, the New York Public Library, New Yorker Hotel, Grand Central Station, and Brooklyn Bridge, among others. A Coney Island–type roller coaster runs completely around the property.

The interior is no less realized thematically than the exterior. Everywhere you look there's a clever replica of another New York icon. Times Square is represented by a rocking pub with dueling pianos and the kind of exuberant crowd that, in New York, would consist of after-theater drinkers and tourists wandering in to ask directions to the Letterman show.

Narrow, crooked, and of course crowded reproductions of Bleecker Street, Hudson Street, Broadway, and others all frame the (Greenwich) Village Eateries area. Multi-story townhouses line the streets, complete with brownstone, fire escapes, and ivy trellises. The roller coaster rumbles overhead like an elevated commuter train.

Details as minor as the lobby phones booths are nonetheless authentic; their swinging glass doors and graffiti on the phone-book holders will make even the most jaded New Yorker misty-eyed.

In short, this is large-scale low-tech virtual reality; instead of head-mounted displays and 3D video, it's achieved with concrete and wrought iron and neon and paint. New York–New York is by far the best reproduction that's ever been seen in Las Vegas, and sets a new standard for thematic accomplishment. *New York–New York, 3790 Las Vegas Boulevard South; (702) 740-6969/(800) 693-6763.*

■ ORLEANS

In December 1996, Coast Hotels (owners of Barbary Coast and Gold Coast) opened Orleans, a $200 million, 760-room locals' hotel on West Tropicana roughly two miles off the Strip. This is a big boxy barn of a casino, with a large bowling alley upstairs, four restaurants, a showroom, a lounge with New Orleans big bands and jazz, and larger rooms with great views of the Strip or the mountains. Plans are to expand Orleans with a multiplex movie theater, large child-care center, bingo parlor, and more rooms. *Orleans, 4500 West Tropicana Avenue; (702) 365-7111/(800) 675-3267.*

■ AND THE CASINOS KEEP ROLLING ALONG

Next up is **Bellagio**, Mirage Resorts' $1.25 billion monument to extravagance, excess, and decadence. Despite the fact that Las Vegas has 70 major hotel-casinos, of which eight are megaresorts built in the past eight years, this town has never had a

five-star or five-diamond hotel. Bellagio is angling to be the first. Located on part of the 122-acre site of the Dunes Hotel and Golf Course, which Steve Wynn bought for $75 million (one of the great Strip bargains in history), Bellagio is named after a resort town in northern Italy. Details are sketchy as yet (it opens in fall 1998), but Bellagio will feature 3,000 hotel rooms (with a rack rate starting at $225 a night: families with children will be encouraged to find accommodations elsewhere), a 12-acre lake complete with a $30 million musical water-jet ballet, and a $70 million Cirque du Soleil production show.

Beyond Bellagio, approximately a dozen casinos are on the drawing board to open through 1999. The latest market segment that Las Vegas hopes to fill in the next few years is the luxury hotel niche. Four Seasons has plans to build a 400-room non-casino hotel on the Hacienda property at the south end of the Strip, next door to Circus Circus's new 3,600-room megaresort, **Paradise**. Seven Circle, a European resort company, plans to open a 400-room hotel surrounded by the three golf courses at Summerlin. Hyatt and Grand Bay (owned by Carnival, the cruise and hotel company) say they'll each build a 400- to 500-room hotel at Lake Las Vegas, the most exclusive development in southern Nevada, just east of Henderson on the way to Lake Mead. Ritz-Carlton has announced plans to build a 400-room hotel-casino at Mountain Spa, a huge new subdivision in the north valley. All five hotels will charge upwards of $250-300 per night for a room. If they happen, that is.

Meanwhile, a handful of other hotels are in the works. A 3,000-room Planet Hollywood might (or might not) be built next to the Desert Inn, in a partnership with ITT. Hilton, which bought Bally's in 1996, assures us that **Paris**, the 2,500-room themed megajoint slated to go up between Bally's and the Aladdin, is still happening, even though it was announced way back in 1995 and nothing has happened since. Countryland U.S.A. might just replace the El Rancho, the only shuttered casino on the Strip (it closed in 1992) after all, that one's been on the drawing board even longer than Paris. And the **Venetian** has also been announced by the owners of the defunct and imploded Sands. They tell us they're building a 6,000-room, all-suite metamegaresort complete with canals and gondolas. And those are the ones most likely to succeed! Another half dozen are too speculative to mention.

(previous pages) The first drop of the Manhattan Express roller coaster at New York–New York is a doozy. (photo by Kerrick James)

GAMBLING—VICE IS NICE

AT THE VERY CORE OF THE GREAT WESTERN PHILOSOPHIES, religions, and para-digms is a crack, a jagged fault line between fate and free will. The tug of war be-tween the two sides accounts for the continually shifting definitions of right and wrong, good and bad, virtue and sin.

At one extreme is superdeterminism, the belief that *everything*, from whom you marry to reading this . . . next . . . word . . . has already been fated by the Great Scriptwriter in the Sky. A lesser variation on the fate side of the fault line holds that the One True God strictly observes and sternly judges your every move, and rewards or punishes you accordingly. A more interactive interpretation rests with the many goddesses of fortune, cavorting among the deities atop the mythical mountains, all of whom can be influenced by the proper prayer, behavior, and bribery.

At the other extreme is pure atheism, in which nothing that occurs is influ-enced by anything other than chance, luck, or choice. Lesser variations on the free-will side involve a God whose critical notice only reflects one's personal morality, or libertine deities whose anything-goes-on-Earth policies are devised simply to promote their amoral entertainment.

The crack separating the two extremes is sometimes thought to be an uncross-able abyss, trapping attitudes on one side or the other. Other times, the fault is believed to divide closely parallel lines, like narrow-gauge railroad tracks, which attitudes can follow singly, or switch, or straddle. But there is a place where both fate and free will co-exist, where they achieve a perfect balance. That's known as destiny.

That balance point can be illustrated with the simple sticks-and-bones game played by the Las Vegas Paiute Indians for hundreds of years. Two players faced each other, each with five sticks. One player held a plain bleached bone and a black-banded bone in one or the other fist. The second player guessed in which hand or hands the bones hid. Sticks were exchanged over each right or wrong play. Then the guesser became the holder. This "handgame" combined all the elements on both sides of the crack. The guessing game in its simplest form lent itself to the fate side. Intellectual exercise was provided by the endless opportunity to psych out the opponent. The gods and goddesses certainly watched and chose sides,

THE GREATEST GAMBLER

*G*ronevelt gambled better than any man he had ever seen. At the crap table he made all the bets that cut down the percentage of the house. He seemed to divine the ebb and flow of luck. When the dice ran cold, he switched sides. When the dice got hot, he pressed every bet to the limit. At baccarat he could smell out when the shoe would turn Banker and when the shoe would turn Player and ride the waves. At blackjack he dropped his bets to five dollars when the dealer hit a lucky streak and brought it up to the limit when the dealer was cold.

In the middle of the week Gronevelt was five hundred thousand dollars ahead. By the end of the week he was six hundred thousand dollars ahead. He kept going, Cully by his side. They would eat dinner together and gamble only until midnight. Gronevelt said you had to be in good shape to gamble. You couldn't push, you had to get a good night's sleep. You had to watch your diet and you should only get laid once every three or four nights.

By the middle of the second week Gronevelt, despite all his skill, was sliding downhill. The percentages were grinding him into dust. And at the end of two weeks he had lost his million dollars. When he bet his last stack of chips and lost, Gronevelt turned to Cully and smiled. He seemed to be delighted, which struck Cully as ominous. "It's the only way to live," Gronevelt said. "You have to live going with the percentage. Otherwise, life is not worthwhile. Always remember that," he told Cully. "Everything you do in life, use percentage as your god."

—Mario Puzo, *Fool's Die,* 1978

tried to send signals to players, and gambled among themselves. In turn, one's deities were beseeched by chants; the opponent (and his deities) were distracted by insults and jokes and nonsense. Often, the contest developed an intensity in which the players seemed inspired by a supernatural force, possessed of a powerful magic (probably determined by the size of the stakes). Finally, side bettors had no opportunity to influence the outcome. Somehow these "primitive" desert Paiute hit upon and preferred to play a completely honest and fair game.

A variation of the handgame with teams, however, lent itself to the free-will side of the track. Five players faced each other, two to hold the bones, the other three to guard the stakes. The choices, the psyching out, the distractions, and the magic intensified. Side bets gained a power of their own, and introduced the possibility

(opposite) Vegas Vickie kicks up her heels. (photo by Kerrick James)

of tampering with the game. Bettors and players could now appropriate the role of the gods by manipulating the outcome. This required a trivializing of divine influence, or a rationalization that the gods would find the cheating acceptable. A secretly rigged game always indicates ungodliness.

A publicly rigged game, on the other hand, always points to providence. Nevada casino gambling, for example, is by all accounts a mostly *honest* game, but it's not a *fair* game. The house makes the rules, and the rules are made so that the advantage remains, eternally, with the house. The odds against the player vary according to the game, but that One True God, that all-powerful, all-knowing, all-controlling Boss Gambler in the Heavens, possesses the ultimate instrument: the Percentage. Slavish mortals can pray, curse, apply every superstition on Earth, try to cheat, play with the highest skill, and even enjoy a streak of good luck every now and then. But in the long run, nothing can overcome the Edge. Because the omnipotent Percentage takes the whole wager when you lose, *and* some spare change when you win. And ultimately, the spare change adds up to the whole wager.

But *all* doesn't have to be lost. What's gained is a matter of choice. For one thing, the odds of the games are well-known and therefore dependable. Since the danger of the Edge is built in, it adds to the challenge of playing and the excitement of winning. So the choice is in favor of the magic over the money. For another thing, losing is actually a very pure and appropriate payment to a God that fulfills, in return, many human desires: pageantry, exhilaration, transcendence, to say nothing of the potential for unearned income—the joy of a small profit or the ecstasy of a celestial jackpot. Finally, only the weakest can't control how much to sacrifice to this God. The vast majority of players successfully withstand divine determinism with the shield of free will. So whether they're ahead or behind, these millions of minions always walk away winners.

■ GAMBLING THROUGH THE AGES

"Human mortality renders life itself a game of chance," writes Jerome Skolnick in *House of Cards*. The notion of free will—the risk-taking and unpredictability inherent in existence—has always suited the gambler's instinct better than fate. "In our womb-to-tomb progress we never stop gambling, for we cannot know the outcome of many small decisions we must make every day," according to Alan Wykes.

And in *Inside Las Vegas,* Mario Puzo claims, "Gambling is a primitive religious instinct, peculiar to our species, that has existed since the beginning of recorded history in every society, from the most primitive to the most complex."

Exactly when gambling began is impossible to establish. It's known that lotteries—using lots to choose a person for a position, task, or even human sacrifice—were practiced by earliest cultures, as were trials by ordeal, wherein chance outcome decided innocence or guilt. God instructed Moses to divvy up the Promised Land with a lottery. Hieroglyphs at Cheops Pyramid at Giza report that Thoth, the god of night, gambled with the moon and won five new days that were added to the Egyptian calendar, marking the transition from a lunar to a solar year. A checkerboard was found in the sarcophagus of Egyptian Queen Hatasu, dating from 1600 B.C.; square ivory dice found at nearby Thebes turned out to be only 25 years younger.

Chinese records indicate that an ancestor of chess was invented by an emperor in 2300 B.C. to simulate war games for young military students. When the Chinese invented paper in 200 B.C., one of the first applications was to make playing cards. The Indian Vedic hymns from 2000 B.C. contain numerous references to the people's chief amusements—chariot racing and dice throwing. Their dice were made of *astragal,* or sheep anklebones, and cheating with loaded dice or sleight of hand was commonplace. In fact, the Vedas include the first recorded mention of a crooked crap marathon in which the victim, after losing everything else, wagered his wife and lost her, too. The Greek gods shot dice for the universe: Poseidon won the oceans, Hades the afterlife, and Zeus the heavens (they were Zeus's dice).

Chasing the gamblers down through time, of course, were the moralists—religious leaders, lawmakers, social reformers, sore losers—one of whom summed up the objection succinctly: "The urge to gamble is so universal and its practice so pleasurable that I can only assume it must be evil." Egyptians convicted of gambling were sentenced to hard labor. The Greeks had strict sanctions against gaming, which they believed to be detrimental to the integrity of the state. The Jewish courts excluded gamblers, assumed to be automatically susceptible to corruption, from the entire legal system. The Koran specifically forbids all types of game playing (except chess). But successful gamblers in all ages have possessed the qualities—action oriented, risk taking, portable, mobile, ingenious, pioneering—to consistently remain a step ahead of the civilizers.

By the Renaissance, gambling had developed into a highly organized, stratified,

ALONE IN THE CASINO, JUST ME AND MY MACHINE-O

More than 110 million Americans gamble. Upwards of 105 million of these people gamble for entertainment, recreation, excitement—to satisfy the basic, primal urge of financial risk-taking for fun and profit. For them, losing is a sensation they can live with. If they walk away from the casino with house money in their pockets, they had a great time. If they left some of their money with the house, they had a good time. But three to four million Americans (65 percent men, 35 percent women) are unable to simply walk away having had a good time. For them, gambling becomes compulsive, an addiction, a dangerous and deadly psychiatric disorder.

What makes a group of people turn to gambling for an escape, as opposed to alcohol, drugs, sex, or food, is a matter of endless conjecture. A gambling disorder starts out as a euphoria derived from the excitement of the activity—a more satisfying sensation than anything else these people have experienced. Whether it's the surging adrenaline of a crap game, the hypnotic trance of a video poker machine, or the fast pace and high stakes of a securities market, as long as these people gamble, they're riding the high; stopping means coming down, and they need to gamble again to get back up. The dependence is particularly insidious, since the various house advantages ensure that the longer they play, the more they lose. And the more they lose, the more they start chasing losses. Herein lies the danger signal. Nearly all compulsive gamblers spend their own, and their families', savings. Three out of four sell or hock valuables, and write bad checks. Almost half descend to theft or embezzlement. Finally, in the terminal stages of ruin, despair, fear, and shame, an estimated 20 percent of compulsive gamblers attempt suicide. And only then, if unsuccessful, do most addicts reach a point of seeking treatment.

There are 600 Gamblers Anonymous chapters nationwide, but only a handful of primary treatment facilities. Dr. Robert Custer, considered the father of compulsive-gambling treatment, says that compulsive gambling is the "most under-researched" psychiatric disorder, and the most deadly. "No other psychiatric disorder even approaches" a 20-percent rate of attempted suicide, he points out. However, public perception of compulsive gambling is 20 to 30 years behind that of alcoholism, for example. Though the ranks of addicted gamblers have swelled in the last few years, mostly due to the highly addictive nature of video poker machines, serious treatment remains hard to come by, and is often a case of too little, too late.

It's no accident that most compulsive gamblers kick the habit by turning to some form of religion. Religion and gambling do have a few things in common. In fact, gambling practices, both outward in form and inward in attitude, can be a kind of secular emulation of religious practices. A casino, after all, is not unlike a church. Both are lavishly appointed; both are far removed from ordinary activity. Both involve highly arcane social rituals, vernacular styles, material objects, and belief systems. Both invite prayers and invocations to some higher power, whether it be chance or God. And both offer rewards, in the form of prizes and miracles, to those of strong and unquestionable faith.

Compulsive gambling is a highly complex disorder, and those trying to quit often find themselves desperately missing not only the addictive "high," but also the meaningful rituals and the sense of purpose, hope, and belonging which, like a secular religion, gambling has given them. The premise of Gamblers Anonymous is straightforward: by providing an escape from daily life, a supportive social network, a set of bonding "steps," and a belief in a "higher power," GA helps fill the void left when the community and the catechism of the casino are gone.

A fool and his money are soon parted.

somewhat degenerate, and morally ambiguous element of society. Pre-colonial Britain, for example, became gripped by gambling fever as it was transformed from an agricultural to an industrial state, with a more affluent and leisurely population. The English played for dangerously high stakes, which only noblemen and upper classes could sustain over the long run. Besides, gambling was a sensual pleasure—one, therefore, to deny the lower classes. Public displays of enormous wagers in exclusive London clubs were considered *de rigueur* for high society. Men won and lost and won back and lost again thousands of pounds sterling in single sittings. Bust-out women reportedly paid gambling debts with their honor; the higher the debt, the more deviant the payment. These gambling "infernos" proved to be the downfall of thousands of aristocrats and their family fortunes.

Even the British government turned bookmaker by sponsoring large public lotteries. Smaller private lotteries also raised funds for business, industry, and especially wild, harebrained, entrepreneurial schemes—such as financing the colonizing of the New World. In fact, from 1612 to 1621 the Virginia Company of England relied almost exclusively on continuous lotteries to supply and resupply the Chesapeake colonists—adventurers and gamblers every last one. But when King James outlawed private lotteries (too much competition), the Virginia Company immediately went bankrupt, and the American settlers had to curtail their idle handgames with the Indians and start thinking about making a living.

■ GAMBLING COMES TO AMERICA

Meanwhile, the moralist Puritans in England were making little headway in their efforts to stem the tide of gambling lust, so they boarded boats, sailed the bounding main, and instilled New England with their righteousness. Gradually, the colonies divided along lines determined by attitudes toward gambling. Yankees considered all forms of betting to be sinful, while Southerners objected only when wagering was taken to extremes. In his epic survey of the evolution of American gambling, John Findlay explains that to Puritans, gambling was "akin to taking the Lord's name in vain; both were appeals to God to pass judgments on insignificant events." But the Virginians mildly counseled against "offending God by blaming Him for losses, while not crediting Him for gains."

Of course, gambling flourished in many forms from Boston to Savannah throughout colonial times. Horse racing and cock fighting occupied the landed gentry of the South, while card playing and dice games were favored by the common classes of the North. The lottery craze that had been carried over from England barely subsided. Small, personal lotteries, such as the one sponsored by Benjamin Franklin to finance the defense of Philadelphia, proved more successful than large-scale, public lotteries, such as the one sponsored by the Continental Congress to raise its own funds for the upcoming confrontation with the British. Indeed, the Crown's attempts to regulate colonial lotteries provided a major spark for the Revolutionary conflagration.

Within one generation of the end of the War of Independence, civilization had emphatically replaced the colonial permissiveness of the Eastern Seaboard, and only "genteel" gaming had a place in the states. The Louisiana Purchase from France in 1803 added the enormous "Old Southwest" to American continental territory, and within a dozen years, this western frontier had been penetrated from Louisville (on the Ohio) and St. Louis (on the Mississippi) down to the notorious gamblers' stronghold of Natchez, upriver from New Orleans. A colorful polyglot

OLD GAMBLERS DON'T DIE

*R*ight now, finally, I have "aged out" as the dope addicts are said to do. I no longer really enjoy gambling, but the infantile lust can return. When I am too old for sex, when age withers my appetite for pizza and Peking duck, when my paranoia reaches the point that no human being arouses my trust or love, when my mind dries up so that I will no longer be interested in reading books, I will settle in Las Vegas. I will watch the ivory roulette ball spin, place my tiny bets on red and black numbers and some sort of magic will return again. I will throw the square red dice and hold my breath as they roll and roll along the green felt. I will sit down at the blackjack table and baccarat and wait for my magical Ace of Spades to appear and I will be a lucky child again.

Should I go to heaven, give me no haloed angels riding snow-white clouds, no, not even the sultry houris of the Moslems. Give me rather a vaulting red-walled casino with bright lights, bring on horned devils as dealers. Let there be a Pit Boss in the Sky who will give me unlimited credit. And if there is a merciful God in our Universe, he will decree that the Player have, for *all* eternity, an Edge against the House.

—Mario Puzo, *Inside Las Vegas,* 1976

DEGENERATE GAMBLING

*T*he care, feeding, and stroking of the big player extends across the board . . . By the same token, when a man goes bust, they don't want him to dirty up their carpet. Like little Frankie Polovsky . . . .

Little Frankie was married to a wealthy woman who gave him a white Rolls Royce as a birthday present, and with that kind of a start they decided to drive across the country. When they got to Vegas he lost all their money, sold the Rolls, and came right back and blew that money, too.

It went on like that for two years. Frankie went through his wife's money and, when he sold their house, she left him. He lost that money too, of course, and then went into such debt that his business was taken away from him. "And now," Julie said, "he's in such serious trouble down here that he's like a bum."

"He's worse than a bum," Stan said. "A bum knows he's a bum."

"He has nothing. All his self-respect and everything else is gone. And everybody looks at him like he was a nothing human being."

"And now he's a mooch," Barbara said. "When he had money he was everybody's buddy. Now that he owes all over town, when he shows up at Caesars, they say what's that bum doing here again."

They beat little Frankie for maybe a million dollars and he was around the other day asking to borrow a couple of hundred. "I gave him fifty," Julie says, "and if you want to call it conscience money, how could I argue with you? I don't want to see him around, either. I admit it. I don't want to have to look at the guy when he sinks to where he's asking for ten."

—Edward Linn, *Big Julie of Las Vegas*, 1974

of cultures—Spanish and Mexican, New England and Dixie, French and English, Caribbean and African—all converged on the recently opened waterways, and contributed various influences to novel styles of gambling on the new edge of civilization: roulette, faro, *vingt-et-un* (twenty-one), three-card monte, poker. The rigged wheels and the fast card games lent themselves to the genesis of a large class of professional, mostly dishonest, gamblers who came to be called "blacklegs." Often working in teams, and thereby advancing a new concept of organized crime, the blacklegs suckered and fleeced all comers. At the same time, gambling operations in saloons and storefronts introduced the concept of public gaming houses to America; their licensing and taxing lent a certain legitimacy both to the enterprises and to the proprietors. The New World's first prominent and elegant

"casino" opened in 1827 in New Orleans.

But once again, within one generation, a substantial migration of settlers to the Mississippi River region had imposed civilization, that time-honored enemy of the frontier fringe elements. Citizens cleaned up the port towns with laws and vigilantism. The famous lynching of five blacklegs in Vicksburg in 1835 triggered a wave of reform up and down the river valleys, forcing the gamblers into motion. The increasingly prevalent and luxurious passenger riverboats provided the perfect new setting for the gamblers' operations. Railroads and the Civil War curtailed steamboat travel after the 1850s, but not before the "riverboat gambler" had spread the new games and practices far and wide along the frontier, and had achieved near-mythical status up till then reserved for the riverboat pilot or the mountain man.

The gold rush to California toward the end of the Mississippi steamboat era immediately attracted, in John Findlay's words, "hordes of sojourners whose restless and acquisitive spirit came to typify the entire society." The new styles of gambling

Whether on a hotel marquee or in the sign graveyard, luck is always a lady.

developed by the blacklegs accompanied the hordes, and were quickly emplaced and refined according to the requirements of the far Western frontier. Public gambling houses were prevalent in the heart of San Francisco throughout the 1850s. Clubs were licensed and taxed, operators were known as "dealers," and the games and rituals evolved into a high-volume business dependent as much on percentages favorable to the house as on outright cheating and stealing. But casino betting was only one manifestation of the deeply ingrained high-risk instincts of the new Westerners. The wide-open frontier presented many opportunities to gamble and hit a jackpot: mining gold, contesting claims, manipulating stocks, trading property, cornering commodities. Prospectors, miners, speculators, traders, and card players fanned out from the Mother Lode throughout the West, from British Columbia to Colorado, from Montana to Arizona, installing California's trendsetting styles of work, play, law and order, and inherent risk taking. But nowhere was the influence stronger, the connection more direct, than in Virginia City, home of the Comstock Lode, in the new state next door.

■ NEVADA—THE GAMBLE STATE

Civilization caught up to San Francisco surprisingly fast, at least in terms of the suppression of wide-open gaming. But a new form of public gambling began sweeping through the young city in the early 1860s, which appealed to all classes, ages, and sexes of residents. Over the Sierra Nevada, just east of the California state line, prospectors had located what would, in a very short time, turn out to be the richest place on Earth—the Comstock Lode. The vast silver strike immediately attracted a throng of gamblers—con men, highway robbers, murderers, fugitives, idlers, drunkards, prostitutes, speculators, and lawyers—as well as miners, freighters, traders, merchants, and journeymen. The thousands of claims staked, badly recorded according to vague laws enforced by Darwin's Theory, overlapped to the extent that the Comstock was "owned" in its entirety three or four times over. By 1863, at the height of the initial wildcat boom in Virginia City, you could stroll up Mt. Davidson, dig in the ground for an hour or so, post a claim notice with a high-falutin' name, print up stock certificates, and be in the silver business. Speculation fever, heavy and sweaty, gripped Virginia City. Deeds were discussed, titles examined, claims traded, stocks bought and sold—one vast gamble, all

*(top) This lady is waiting—for a jackpot winner at Harrah's Laughlin, or a photographer.
(bottom) Las Vegas is full of good luck charms.*

dependent on the fluctuating value of the famed "feet" of Comstock pay dirt. A parade of lawsuits to determine ultimate possession of hundreds of millions of dollars was up for grabs: testimonies were bought cheaply; juries freely admitted to taking bribes; opponents were routinely threatened, slandered, and occasionally eliminated; the distinction between judge and auctioneer was rhetorical.

In order to handle the mining companies' stocks with some semblance of order and law, the San Francisco Mining and Stock Exchange Board was created in 1863. Speculation ran as rampant in the City by the Bay as it did in Virginia Town, especially since the enormous capital required to mine and mill the Comstock metals was supplied mostly by California money markets. Thousands of investors, big and small, clogged the Exchange and even the streets outside, gambling their savings on mining stock rumored or manipulated to be representative of valuable ore rising from the depths of the Lode. Thousands were enriched or impoverished daily, depending on the outcomes of explorations, lawsuits, swindles, mergers, bankruptcies, and the like. In fact, the Stock Exchange provided a similar excitement on the silvery streets above the Lode itself, where gamblers invested more according to the market situation in San Francisco than the mining situation in Virginia City.

Nevada became a state in 1864, and the Comstock's five-year-old legal gridlock was unsnarled by a battery of new and unimpeachable federal appointees—just in time for the first *borrasca* (major bust) on the Lode. Most of the wildcat operations succumbed, the stock market crashed, and mining in even the largest, most California-capitalized claims was suspended. The small-time quick-buck scammers and lawyers left town, to be replaced by the big-time, big-stakes swindlers and bankers. William Ralston, president of the Bank of California, dispatched a petty tyrant named William Sharon to Virginia City to gain control of the desperate situation. Both Ralston and Sharon had been born in Ohio in the 1820s; both had started out in the riverboat business; both were gamblers and empire builders. Sharon immediately began consolidating the bank's interests: buying out claim-holders for pennies on the dollar; approving loans liberally and accumulating collateral; exploring the shafts, tunnels and drifts; conducting numerous and systematic assays. He studied geology, mineralogy, and ore bodies; the hoisting, pumping, and communications mechanisms of the mines and mills; timbering and teaming and transportation; the town's water and gas systems. Driven by determination, plus a natural greed and streak of ruthlessness, William

Sharon, by spring of 1865, had emerged as the ultimate expert on the Comstock, the possessor of the big picture, the maestro of the maelstrom.

For the next seven years, "Ralston's Ring" ruled the Lode. Sharon accumulated a huge monopoly of mines, mills, transportation, utilities, and stock. He unearthed bonanzas from the deepening mines and became quite adept at squeezing the stock market to fleece the gamblers, little or large. Even the swindlers had never imagined such a grand scale. All Sharon had to do, for example, was quietly buy up the stock of an unproductive mine at $10 a share, then plant a rumor of a possible bonanza at that mine. This would drive the price of shares up to exalted heights, when he'd sell them off and fill the vault. Then the vault itself was no longer large enough. In June 1867, the Bank of California moved into its new palatial headquarters at the corner of California and Sansome streets in San Francisco. The building immediately earned the subtitle, "The Wonder of the Silver Age."

Eventually, this new style of public gaming gripped the whole country, west and east. Americans went mad for Comstock stock. The game, of course, was as rigged as a stacked deck, and the rich got richer while ordinary players in the hundreds of thousands were humbled by the house advantage. Even genteel society, as it caught up to *this* new frontier, embraced the vast shell game as legitimate. Ultimately, McKay, Fair, Flood, and O'Brien, the "Silver Kings" of the Big Bonanza —gamblers even shrewder and more poker-faced than Sharon and Ralston—beat them at their own game and manipulated perhaps the largest stock-market boom and bust of all time. In the end, the great gamble of the Comstock Lode left the state of Nevada with such a large and long-lasting legacy that civilization itself, with all its powers, pressures, and practices, could not and has not overcome it.

■ THE GAMBLE OF LEGALIZED GAMBLING

The first territorial governor of Nevada, James Nye, was an ex-police chief of New York City. In one of his first speeches to the new territorial assembly, he proclaimed, "I particularly recommend that you pass stringent laws to prevent gambling. Of all the seductive vices extant, I regard that of gambling as the worst. It captivates and ensnares the young, blunts all the moral sensibilities, and ends in utter ruin." Dutifully, the assembly ruled that violators of the prohibition of all

games of chance were subject to two years imprisonment and/or a $500 fine. The law was promptly dismissed by the vast gambling public, ignored by marshals, and forgotten by legislators.

In 1864, President Abraham Lincoln wanted Nevada to become a state. He needed Comstock silver to finance the Civil War. He needed two additional anti-slavery votes. And he needed to keep a check on the "secesh" leanings of California. The law required 120,000 certified residents, but Nevada had less than 40,000. When Congress voted, the outcome was Nevada one, the law zero. Thus Nevada became a state. Nye remained governor, but a new legislature was elected, which passed a bill allowing wide-open gambling. Governor Nye vetoed it, but the lawmakers overrode his veto. In 1869 they instituted license fees for all gambling houses—of which Virginia City claimed 120 (and one library).

As mining in Nevada declined, then died, during the last two decades of the nineteenth century, the state became more and more dependent on gambling taxes. But with a new and major gold-, silver-, and copper-mining boom at the turn of the twentieth century, revenues from gambling decreased in importance. John Findlay points out that "the return of prosperity in mining enabled the state to afford to follow the nation's progressive impulse. Seeking greater respectability in the eyes of other states, Nevada outlawed gambling in 1910." This law succeeded primarily in moving the games into back rooms, turning front rooms into cigar stores, barber shops, and candy counters. Combined with national liquor Prohibition, the laws created a "brotherhood" of drinkers and gamblers. In *Gambler's Money*, Wally Turner writes, "One of the by-products of all this was the creation of a lawlessness in attitude for a whole generation of Americans, and a class of dishonest law enforcement officers and public officeholders such as the nation had never known before."

Furthermore, the state *and* society turned out to be the big losers. Fees and taxes declined, payoffs and corruption increased, crooked games and rigged equipment operated by undesirable characters preyed on the weak and naive. In 1913 and 1915, the law was watered down slightly to allow social card playing, but matters generally stood pat for another 16 years, until the height of the Great Depression.

It's often been repeated that re-legalizing wide-open gambling was Nevada's answer to the collapse of the nation's economy. But Wally Turner argues effectively

(opposite) Roulette means "little wheel."

that distaste for the system that had produced speakeasies and back-room gambling prepared Nevadans to accept legal gambling. On February 13, 1931, Republican Philip Tobin, a rancher from Winnemucca, introduced a bill in the state legislature that provided for the licensing of gambling houses and the collection of fees ($25 per gaming table and $10 per slot machine) by the county sheriffs. Licenses could not be granted to non-citizens. Cheating was forbidden, minors prohibited, and applicants had to pay three months' fees in advance. That was it.

Again, Wally Turner: "How is the program to be controlled? Who is responsible for seeing that no cheating occurs? The sheriff? Who keeps the sheriff honest? Where is a provision barring ex-convicts? Who licenses the dealers? Who sees that the gambling house is financially capable of paying off winners? In short, who is responsible?

"The answer. Nobody.

"The legislature of Nevada turned loose a group of professional gamblers on its people and their guests, and then spent the next three decades trying to control them."

For another 15 years, the state seemed content to allow the gambling industry to evolve organically, with no additional taxes or regulations. Those were the days! Exactly like the first few wildcat years on the Comstock. Before big business, the law, and civilization installed their dampers. Gambling was so wide open that notorious operators such as Guy McAfee and Tony Cornero from Los Angeles, Benny Binion from Texas, and Ben Siegel from New York were handed licenses with barely a question asked. Downtown Las Vegas was almost completely transformed into wall-to-wall casinos, and two casino-resorts occupied the new Strip, with two more under construction. Still, in 1945, when the state finally delegated casino taxation and licensing responsibilities to the Tax Commission, the reasons had more to do with the end of World War II and the loss of Nevada's big military payroll than with any squeamishness about a pariah industry or boss gamblers. It finally required the national headline splash of Siegel's gruesome murder in 1947 to shake the state out of its innocent lethargy.

In 1949, the Nevada Tax Commission assumed greater powers in the investigating of applicants and enforcing of stricter regulations; its agents were granted the authority of peace officers. In 1955, the state Gaming Control Board was spun off the Tax Commission, and in 1959 the state Gaming Commission was created to formulate policy and oversee the Control Board. It had only taken almost 30 years for Nevada to install its permanent casino regulatory system and it took another 35 years until all the undesirables had been driven out (or so far underground as to render the point moot). But finally the industry achieved a respectability nearly unknown in gambling history. And today it's a giant corporate numbers game—high volume, quick turnover, and an absolute reliance on the One True God: the Percentage, the P.C., the Edge, the Vig or Vigorish. The omnipotent House Advantage.

■ NEGATIVE EXPECTATION

In today's terms, gambling is considered entertainment, and modern casinos define the house advantage as the price of admission. In 1996, Las Vegas's gross gaming revenues (the "hold") totaled nearly $6 billion, which translates into nearly $200 dollars in profit every second! From whom do the casinos win almost $12,000 a minute? Losers. How do the casinos win it? Favorable odds. Since the casinos make the rules of the games, they simply give themselves a mathematical advantage.

The game of roulette best illustrates the house advantage. There are 38 numbers on the wheel: 1 through 36, plus a zero and double zero. If the ball drops into number 23 and you have a dollar on it, the correct payoff would be $37 (37 to 1, which equals the 38 numbers). However, the house only pays $35. It withholds 2 out of 38 units, which translates to a 5.26-percent advantage for the house. Now, this 5.26-percent advantage can be looked at in different ways. For every $100 you bet on roulette, on average you can expect to lose $5.26. Or, out of every hundred spins of the roulette wheel, you can expect to lose 52.63 of them. Or, in the long run, you'll lose your money nearly four times faster at roulette than by making pass-line bets at craps (which have a 1.4-percent house advantage). Of course, luck will play a significant part in the gambling proceedings in the short run, but the longer you play craps, roulette, or any casino game where the house holds the advantage, the more your losses will add up to the percentage.

The house advantage is the single most important concept to be aware of in order to understand the secret behind casino gambling, and in order to determine how much "admission" you'll pay for the various forms of "recreation."

■ WHEEL GAMES

Some form of wheel wagering has been in existence since the earliest "spin the stick" games for choosing contestants, combatants, victims, and the like. The **big six**, or **wheel of fortune**, or **money wheel** is one of the oldest carnival games. The Wheel is partitioned into 54 slots of different denominations: 24 $1 slots, 15 $2 slots, seven $5 slots, four $10 slots, two $20 slots, and two slots with a joker, casino logo, American flag, or other symbol. You lay your bet on the corresponding unit on the layout; the odds are the same as the denomination. For example, a $1 bet on the $20 pays $20, and the joker pays 40 to 1. The house advantage starts at a prohibitive 11.1 percent for the even-money bet and rockets to 24 percent on the joker. This explains why most wheel attendants could compete with the Maytag repairman for loneliness on the job. Two things recommend the wheel of fortune: it's the easiest table game to play and the clicking of the wheel pegs against the leather or wooden flapper is hypnotic.

Keno, like the wheel (and roulette), is a slow-paced, bad-odds, easy-to-learn numbers game for first-timers, suckers, drinkers, long-shot artists, and promotion exploiters. This "solitaire bingo" dates from the Chinese Han Dynasty, when it had 120 ideograms to choose from. Immigrants brought it to Nevada in the 1860s; Warren Nelson of Reno's Cal-Neva Casino transformed it into the game that's played today. Pull up a public school–type desk under the big numbers board in the easily identifiable keno lounge, then simply mark your numbers (one to 20 of them) with the black crayon on the paper ticket according to the instructions in the ubiquitous instruction booklets. Be sure to understand about minimum bets (usually 70 cents or $1), but don't worry about the variety of tickets (straight, way, and combination)—a keno runner or ticket writer will show you how to bet if you want to play more than one game at a time.

According to Anthony Curtis in *Bargain City—Booking, Betting, and Beating the New Las Vegas,* the range of the house advantage on an eight-spot ticket (and this is the best-odds play at keno) is between 21 and 33 percent (depending on the payout schedules at the different casinos). It gets worse from there. But since each keno "race" takes about 10 minutes to run, this is a good game to play in the coffeeshop, or if you're killing time in a casino, or if you want to rest from other games in relative stress-free comfort, or if you want to drink (cocktail waitresses are usually attentive to the keno-lounge drinkers), or if you're looking for a shot at a

Riding the roller coaster at Circus Circus's Grand Slam Canyon may be the perfect antidote to a nerve-wracking day of gambling. (photo by Kerrick James)

jackpot risking only a small spot. Keno is also promotion intensive and you can find coupons and specials for keno at many casinos around town.

Roulette is French for "little wheel." The invention of roulette as we know it today is often attributed to the seventeenth-century French philosopher-mathematician Blaise Pascal, who is also credited with originating probability theory and the laws of perpetual motion. But the forerunners of roulette—called *hoca, boule,* and even-odd—were all in use throughout Europe in the pre-Pascal 1600s. The

---

CASINOS TO SEE

Do you think that all casinos look alike? Or that they all equally cause an advanced case of casinility? Or would you like to sightsee casinos but don't know what to look for? The following are some suggestions to enhance your experience of Gambleville.

At the southeast corner of Fremont and Sixth is the original casino wing of the **El Cortez**, built in 1941. The exterior has remained unchanged since, and even inside you might think you're back in the 1940s.

When it opened in 1946, the **Golden Nugget** (between Casino Center and First) was the classiest joint downtown, with a Barbary Coast motif, carpeting, and large nudes gracing the walls. Since Steve Wynn remodeled the casino in the mid-1980s, it has been returned to its former glory, and is once again the elegant establishment on Fremont Street. Don't miss the largest gold nuggets in the world, displayed across from California Pizza Kitchen.

At the **Horseshoe**, right across Glitter Gulch from the Golden Nugget, is an unmistakable contrast between the solid Wild West motif of the early 1950s and the predominant glitz of the mid-1960s. The casino in the original Horseshoe is connected now to the casino in the old Mint or "west Horseshoe. The old wing's wood, brick, and ornate chandeliers clash a bit with the new wing's brass, glass, and flickering lights. But in either casino you can still, after 45 years, place a million dollars on one roll of the dice or deal of the cards. And even if you don't have that kind of money, you can see a million dollars on display in back of the old casino and have your picture taken in front of it.

Jackie Gaughan's **Plaza**, at the corner of Fremont and Main, has a bank of penny slot machines near the south entrance. At East Ogden and Fourth, Jackie Gaughan's **Gold Spike** has a bank of penny video poker machines (the only ones in existence, I believe) against the back wall; this hard-hat area is known as the "Copper Mine."

The venerable **Las Vegas Club**, at Fremont and Main, has a good multi-deck blackjack game and a baseball theme, with photos lining the walls and memorabilia in display cases in the lobby.

The **California** caters quite single-mindedly to the Hawaiian market, so this casino (East Ogden near First) has a distinctive aloha vibration. The dealers wear Hawaiian shirts, the carpet has a tropically floral motif, and the Cal Club Snack Bar serves excellent saimin soup, fried saimin, bento, and teri sandwiches.

Over on the Strip, **Circus Circus**, with veritable hordes of grinds, tinhorns, low rollers, suckers, and kids, is one of the best casinos in town for people-watching (Las Vegas Boulevard South and Circus Circus Lane). Next door, **Slots-A-Fun** is the ultimate low-roller haven on the Strip: dollar blackjack, 75-cent Heinekens, and free popcorn.

At Desert Inn Road is the **Desert Inn**, where you can easily pretend to be in Monte Carlo, or even Las Vegas in the jacket-and-tie 1950s. Quiet, roomy, elegant.

In the **Mirage** casino (Las Vegas Boulevard at Dauphine), the action is always hot and heavy. Average bets that would make most downtown pit bosses break into a sweat barely get you a buffet comp here. Check out the $100 video poker machines (with a $100,000 royal-flush jackpot for a $500-max coin bet) and the $500 slots.

One block down, you can spend at least several hours ogling the internationally renowned **Caesars Palace**, which is a palace for all Caesars, the Casino of Casinos. And be sure to walk next door and spend another several more at the Forum Shops at Caesars, the Mall of Malls.

Tasteful stained-glass signs and a 30-foot Tiffany-style mural, *The Garden of Earthly Delights,* set the **Barbary Coast** (across the Strip from Caesars) apart from the madding crowd.

Across Tropicana from the MGM, the million-dollar, 4,000-square-foot leaded stained-glass dome at the **Tropicana** is the great Las Vegas casino breathtaker. It's suspended on pneumatic shock absorbers to withstand building vibration from the air conditioning; the ceiling remains stationary and the building vibrates around it.

Luxor's air-filtration system had to be so powerful to process the 29 million cubic feet of interior atmosphere that it's the least smoky joint in Las Vegas. You'll find it on the Strip, at Hacienda.

To attract gamblers to the no-man's-land location of **Stratosphere** (at Las Vegas Boulevard South, two blocks north of Sahara), the casino has to offer a little extra gambling incentive. Dozens of video poker machines have a better-than-100-percent return percentage, all roulette wheels are single zero, all dollar slots pay back 98 percent, and you can take 100 times odds on the crap tables.

earliest gambling action in Monaco consisted of two roulette wheels in a barn. European wheels utilized (and still do) one zero, which put the players at a 2.7 percent disadvantage; they also offer another concession, called *en prison*, which lowers the casino edge to 1.35 percent.

You can make a total of 14 bets on a roulette layout, 13 of which carry a disadvantage of $5.26 out of every $100 bet. You can bet on one number ("straight"), two numbers ("split"), three numbers ("street"), four numbers ("corner" or "square"), five numbers (this bet covers 1, 2, 3, 0, and 00, and has a house advantage of 7.89 percent), six numbers ("line"), 12 numbers ("column" or "dozen"), high or low (1-18, 19-36), red or black, and even or odd. Though you can play roulette with regular casino checks (chips), you can also buy "wheel chips," which come in half a dozen different colors—to differentiate among players. You must specify to the dealer which denomination your personal wheel chips represent, and you *must* redeem them for regular checks before you leave the table.

Countless systems have been in use for centuries to try and beat the wheel: the famous Martingale, which doubles the wager after a loss, and its counterparts Reverse and Great Martingales; the D'Alembert; the Biarritz; Cuban; Cross-Out or

At craps, you have a manual connection with the primary equipment.

Cancellation; Third Column or Perfect; and the Biased Wheel. This last was first used successfully by an English engineer named Jaggers in Monte Carlo in the late 1800s. He noticed that a slight inaccuracy in the wheels would favor certain numbers, and he employed half a dozen assistants to watch and note the numbers. Then he analyzed the results, used them as a basis for betting, and walked away a $180,000 winner after five days of casual gambling. The Biased Wheel system has been used successfully ever since.

A high-tech variation on this theme was developed by a group of physics gradu-ate-student hippies at University of California, Santa Cruz in the late 1970s. They undertook to predict the outcome of each spin of the wheel by determining the dozen or so variables that make up the physics of roulette. They wrote a computer program which would analyze the various physical elements of any wheel at any casino, and then project, in two seconds, the quadrant into which the spinning ball would drop 15 seconds later. Then they built a tiny computer that fit into a shoe, which could be programmed and decoded by means of the big toe of the programmer, who would then transmit the signal to the bet placer. The whole scheme, as well as everything else you ever wanted to know about roulette, is

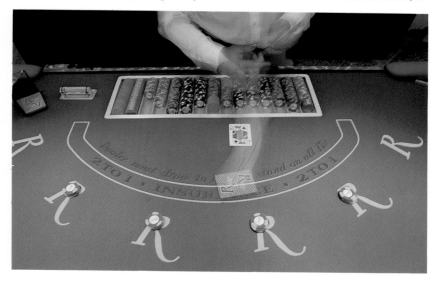

Pitching cards.

covered in *The Eudaemonic Pie* by Thomas Bass. Shortly after the book was published in 1985, the Nevada Legislature passed a law prohibiting the use of any device that could project the outcome of any casino games—punishable by up to 10 years and $10,000.

Various methods have been employed to "gaff" or rig roulette wheels. Magnets and steel-centered balls have controlled the outcome, as have tiny needles that pop up in all the red or black cups or around the back track to steer the ball toward the zeros. Other techniques include "screening out"—blocking the view of the wheel while a dealer uses sleight-of-hand to switch the number—and the old standby of short payoffs. One of the most prevalent myths of cheating at roulette, however, is entirely spurious: that the dealer can control where the ball will drop into the wheel. Forget it.

Even though the house advantage is 5.26 percent, the hold for roulette tends to hover at upwards of 30 percent. You can see for yourself why this is true by just observing the game for a few minutes. Watch how the dealer marks the winning number of a spin with a pointer, and then shovels in, with both hands and arms, the ton of losing bets on the layout. John Scarne concluded, "The best way to avoid losing at roulette is to stop playing." But most gambling experts simply recommend that if you play for small stakes, you can relax and enjoy the leisurely pace, the pageantry of the wheel and layout, and the history and glamour of the game.

■ SLOTS

At the same time that the San Pedro, Los Angeles and Salt Lake Railroad was envisioning a company town in the middle of Las Vegas Valley, and a French chemist was discovering the illuminating properties of neon gas, a Bavarian immigrant living in San Francisco was inventing a machine that would ultimately dominate the Nevada gambling industry. Charlie Fey, the twenty-first (and last) offspring of a West German family, hit the road to adventure in 1876 when he was 14, winding up in England as an apprentice scientific-instrument maker. In 1882 he continued west to Wisconsin, where he worked on delicate measuring equipment and dabbled in gambling equipment such as punchboards and wheels. Finally, his restless spirit carried him to San Francisco in the mid-1890s, where the Barbary Coast gambling clubs inspired him to invent the mechanical three-reel slot machine.

The slot's instant popularity created a new industry in San Francisco, and soon slot machines proliferated in the city's saloons. Though some of the machines' gimmicks changed slightly over the years, the basic concept and design (single coin, stiff handle, fruit symbols) remained firmly in place until as recently as the mid-1960s, when Bally's introduced electrical slots with light-and-sound effects, multiple-coin betting, and triple-pay lines. The new machines finally attracted action from participants other than the proverbial wives of crap shooters and twenty-one players. Still, these quarter slots held a substantial 20 percent of the drop, paying off in sporadic, though sizable, jackpots—perpetuating their reputation as sucker bait. Slots accounted for a minimal 30 percent of gambling revenues up until 1975.

Then dollar slots appeared on the casino scene. Since these machines handled much larger action, they could be set on a much lower hold, starting at 10 percent, and even dropping down to five without compromising the house advantage. (Five percent of a buck is equal to 20 percent of a quarter.) With more frequent and bigger payoffs, slots began to account for higher percentages of the gross (42 percent in 1980) and more space on the casino floor.

In the last ten years, microchips have added an incredible variety to reel slots and video machines. Electronic slot machines come in many varieties with all the bells and whistles; multi-game video machines actually give you your choice of reel slots and other video variations. Reel slots, video poker, video keno, blackjack, roulette, and even greyhound racing these days contribute to the coin-operated machines' average of 60 percent of casino floor space, and up to 70 percent of revenues, which means more profits for the casinos than all table games combined. Progressive reel slots, such as Quartermania and Megabucks, are linked throughout the state by modem and have multiplied jackpots into the millions of dollars, competing with state lotteries. And new models now take tokens worth $100 and even $500.

Slots are particularly popular with first-timers, as well as players somewhat intimidated by the fast pace and high pressure of the table games. They're particularly *un*popular with old-timers and professionals, who consider them machines to take your money. This is true of spinning-reel slots, whose main problem is that you

(top) Arrivals lighten their loads at McCarran Airport . . . (bottom) but in Las Vegas, it all comes out in the wash.

simply can't fathom the odds against you, which can be anywhere from two percent to 25 percent (by law in Nevada). So how do you locate a "loose" slot? First, generally, the higher the bet, the lower the hold. Nickel machines keep an average of 20 percent, quarter machines around 10 percent, dollar machines roughly five. So, depending on your bankroll, play the dollar slots for an increased expectation, and the nickel slots for more action or less risk.

One of the great myths about gambling is that a slot machine comes "due" for a jackpot. The truth is that the odds at slots are permanently and unalterably fixed. If the odds of lining up three sevens on a 25-cent slot machine have been set by the casino at one in 10,000 spins, then those odds remain one in 10,000 whether the three sevens have been hit three times in a row or haven't been hit for the last 30 years. Don't waste a lot of time playing a machine that you suspect is "ready," and don't think that if someone hits a jackpot on a particular machine only minutes after you've finished playing on it that it was "yours."

If you have the hots for slots, remember to join as many slot clubs as you can. Slot clubs are akin to airline frequent-flyer programs: they reward you with prizes, comps, even cash rebates for your playing time on slot machines.

■ CRAPS

Walk into any casino anywhere in the world and follow your ears toward the locale where humans (as opposed to machines) are making the loudest or rowdiest sound —you can bet the rent money that it emanates from the crap tables. Craps generates the most action and excitement of all casino games, for several reasons. It's extremely fast. Selected bets have one of the lowest house advantages in the casino, and the variety of wagers is extremely enticing. Craps is a game in which the players, especially the shooter, have a personal connection with the primary equipment, the magical dice. And it's a *group* game, in which you can bet with or against the shooter, and hot streaks can literally raise the temperature of the casino. When a new shooter steps up to roll, one who looks as if he or she couldn't "make a point with a pencil sharpener," you can bet against. But when the dice keep rolling and the players keep winning and the crowds keep gathering (on both sides of the pit), there's no excitement like it anywhere else in the casino.

Dice, in one form or another, have been used for gambling for thousands of years. But America's game of "bank craps" evolved from hazard, a dice game that gripped Europe for a thousand years. Hazard was introduced to Europe in the eighth century by Muslims who conquered Corsica; from there it spread quickly through Italy, and over to Spain, France, and England. The French word *hasard* derives from the Arabic *az-zahr*, which means "dice." The French also referred to the two spot and three spot as "crabs." Hazard entered the United States through New Orleans in the early nineteenth century and was transformed by Southern slaves into a primitive form of "private craps." The game spread up the Mississippi River and out from there. Around the turn of the twentieth century, a dicemaker, John Winn, introduced the crap bank, wherein the players, instead of betting against each other, bet against the bank. Winn collected a half-percent commission on each bet, and allowed wagers with and against the shooter. Other dice players immediately booked crap games, and additional refinements were made. According to John Scarne, by 1910, bank craps had overtaken faro as the most popular casino game in America.

Craps is a complicated game to learn completely, and the hardest to step up to the first time. Luckily, with only a partial knowledge of the rules and percentages, you can still play an intelligent and exciting game of craps. By making the first and simplest wager (on the pass or don't-pass line), and backing the bet with odds (usually single and double), you're bucking one of the lowest percentages in the house: .6 percent. (A few casinos offer triple odds, with a .4 percent vig; the Horseshoe, Stratosphere, and Frontier casinos now offer 100 times odds for a .2 percent house advantage.) Simply placing your checks on the "line," you also remain blissfully ignorant of all the sucker bets, while still participating in a fast and fun game.

Other wagers include come and don't come, field, big six and eight, place and buy, and proposition. To fully understand the game, it's necessary to spend a couple of hours reading about the bets, rules, and procedures, a couple more hours practicing with the dice and memorizing the odds, and a few more making tinhorn bets at the live action (though preferably at a relatively quiet table) while familiarizing yourself with the well-defined crap subculture.

Craps, like the wheel of fortune, keno, roulette, and slot machines, falls under the "independent-event" category of gambling. In plain English, this means that the wheel, reels, balls, and dice have no memory. Each roll of the bones has nothing to do with the roll preceding it, nor the roll following. The roulette ball

(opposite) Stickman, boxman, and yo'leven—stick with the line bets and odds.

simply does not have the capacity to say to itself, "Well, I haven't hit number 23 for 114 spins, so it must be time." The same is true for slots, which immediately dispels a myth in which the majority of slot players, even those who understand gambling theory, believe: that a machine comes due for a jackpot. We know that the theoretical odds of a reel slot lining up three sevens remain the same for every hand. Thus, "systems" at craps, like roulette, are mostly wishful thinking. The crap-systems literature tends to record and analyze thousands of consecutive rolls, instructs how to follow hunches, and describes various money-management strategies, from conservative stakes at a "cold" table to aggressive betting on a long roll. The final word on crap systems was delivered by Nick "The Greek" Dandelos, one of the all-time great gamblers. "The best long-term attack I know of at craps," he said, "is to play the don't pass line and lay the odds. Using that system I've lost millions of dollars."

On that note, a final caveat. In spite of the low house advantage, craps still retains nearly 20 percent of the drop. Why? Sucker bets, certainly: proposition wagers have a 9.09- to 16.7-percent advantage. But also, the game is played so fast and the betting reaches such precipitous elevations with Old Man Percentage collecting his commission on every last check, that you can lose your bankroll faster, though arguably with more enjoyment, than at probably any other game in the casino. To ensure the enjoyment and reduce the risk, study the odds carefully, and do not deviate from a strict and well-planned betting strategy based on the size of your bankroll.

■ VIDEO POKER

With the introduction of video poker machines in the late 1970s, a whole new dimension was added to coin-operated gambling machines. Finally, here was an interactive machine with which one could make decisions, play hunches, and have a whole level of enjoyment beyond the "idiot pull." Video poker immediately carved a large new class of casino customers out of local Nevadans and frequent visitors, and greatly swelled the ranks at Gamblers Anonymous meetings. Women especially seem to develop intense love affairs with video poker machines. Today, video poker is a mainstay in bars, lobbies, supermarkets, laundromats, and convenience stores, in addition to casinos.

You can play video poker machines with pennies, nickels, quarters, dollars, "big nickels" ($5 tokens), $25 tokens, even $100 tokens. The variations of games have grown tremendously over the past few years. You now have your choice of jacks or better, deuces and jokers wild, bonus, double bonus, double double bonus, and triple bonus; progressive meters on all the versions, and dozens of different payback schedules for each variation.

Video poker machines can be handicapped (meaning you can determine the exact house advantage) by analyzing the payout schedules posted on the machines themselves. Some video poker machines, in fact, give the player a slight advantage (assuming that the player doesn't make any mistakes). Because it's a game that can, in some instances, be beaten, video poker has approached the exalted level of blackjack when it comes to being analyzed and computerized. Basic strategies have been developed for maximizing the expected value; several books and computer programs teach you how to excel at video poker.

■ BACCARAT

The origins of baccarat are obscure. Some gambling historians say it originated in Sicily, others insist on Corsica. Still others claim that a form of baccarat was played by peasants in Paris during the reign of Louis XIV, during the late seventeenth century. Wherever it came from, the original version of today's baccarat was a simple numbers game. There were two participants, a player and a dealer. The dealer gave the player two cards and took two for himself. The player whose cards totaled the closest to nine won. Tens and face cards counted as zero, hence the name of the game, baccarat, which in Italian means zero.

This simple street "game of nines" was combined with a game called "chemin de fer," or "shimmy," which was played only by the highest ranking of the French nobility in their private gambling salons. Shimmy was also a game of nines, but each player could take a third card. A number of rules pertaining to the third card, as well as the practice of collecting a commission from players, evolved over the centuries, until modern chemin de fer found its way to the casinos of pre-Castro Havana in the late 1950s, where it was known as Cuban baccarat. From there, it was a short hop to the casinos of Las Vegas.

The Sands introduced the game to the American gambling public in November 1959, shortening the name to baccarat. The Sands, and later the other Nevada casinos, retained the aura of glamour and exclusivity that had clung to the game since the time of the French nobility, by segregating the tables in a hushed pit off the main casino, costuming the dealers in tuxedos, employing well-dressed attractive shills, and imposing high minimums on the betting action.

Today, baccarat is played for higher stakes than any game in the casino. Most baccarat games require a lofty minimum bet of $100. And some players, usually from the Far and Middle East, have been known to wager in excess of $100,000 per hand. These "whales," as they are referred to, are both coveted and feared by the casinos. The results of play in casino baccarat pits can often mean the difference between a profitable and unprofitable month for a casino company.

Of course, you don't really have to be an Arab oil dealer to sit down at a baccarat game. Many casinos offer mini-baccarat tables in the main pit. Mini-baccarat is played on an undersized table (often just a blackjack table with a baccarat layout). The rules are the same, but there's less protocol and bets are as low as $5 per hand.

■ BLACKJACK

If craps is the hottest and most extrovert game in the casino, then blackjack is the coolest and most cerebral. Blackjack is the only game in the casino that has a memory, which means that cards removed from play can be remembered and cards remaining to be played can be determined. The house advantage for twenty-one actually changes after every hand, depending on the cards already used. Thus, aside from video poker, blackjack is the only casino "bank" game (played against the house) that invites various levels of skill into play. It's not easy, but world-class blackjack players can and do earn six-figure salaries working full-time at it. Consequently, blackjack has been analyzed, computerized, theorized, strategized, advertised, epitomized—in short, *scrutinized*—by a legion of hackers, mathematicians, writers, and professional players down to its last obsessive detail. If craps and slots are subcultures, blackjack is an entire universe.

Naturally, the casinos have a difficult time tolerating a game at which they can be beaten, and at one edge of the blackjack universe, the player-pit relationship has become extremely polarized. Card counters (skilled players who can track the cards and calculate the corresponding advantages and disadvantages at a high speed and degree of accuracy) have been receiving the bum's rush since the advanced and highly effective systems began showing up in the early 1970s. But even if you have no interest in casing the deck, a lesser level of skill, known as basic strategy, can be learned in just a few hours of study and practice. Basic strategy reduces the house advantage to near, or even below, the best odds at craps. In a massive study of players and hands conducted during the blackjack card-counting controversy in Atlantic City in the early 1980s, players were categorized as novice, experienced, basic strategist, and card counter. Players using basic strategy bucked an average .5 percent edge, while the best card counters enjoyed a 1-percent to 1.5-percent long-term advantage over the house, with some situations achieving mythical sure-thing status. Novice and experienced (or general public) were at a 1.5- to 2-percent disadvantage (2 percent is the number the casinos tend to use when figuring their edge at blackjack, primarily for purposes of rewarding comps to blackjack players). Even if you don't count cards, don't practice basic strategy, and simply are familiar with the rules of the game, your expected loss per wager is less than half what it is at roulette.

The origins of twenty-one are as obscure as the origin of playing cards themselves. Some historians trace the symbols on cards to the eighth-century Chinese T'ang Dynasty, whose paper money used pictures of princesses, emperors, and governors to signify value. The first mention of playing cards in Europe appears in the writings of a Swiss monk in the mid-fourteenth century, and by the late 1500s, a card game called *bassette* had taken the Continent by storm. Bassette was played with the Italian tarot deck, which consisted of 78 cards in four suits: four face cards in each suit (knight, jack, queen, king), 10 "spot" or numbered cards, and 21 trumps (from the French *triomphe*); this is generally considered to be the direct ancestor of today's 52-card deck. Bassette gave way to faro in Europe by the early 1700s, basically a guessing game as to which cards of the deck would appear next.

Faro made its way to America, as usual, via New Orleans and the Mississippi River following the Louisiana Purchase of 1803. Faro remained the most popular betting game in the U.S. throughout the nineteenth century and into the twentieth; at the time of the Comstock, 300 faro banks were in operation in Nevada. There are as many theories as to why faro died out in Nevada by the 1950s as there are why the Anasazi abandoned Pueblo Grande de Nevada in the early twelfth century. But by 1963, Major Riddle, then president of the Dunes, reported in his *Weekend Gambler's Guide* that only the Stardust sponsored a faro game, between midnight and 9 A.M., and the Fremont ran one for a few hours a day. The Reno Ramada tried to revive faro in 1987, to major indifference.

The French claim blackjack as a direct descendant of their *vingt-et-un,* which arrived in America right on schedule and swept through the states in the nineteenth century. Modern-day blackjack has been traced to the early 1900s' backroom gambling dens at race tracks in Evansville, Indiana. Here, dealers paid a $5 bonus for a two-card count of 21 when one card was either the black jack of spades or clubs—hence the nickname. Blackjack made its first public appearance in Nevada casinos as soon as gambling was legalized in 1931, and within 15 years had replaced craps as the most popular bank game.

This is all the more remarkable since neither the casinos nor the players knew much about the game or the odds. Early blackjack literature reflects this ignorance, and relies, for evaluating the undetermined house advantage, on the rule that players draw their cards first, and if they bust they lose, even if the dealer also busts later in the same hand. John Scarne claims to have perfected a form of "card casing" in the late 1940s that effectively got him barred from several unnamed casinos; Scarne's basic strategy for playing blackjack was published in the first edition of his *Complete Guide to Gambling* in 1961. He also figured the house advantage at 5.9 percent (this number has been more accurately calculated to 5.5 percent) if players mimicked the dealer (simply drawing to 17). This could be reduced, he wrote, to 2.15 percent using proper doubling-down and splitting procedures.

But conventional history tends to favor the four Army engineers at Aberdeen Proving Ground in Maryland who played tens of thousands of blackjack hands and produced advanced calculations that determined "basic strategy" for blackjack; their results were published in the September 1956 issue of the *Journal of the American Statistical Association.* Mathematics professor Edward O. Thorp used the results to originate a card-counting technique, and published his notorious *Beat the Dealer* in 1962. The original Thorpe method was extremely difficult to master and implement, and the casinos, though they battened down the hatches and waited for the storm of red ink, actually profited handsomely from the "storm"—of black-ink publicity.

It's approaching four decades since the appearance in print of card-counting techniques, and the refinements, by both the counters and casinos, have been extreme. The counting systems themselves have been fine-tuned by the most powerful computers, simulating billions of hands. A dozen or so competing systems have been developed, tested, and marketed. Most are based on a "plus-minus count" in which cards are assigned values of plus one, minus one, or zero, and are added or subtracted to determine the "running count." This is divided by the approximate number of decks remaining, for the "true count," which is used to calculate the amount of bets. Some systems manage to combine the true count with the running count into what's called an "unbalanced count." Others even employ a "side count," for figuring insurance-play odds, for example.

All the while, card counters must be acutely alert to the dealer and floormen, the casinos' front-line defense against blackjack experts. Much attention has been paid to card handling: shuffling (zone, stutter, stripping), cutting and loading the deck, tracking the shuffle. Many brilliant minds have concerned themselves with dealer "tells" (mannerisms that reveal the value of the hole card), spooking and front loading (glimpsing the dealer's hole card), and cheating (dealing seconds, clumping, palming). Formulas have been written to determine profit expectations (bet times advantage times hands per hour), and proportional bet-sizing methods developed to maximize bankrolls. Table hopping, depth charging, Wonging, single-, double-, and multi-deck strategies, toking guidelines, team play, credit manipulation, and camouflage have all been applied to the twenty-one pit. Every minuscule variable of the entire experience has been dissected and corrected and perfected—much of it to avoid being detected.

The casinos, of course, haven't been idle in the meantime. Sophisticated detection techniques have been added to the pit personnel's typically intense scrutiny of players, along with tightened security and heightened countermeasures: multi-deck shoes, lowered table limits, unbalanced shuffling, fewer hands between shuffles, intimidation, scrutinized table statistics, dealer resistance, barring, and black lists. Many casinos feel they're at war with counters. Others are more patient. All casinos are observed and rated by periodicals, such as *Blackjack Monthly*, for levels of card-counting cooperation.

Doubtless, the myriad hoops that card counters must pass through discourage even serious blackjack players. But learning basic strategy is only slightly more challenging than learning the rules and options of the game itself, and can quickly, legitimately, and painlessly reduce your disadvantage from 5.5 percent by mimicking the dealer or nearly 2 percent calculated against the general public to an average .8 percent—without in the least jeopardizing your enjoyment of the game. Isn't that, after all, what gambling is all about?

SEX, LIES, AND LAS VEGAS

(**Note:** This chapter follows local sex industry practice in its use of the term "girls" as an acceptable label for women who practice prostitution.)

CASINO GAMBLING IS ACCESSIBLE, ACCOUNTABLE, and accepted. With books, videotapes, even lessons provided free by the casinos themselves, you can participate in the games, manage your bankroll, and maintain the proper attitude—in short, *play intelligently*—in a very short time. On the other side of the tables, the house advantage, that intractable swindle behind your predictable dwindle, is the worst-kept secret in Nevada. The second worst-kept secret is that sex is nearly as prevalent an illegal business in Las Vegas as gambling is a legal one. But there's one main difference. The mathematically exact and publicly acknowledged gambling business is inversely proportional to the profoundly enigmatic and unspoken scope of the business of sex in Las Vegas.

■ BLOCK 16

At the turn of the century, red-light districts were common all over the country. They were confined and adequately policed. By the time Las Vegas was founded in 1905, Nevada's tradition of flesh peddling in mining boomtowns was nearly 50 years old, as old as the state itself.

Las Vegas's original sex market, known as Block 16 (downtown between First and Second, and Ogden and Stewart streets) was typical. A mere block from the staid and proper First State Bank, the Block was established in 1905 by conservative town planners working for the San Pedro, Los Angeles and Salt Lake Railroad, as the predictable byproduct of the company's liquor-containment policy. Immediately after purchasing Block 16 lots at the railroad auction, two saloon owners hitched their establishments to freight teams and dragged them over from Ragtown to the Block—with the working girls trailing right behind. Hastily erected lean-tos were eventually replaced by a row of cribs behind the saloons, and finally by rooms upstairs, all in a "line" facing Second Street. The Block, sleepy and deserted during the daytime, woke up at night, when its well-known vices, gambling and whoring, temporarily banished the dried-up, small-town desolation. When the train pulled in, no matter what time of day, savvy travelers used the 45-minute stop, as the engines were serviced with coal and water, to re-fuel themselves. This group of men daily huffed the few blocks to the Block for a couple of drinks, a little faro, maybe even a quickie.

In a twilight zone not quite illegal, Block 16 was not quite legal either. During the early years, saloons operating brothels were required to buy $500 licenses. Later, regular raids and shakedowns helped finance local government. The 40 or so "darlings of the desert" were required to undergo weekly medical exams; at $2 per, the city physician held a plum position! Law and order were maintained by the steely eyes and quick fists of six-foot-three, 250-pound Sam Gay, the one en-during character from the Block, who went from bouncer to five-term sheriff.

Even with an occasional spirited civic campaign to eliminate it, Block 16's activities were barely interrupted by the state's 1911 ban on gambling. It also man-aged to survive the tidal wave of shutdowns nationwide during the Progressive years of this century's second decade. The wave did touch Las Vegas in the 1920s, however, when a grand jury instructed city commissioners that "occupants of houses of ill fame not be allowed on the streets, unless properly clothed." On hot summer nights it wasn't uncommon to see scantily clad women sitting in second-floor windows along the Line while young boys on bikes rode by for a peek. The Block fared well during the tricky years of Prohibition, with booze provided by bootleggers from the boonies of North Las Vegas. And even during the federal years of Boulder Dam and the New Deal, amorality thrived, and Block 16 housed more than 300 working girls without undue interference.

Ironically, the re-legalization of wide-open gambling in 1931 foreshadowed an end to the Line, and kindled the enduring opposition of casino operators to bla-tant prostitution. The clubs, casinos, and hotels along Fremont Street were bright, boisterous, and (mostly) benign, but the Second Street approach to the Line was suitably subdued, sequestered, slightly sinister. Respectable residents now only ventured into the Block while acting as guides to visiting friends. At least one practical joker arranged for a shady lady to emerge and greet, familiarly, the visit-ing friend, wife at his side! To the dismay of local boosters, the prosaically named Block 16 began to gain a measure of fame, as word spread about this last holdout of the Wild West, and tourists to the dam site and Lake Mead visited Las Vegas to

Rare photo taken in the '30s of Block 16's working ladies outside the Arizona Club.

rubberneck the saloons and casinos and bordellos. It was no accident that the downtown sawdust joints, and even the first two hotels on the Strip, adopted strictly frontier motifs.

What finally killed Block 16 was World War II. The War Department had many reasons to want open prostitution closed. With soldiers at the gunnery range coming up for off-duty passes in rotations of hundreds per night, the road to downtown Las Vegas could become Intercourse Boulevard and Block 16 would turn into the "pubic center of the West—this at a time when syphilis took weeks to check, and when gonorrhea could cripple a company," Gabriel Vogliotti wrote in his fascinating *Girls of Nevada*. The voices of the wives of men assigned to bases near notorious Las Vegas (and Reno) were heard loud and clear in Washington: by allowing uninhibited sex for sale in the vicinity, the government was offering federal help in sex betrayal to men who'd been called to arms. Thus, these women believed, the War Department was "debauching men and cheapening womanhood." When the commander of the Las Vegas Aerial and Gunnery Range threatened to declare the whole town off-limits to servicemen, local officials immediately revoked the liquor licenses and slot-machine permits of the casinos on Block 16.

These fronts financed the prostitution, which by itself could not finance the fronts, and the Block's illustrious 35-year alternating current finally ran out of juice. (Today it's occupied by a parking structure for Binion's Horseshoe, fronted by a statue of Benny himself astride his trusty steed.

■ ROXIE'S

Las Vegas's era of centralized and destigmatized prostitution was officially eulogized, but another 30 years would pass before it would become unquestionably illegal. In fact, many Las Vegans opposed the Block's demise. A petition was submitted to city officials, with 395 signatures, to reopen it—not only to satisfy clients' needs and enhance the community's economic health, but also to keep the single men away from married women and high school girls. The brief movement failed, however. Some of the pros relocated to Skid Row on First Street, a block away, while others settled at the Little and Kit-Kat clubs out on Boulder Highway.

After the war, a few of the old proprietors attempted to revive the Block, which had gone to seed with cheap rooming houses, but the city condemned most of the buildings in 1946. Another nail in the coffin of brothel prostitution in Las Vegas was hammered into place in 1949, only two years after Bugsy's untimely demise. State Senator A. V. Tallman of Winnemucca introduced legislation totally legalizing brothels in Nevada. The measure passed both houses, but Governor Vail Pittman vetoed it after powerful prodding by the increasingly influential hotel-casino owners. The veto fell short of being overturned by only a few votes.

Meanwhile, Las Vegas brothels refused to be laid to rest. Organized prostitution expanded beyond the city limits. The Kassabian Ranch and C-Bar-C were located in Paradise Valley a little off the Strip, while Roxie's squatted on Boulder Highway (near the intersection of today's Sahara Avenue) in a section known as Formyle. The Kassabian was shut down by the county vice squad in 1946, and the C-Bar-C burned to the ground in a mysterious fire shortly thereafter. But Roxie's survived well into the 1950s. The owners, Eddie and Roxie Clippinger, surrounded themselves with strong juice by paying off, year after year, the county sheriff, two county commissioners, and a law firm, one of whose partners was the state lieutenant governor.

(previous pages) Inside the Mirage.

The FBI finally raided Roxie's in April 1954, charging the Clippingers with violation of the Mann Act (transporting girls across state lines for immoral purposes). Disclosures during the trial in Los Angeles, combined with a sting operation contrived by local crime reporter Ed Reid (covered in detail in *Green Felt Jungle*), produced indictments against the sheriff and a county commissioner, disgraced the lieutenant governor, contributed to the governor's subsequent defeat, and revealed Jake Lansky's hidden ownership in the Thunderbird, which led to the revocation of its license by the Tax Commission a year later. Among other revelations about Roxie's were payoffs to the county vice squad to discourage prostitution on the Strip and eliminate competition, a dollar-a-head kickback to cabbies who delivered tricks to Roxie's (members of Teamsters Local 631, the cab drivers once officially petitioned Eddie Clippinger for $2 a head), and the presence of TV cameras in the cribs. When Roxie's was finally driven under, it was one more nail in the old coffin. But it was by no means the last.

Because meanwhile, a new system of cash and carry was evolving as Las Vegas developed into the city with the most hotel rooms—all those beds!—in the world. And it all started, naturally enough, in the feverish dreams of that prominent pioneer and private pimp, Benjamin "Bugsy" Siegel.

■ MOE, BUGSY, AND GIRLIE

The sex business had been part of Siegel's overall vision from the beginning. An inveterate ladies' man, he instinctively wanted to provide easy sex to seduce, service, and presumably satisfy the suckers. His Flamingo established two traditions of sex Las Vegas–style. First, he designed the hotel with separate modular wings, accessible without ever having to pass through a lobby or main entrance. This was at a time, in the late 1940s, when the men who ran hotels actively barred pros: grim, gray-haired matrons guarded elevators, and Mack Sennet–type house detectives roamed the halls, listening for the telltale evidence. At the Flamingo, a guy could spend every night with a different girl and never be seen by anybody.

The second tradition was that casinos should be "dressed up" with girls. Young and pretty. Suggestively attired. Everywhere! Coat-check girls. Hat-check girls. Cigarette girls. Shills. Escorts. Loungers. Showgirls. And the ultimate juice girls:

girls: the pit cocktail waitresses. Some working girls were hired as hotel help to be at the beck and call of the house; they quickly and quietly introduced other receptive workers to the lucrative sideline and simple system of being procured. Unfortunately, Bugsy left the hotel business before he had the opportunity to extend and fine-tune his sex agenda. But he laid the foundation of a program that would develop quickly and manage to maintain a delicate balance between passionately opposing policies for the next 20 years.

Though many operators no doubt contributed, it's conceivable that Moe Dalitz, owner of the Desert Inn and the man who first organized modern Las Vegas, originated the ultimate methods of supplying sex to guests. Dalitz was 50 when he came to Las Vegas, and he knew many things. He knew, like Bugsy, the sexual excitement implicit in gambling, and that women were integral to the casino scenery. But Dalitz had faced down the Kefauver Commission during his second year as an owner, and was aware of the growing distaste of the public for prostitution, so he knew the imperative of keeping it discreet. He also knew that countless women, of every description, were attracted to Las Vegas, and that uncontrolled prostitution became very dangerous in urban areas because of its association with pimps, drugs, white slavery, theft, and violence.

Finally, Dalitz knew that all the conflicting realities boiled down to two basic truths. First, gamblers needed sex: the suggestion of it, with women parading around on stage and decorating the floor; the mysterious myth of its ready availability with gorgeous and expensive pros; and the eventual consummation—prescribed, safe, hidden—that gets the guy to sleep or wakes him up, makes him feel lucky when he wins or consoles him when he loses, keeps him around the tables a little longer, and sends him home having experienced what has been called the "Las Vegas total." But second, the sex trade had to be directly and carefully choreographed, from start to finish, in order to avoid any chance of offending the millions of straights that filled the hotels, of becoming so obvious or vulgar or hazardous that it menaced in any way the smooth and consistent workings of the great god Percentage.

So Dalitz passed the word. Around the Desert Inn. Through his managers. To the front-line staff—the hosts, the pit bosses, the dealers, the bell captains, the bartenders. And to the other owners, to be passed down to their staffs. The rules, as usual, mostly revolved around juice. The girl had to be connected. She had to work for the hotel, be hired as a hooker and given a straight job for a front, or asked, after being hired, whether she was interested in turning tricks. Or she had to be recommended by a trusted employee who could vouch for her. The girl had to be cooperative. Her main objective was to see that the player spent more time at the tables and less time in the hotel room. She had to be reliable. And she'd better be honest. After all, the money that wallet thieves and chip hustlers stole belonged, in the words of Mario Puzo, "to the gambling casinos, and was just being temporarily held by the john." In the attitude of the gaming bosses, "larcenous girls were really stealing casino money."

Charges were standardized, from a quickie French up to the full trick, which was to cost no more than a "honeybee," "a bill"—a hundred dollars. Any deviation would be immediately and summarily rectified, by any one of the number of private and public security forces that surrounded, in concentric circles, the casino counting rooms. Similarly, freelancers were actively discouraged. Any girl found hanging around the casino, restaurants, or lounges too long was earnestly apprised of the rules and either driven away or registered, as the case might be. Streetwalkers, part-time call girls, divorcees doing their "friendly forty-two," swinging coeds or housewives, cocktail waitresses, showgirls—any woman with enough beauty, body, or appeal to sell, and the capability of successfully compartmentalizing sex into a purely business transaction—all translated Bugsy Siegel's vision, and Moe Dalitz's version, into a vast and well-managed sex market in Las Vegas, throughout the 1950s and 1960s.

The personal connection extended to the solicitor as well. A man who wanted sex, from a high roller to a tinhorn, had to use the proper channels. The major plungers, well known to owners and executives, were supplied with a showgirl or a high-class courtesan as a matter of course. Lesser players, if well known to the cocktail waitresses and registered cruisers, could have their pick of the pit girls. Hotel guests were fired on by the bell captain or one of his boys; casino customers could become familiar enough with a pit boss or bartender to make a circumspect inquiry. Cab drivers and motel clerks carved their own niche within the system, but professional pimps were quickly discouraged. The word spread among the legions of male Las Vegas patrons: follow established protocol. Accrue some juice and use it judiciously. Thus the whole path was a procession of pedigree, from the whispered word to the soft knock on the door. It had to be man to man before it could be man to woman.

If you didn't know the procedure, however, you might walk away thinking that Las Vegas's fabled copious commercial copulation was one of the great myths of the day. Because above all, the pandering, procuring, and coupling had to be *illegal*. Herein lay the true beauty of the system, and the unmistakable signature of Siegel, Dalitz, and all the other racketeers-turned-executives. For propriety, for privacy, and ultimately to protect the reputation of legal gambling, the whole delicate system, its makeup, mechanics, and management, had to operate outside the law. One false step, one loose lip, and the whole precarious structure could collapse like a house of cards.

■ IS THERE OR ISN'T THERE?

This code of silence, second nature to the gamblers, was imposed upon the vast industry of retail sex in Las Vegas, one that continued to invite equal measures of fascination and condemnation. The system reigned supreme for almost 20 years, and worked so well that wildly differing impressions of it were reported. Writing in 1953, Paul Ralli commented naively, "One of the best proofs that Las Vegas is reasonably outside the control of mob influence is the almost total absence of organized prostitution. Ten years ago, prostitution constituted the town's main attraction, next to gambling. But today, it's as though the call of Las Vegas is to the appetite of the pocketbook rather than that of the flesh." Hillyer and Best, otherwise far from priggish or censorious, wrote in 1955, "Las Vegas today is probably as clear of professional female enterprise as any other resort area its size. Maybe more so. Gambling is the greatest deterrent to sex since man invented the chastity belt."

Other writers, however, had different ideas. Typically, *Green Felt Jungle* established the negative extreme. "Money mysteriously breeds prostitutes the way decaying flesh breeds maggots. Where there's easy money there's whores; it's that basic. And where there's gambling, there's easy money." Reid and Demaris claimed that of Las Vegas's 1962 population of 65,000 residents, "a conservative 10 percent are in one way or another engaged in prostitution. Cabbies, bartenders, bellhops, newsboys, proprietors of various establishments (liquor stores, motels, etc.), gamblers, special deputies, and professional pimps make a sizable income by procuring for a veritable army of prostitutes."

In *Gambler's Money* (1965), Wally Turner saw the system a bit more objectively:

Every night lovely long-legged dancers appear on stage, contributing to the air of suppressed excitement that the gambling operators seek to create. Are there prostitutes among them? Las Vegas being what it is, undoubtedly some of the girls sell themselves for money on occasion. To some of the [bosses], sex is just another commodity and they would insist that it be sold. But prostitution in Las Vegas has changed in the past few years. There are no houses where prostitutes live together. There are no streetwalkers. But there are many call girls, and frequently they do business only through the staff of one or more of the casinos. Some share their fees with the employees who called them. Others may be called directly by management to deal with a heavy winner and distract him, or at least keep him in town until the pendulum of the percentages swings again to the house and he is relieved of his winnings.

Vogliotti reported that a magazine writer came to Las Vegas to do a story on prostitution at the height of the Dalitz system, but didn't get very far. His parting judgment? "Only a Senate investigating committee could extract any truth." The writer found that "call girls, showgirls, cocktail waitresses all gave the same 'Who me?' as did the owners, lawyers, and police. It is a vast, smooth mendacity, a universal conspiracy to deny." Vogliotti declared that "the amount of prostitution in Las Vegas is, safely, that of Paris or Amsterdam, but the whole thing has been so beautifully distorted by writers that few men really know the picture."

Finally, Howard Hughes entered the picture, and all the careful construction, all the distinct lines, bled together like a watercolor in the rain.

■ HOWARD AND JOE

On one hand, it's possible to ascribe a direct cause and effect—from the Hughes whirlwind to the Great Las Vegas Working Girl Invasion of the 1970s. Certainly the owners of the Desert Inn, Sands, Frontier, Castaways, and Silver Slipper were bought out, and Hughes's staff was in. Certainly Hughes's ultimate Las Vegas chief of staff, Robert Maheu, installed a security team so huge that it constituted a sort

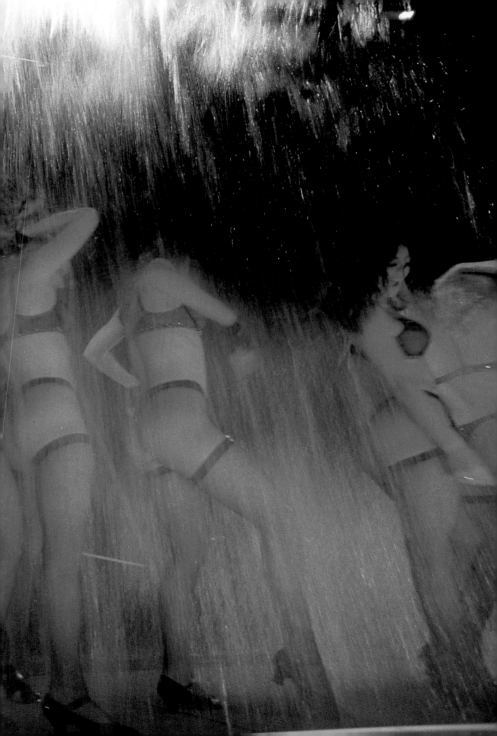

of private army, and he took many emergency steps to erase anything even remotely notorious—skimming, cheating, bribing, racketeering, aiding and abetting, and of course, girl-running. Certainly the old rules were deteriorating and the new rules, strictly enforced, were less than permissive.

On the other hand, the owners may have changed at the Hughes properties, but many bosses stayed on as advisors. And the management of the many non-Hughes hotels—Trop, Stardust, Riviera, Dunes, Sahara, Hacienda, Fremont, Horseshoe, Mint, and a dozen other small casinos and hotels—remained, except for the usual turnover, the same. In 3,000 phone conversations with Hughes during his four years in Las Vegas, Maheu claimed he never once received instructions from his boss on the working-girl situation. Finally, documents exist written by aides to Maheu that read, "When you get into the hotel business, you back into the whore business. Every man who enters the business must decide how he feels about pandering or, at least, supplying the furniture of love."

Maheu subsequently retreated from his staunchly puritan position concerning prostitution in his hotels, but the die had been cast; a strangeness and uncertainty, similar to the period just after the closing of Block 16, crept into the sex business.

This vacuum was quickly filled by Joe Conforte, without whom no chapter on sex in Nevada could be complete. Conforte, who owned the world-famous Mustang Ranch in northern Nevada, had been crusading for more than 15 years for prostitution to emerge from its twilight zone of quasi-legal status into full acceptance within state law. By this time, houses of ill repute had been servicing Nevada for more than 100 years, and nearly 50 rules and regulations had been entered into the state statutes governing the brothel business. For example, no brothel could operate on a main street, or within 400 yards of a church; no advertising was permitted; minors could not be employed in brothels, nor anyone with venereal disease; public opinion could be used by city councils and county commissioners to close brothels as a public nuisance, or to tax and regulate them. In short, 50 convenings of the state legislature hadcontinually added to the control of whorehouses, without finally outlawing them altogether.

Conforte had fought for legalized prostitution in Washoe County's Reno for many years, doing battle with another crusader, District Attorney Bill Raggio (now majority leader of the State Assembly), who finally succeeded in jailing Conforte for a number of years on charges relating to their disagreements. After serv-

(previous pages) Sex on parade, during the "Splash" revue at the Riviera.

ing his time (and running a prostitution ring inside the Carson City prison!), Conforte set up shop at a ranch, known as Mustang, just across the Washoe County line in tiny Storey County (population 1,500), and did a booming business in relative peace and quiet—until charges of "paying off" the county officials started to rankle him. By then, Mustang Ranch was the county's largest taxpayer, which gave Joe a certain amount of juice in local politics. In 1971, Conforte convinced the commissioners to pass Ordinance 38, which legalized, once and for all, prostitution in Storey, the first county in the country ever to do so.

Meanwhile, a young politician named Roy Woofter, whom Conforte had befriended and staked to a law-school education, was elected district attorney of Clark County. Woofter quickly introduced an ordinance allowing one brothel to operate in Las Vegas in a high-walled security compound in a specified area of town, with experienced management, and medical, police, and community clearance—in short, all the features that recommended legalized prostitution. Woofter actually managed to gather a fair amount of local support for the bill, including that of more than one county commissioner, and a surprising number of locals. Immediately, however, the hotel owners and convention bureau officials let out a howl that was heard all the way to the state capital. The owners, as always, wanted prostitution to be available but discreet, so as not to tarnish the already questionable image of the world's gambling capital (they also believed that a brothel would compete with a casino). The convention managers, similarly, insisted that nothing could be more detrimental to their business than a legalized whorehouse nearby (though the illegal working-girls' connection to conventions across the country is truistic).

State legislators wanted to keep Conforte out of Las Vegas, largely to safeguard the image of and revenues from gambling. In 1971, they passed Statute 244-345 (8), rendering prostitution illegal in counties with a population of more than 250,000—which applied, in that year, only to Clark County. This effectively ended the local brothel movement, gave jurisdiction to state law-enforcement agencies, and once and for all pounded the proverbial last nail in the 20-year-old coffin. Conforte's Mustang Massage operated for a year and then folded.

■ THE SIXTIES CATCH UP TO LAS VEGAS

The presence of Howard Hughes, not to mention the quarter-billion dollars he pumped into the local economy, helped stimulate a boom period, in which the Aladdin, Caesars Palace, Landmark, Circus Circus, Four Queens, International, Holiday Inn, and MGM Grand opened in a five-year period, and nearly every existing hotel expanded. Increased tourism and gambling revenues reflected the prosperity and full employment of Lyndon Johnson's Great Society and the Vietnam War. Social upheaval, the sexual revolution, and the drug culture also contributed to the transformation of Las Vegas during the short, intense, and uncertain Hughes era.

For all these reasons, suddenly thousands of new hotel workers—bellmen, bartenders, dealers, cocktail waitresses, showgirls—joined the picture, possessing as little idea about the traditional dynamics of the sex industry as did the vast new wave of visitors. Driven to distraction by the tons of female flesh surrounding him in Las Vegas, a single male tourist now found himself in a quandary when deciding whether to ask a bartender, cab driver, or bell captain about how to hire a girl. Vogliotti described it best. He calculated that in 1974, there could be 600 bartenders at work on the evening shift, and:

> . . . *They* have no single attitude on procurement. If a visitor hits one by chance who is sympathetic, the bartender may solve his problem by asking what he thinks of the little redhead six stools down. But the man mopping the bar may be one of the great majority who is content with his $220 a week and irritated that so many glassy-eyed jerks think he will pimp. He may shrug and explain, deadpan, that being married himself, he often wonders just what the hell you *do* do. On the other hand, he is maybe one of a few who work a quiet second business with a string of girls, or even one who, after long and friendly discourse with a customer, figures him good for a few hundred and goes to a phone to call his wife."

With the demand swelling and the old rules increasingly relegated to history, a dilemma of supply suddenly surfaced. Maybe the conventional wisdom that Hughes had bought out the mob opened the door, or maybe the radical '60s finally arrived in Las Vegas. Whatever the causes, hard-core streetwalkers came out of

(photo by Kerrick James)

the woodwork. In addition, weekend warriors—California secretaries, Utah Lolitas, and the like—descended on Las Vegas like locusts. Today, long-time residents still recall the time, in the late 1970s, when a man couldn't walk the long block from the Sahara to the Riviera *with his wife* without getting a couple of bold and lurid solicitations. The corner of Flamingo Avenue and the Strip was so overrun that streetwalkers took turns directing traffic. Some were freelancers; many had pimps. Some were clean, while many were drug addicts and thieves. It was what the cops, the casinos, and Carson City had feared all along: obvious, rampant, defiant, and dangerous prostitution in the city that could now, with some accuracy, be called Sin Central.

Finally, in the early 1980s, John Moran was elected Clark County sheriff on a platform of ridding the county of its highly visible prostitution problem. In 1982, police arrested 13,000 pros, apprehending many of them two or three times a night. The campaign proved mostly successful; in 1984, around 6,000 arrests were made, and in 1985, around 5,000. In 1986, 90 percent of prostitution-related arrests were made *inside* the hotels, as undercover vice cops collared the freelancers in lounges, and at massage parlors, all of which the sheriff managed to shut down. Once again, Las Vegas was relieved of its unsavory image as a whore capital, by removing the most visible evidence. But by then, other systems had been renewed, or invented.

■ TODAY'S MARKET

The best features of the Dalitz system continue to exist in the casino context, though they're difficult to notice, even if one is on the lookout for them. The connection to available and trustworthy call girls has become the province of select executives, primarily casino hosts whose job it is to handle the myriad needs of the casino's best customers. The hotel staffs, as well, could have fingers in the illegal sex pie. It's lucrative but risky; if a host or bellman is busted, it'll cost him his job.

The freelance market hasn't exactly disappeared either. Today's intercourse industry has evolved from a variety of influences, but mostly reflects the dominant local service economy. The seminal year was 1975, when getting your head, straight, full French, Greek, English, Roman, Around the World, half and half, golden shower, S&M, B&D, binaca blast (or crème de menthe, or Alka Seltzer), fetish, even Kermit the Frog became simply a matter of letting your fingers do the walking through —where else? The Yellow Pages.

In 1971, the first sex ads appeared in the phone book under Escort Services —two small display ads with women in discreet, two-piece bathing suits. The other ads in the Escort category were for detective agencies. But by 1975, three whole pages of Escort Services left nothing to guesswork, with companies named Lusty Women, Party Girls, Swinging Companions, and Suzi Wong's Matchmaking. In 1977, Escort Services filled five pages and Massage Parlors also filled five. In 1981, a full page of Dating Services showed up, along with a half page of Adult Maid and Butler services. In 1982, however, as part of new Sheriff Moran's crackdown, Massage ads disappeared entirely (except for the legit bodyworkers), Dating disappeared, but seven pages of Escorts remained. By 1987, the continuing crackdown had mostly eliminated Escort Services, but a new listing had emerged: Entertainers. A hundred and six pages worth in 1997! And when this category is closed? Sex might move to such listings as Bed Accessories, or Temporary Services, or even the all-purpose Rentals.

Topless clubs are alive and well in Las Vegas; several are totally nude. Some jiggle joints, such as Olympic Gardens, cater to an upscale and sophisticated crowd, with modern and airy rooms and state-of-the-art sound and light technology. Others still go for the raunch, such as the venerable Palomino in North Las Vegas, and the Tally-Ho on Highland Drive. The most visible is the Girls of Glitter Gulch, right on Fremont Street between Main and First.

A different form of nightclub, commonly known as "sex-tease" establishments, have come under serious legal fire lately, but seem to be extremely hard to shut down and wipe out completely. These places are strictly sucker bait for unsuspecting tourists, all seduction but no consummation. Yellow Page ads, cab drivers (who are paid a kickback for delivering marks), the bartenders, and the girls, often underage in skimpy costumes, all explicitly promise the availability of sex, right after you buy a bottle of non-alcoholic champagne for anywhere from $100 to $6,000. But when you're ready to get it on, or your money is gone, burly bouncers boot you through the back door. You'll know you're in the wrong kind of place if you can't get a drink with hard liquor; sex-tease clubs can stay in business, but they can't get liquor licenses.

Swingers clubs such as the famous Red Rooster, on the other hand, are quite honest about the activities offered therein. You pay $40 admission to get into a private home where swinging singles and couples might or might not hook up with like-minded people for a particular brand of group therapy. Sex is by no means guaranteed, and most would-be swingers, especially single men, spend their time drinking their own booze, shooting pool, watching TV, or just socializing —sort of an Elks club where some people get naked.

Another current wrinkle comes in the form of anonymously published, garage-printed, girlie rags handed out by leafleteers in various places along the Strip, which exhibit pictures of women in suggestive poses and list local phone numbers. Other cheap newsprint advertises the Nye County legal brothels outside of Pahrump. These fliers and tabloids and even Yellow Page ads are all technically illegal; state law prohibits the advertising of prostitution. On the other hand, tacit Las Vegas tradition is tolerant to that extent. After all, even in the age of AIDS and wholesome Convention and Visitors Authority ad campaigns, as long as there's gambling, and parading showgirls and cocktail waitresses and keno runners, and hotel rooms, and a man and a woman. . . .

Soft porn mags fill sidewalk boxes along Las Vegas Boulevard. (photo by Kerrick James)

D A Y   T R I P S
S L I P P I N G   T H E   G R I P   O F   T H E   S T R I P

FOR MOST VISITORS, THE AREA ENCLOSED BY the Fremont Street Experience (from Main to Fourth) and by Las Vegas Boulevard South from Sahara to Tropicana delineates the limits of Las Vegas—the boundaries beyond which 27 million of more than 30 million annual visitors never venture. The hotels, gambling, shows, and food create an electromagnetic field that most first-timers, and many long-termers, don't want to, or can't, escape. Why bother? You can drink for free, take in a lounge act or revue, scarf the cheap food, people-watch till your eyes pop, and gamble at that place and time where and when you feel luckiest. It's exactly what Las Vegas expects and wants you to do.

According to a recent Las Vegas Visitor Profile Study, 28 million of 29.6 million visitors stayed in Las Vegas for four nights or less. A full 75 percent of visitors' trip time was devoted to the big three: eating, sleeping, and gambling (with an average betting budget of $580). Another eight percent of trip time went to entertainment (though only three of ten visitors attended a headliner or floor show), and only seven percent went sightseeing. Of the five million people who got out of town, two million went to Hoover Dam, one and a quarter million to Laughlin, and only 35,000 to stunning Red Rock Canyon, less than a half hour's drive from the heart of Glitter Gulch.

These surprising statistics certainly confirm the irresistibility of the Las Vegas magnet—especially since within a mere hour of city center are some of the American Southwest's most spectacular natural and man-made scenery and attractions. The variety, as well, is plentiful enough to supply even the most fast-lane sightseers with new experiences every day for weeks. Historical, cultural, recreational, and educational venues are found all over town. In addition, high mountains and low deserts, vast lakes and canyon-rimmed rivers, fiery red hillsides and bucolic green valleys, a massive dam and an Old West theme park, ancient Pueblo ruins and Nevada's newest boomtown all beckon from just beyond the fearsome force field.

■ SIGHTS AROUND TOWN

■ OLD LAS VEGAS MORMON FORT

This tiny museum is the oldest building in Las Vegas and a true "soul survivor." The adobe remnant was part of the original 150-square-foot "fort" constructed by Latter-day Saints missionaries in 1855, the first non-Indian residents in Las Vegas Valley. The Mormons abandoned it in 1858. The remnant served as a storage shed on the original Las Vegas Ranch. After buying the ranch, the San Pedro, Los Angeles and Salt Lake Railroad leased the old fort to various tenants, including the Bureau of Reclamation, which stabilized the shed, and rebuilt parts of it to use as a concrete-testing laboratory for Hoover Dam. In 1955, the railroad sold the old fort to the Elks, who in 1963 demolished all the buildings except for the little remnant, which was bought back by the city in 1971. Since then a number of preservation societies have helped keep the Old Fort in place. Artifacts unearthed in a recent archaeological dig on the Old Fort's grounds are displayed inside. It's immensely refreshing to see some preservation of the past in this city of the ultimate now. *Corner of Las Vegas Boulevard North and Washington; (702) 486-3511.*

Tiny remnant of the Mormon fort, oldest building in Nevada.

■ LAS VEGAS NATURAL HISTORY MUSEUM

This is a fun museum for children—and for adults who appreciate good taxidermy from around the world. North American predators are represented by wolves and foxes; black, brown, and polar bears; lynx and mountain lion; the prey by musk ox, bison, Rocky Mountain bighorn. African predators include lions, tigers, leopards, and cheetahs. An especially exotic exhibit displays African deer species: duiker, steinbok, nyala, big kudu, bush bok, klipspringer, and dik-dik, all with fantastically shaped antlers. The Bird Room also exhibits a wide variety of our feathered—and stuffed—friends. The Shark Room features mounted sharks and a 300-gallon aquarium. In addition, there's an impressive collection of dinosaur fossils, including 14 dinosaur skeletons and a skull and foot of *Tyrannosaurus rex*. Meanwhile, three animated dinosaurs nod their heads and swing their tails while roaring for the crowd.

Best for the kids is the Hands-On Room, with a fossil sandbox and dinosaur call, among other playthings. The gift shop sells posters, postcards, puzzles, stuffed and plastic animals, books, and clothes. *900 Las Vegas Boulevard North; (702) 384-3466.*

■ NEVADA STATE MUSEUM AND HISTORICAL SOCIETY

A comfortable and enjoyable place to spend an hour or two studying Mojave Desert and Spring Mountains ecology, Southern Nevada history, and local art. Three rotating galleries exhibit anything from photographs of the neon night or desert to Nevada textiles or early telephone technology. The Hall of Biological Science has interesting exhibits on life in the desert. Learn how the mighty Spring Mountains are a "biological island surrounded by a sea of desert." The Hall of Regional History has graphic displays on mining, nuclear tests, Hoover Dam construction, politics, ranching, and Indians. *700 Twin Lakes Drive, in back of Lorenzi Park; (702) 486-5205.*

■ MARJORIE BARRICK MUSEUM OF NATURAL HISTORY

This is a good place to bone up on local flora, fauna, and artifacts. First study the vegetation in the arboretum outside the museum entrance, then step inside for the wildlife: small rodents, big snakes, lizards, tortoises, gila monster, iguana, chuckwalla, gecko, spiders, beetles, and cockroaches. Wander through the art gallery into some graphic Las Vegas history. Display cases are full of native baskets, kachina dolls, masks, woven goods, pottery, and jewelry. Mojave Desert fossils and minerals are exhibited, with a huge polar bear incongruously standing in the middle. The centerpiece is a rough skeleton of an ichthyosaur, a whale-sized sea lizard, which is Nevada's state fossil. *On the UNLV campus: go east on Harmon Avenue, which dead-ends at the arena parking lot just beyond the museum; (702) 895-3381.*

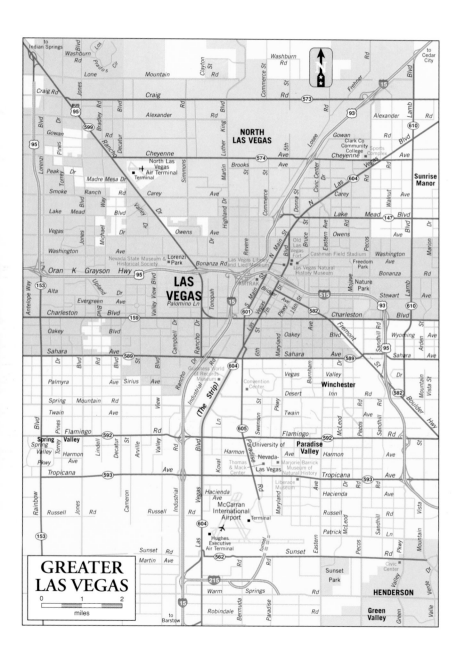

GREATER
LAS VEGAS

0   1   2
miles

Where else but at the Liberace Museum?

■ LIBERACE MUSEUM

Liberace—in life and in death—embodies the heart and soul of Las Vegas. Born in Wisconsin in 1919, third of four children in a musical family, Walter Valentino Liberace (who legally assumed the one name, Liberace, in 1950, and was known as "Lee" to his friends) was a prodigy pianist at age seven and a concert boy wonder at 14. He first played Sin City at age 23. From then on, he was a one-man walking advertisement for the extravagance, flamboyance, and uninhibited tastelessness usually associated with the town he loved so much. Like Las Vegas's surface image, Liberace's costumes began as a means of standing out; then he had to keep topping himself with increasingly outrageous gimmicks. Along the way, he became one of the most popular entertainers of all time. "Mr. Showmanship" racked up six gold records and at one time was entered in the Guinness Book of World Records as the world's highest-paid musician.

The Liberace Museum is the most popular tourist attraction in Las Vegas, outside of the casinos. You can bet the rent that at least two tour buses will be parked out front with hundreds of retirees paying tribute to the man who, his passable playing and uncontrollable clothing notwithstanding, was possessed of a certain charisma, generosity, and genuine rapport with his audiences and inspired mass displays of devotion.

The main building preserves Liberace's costumes: Uncle Sam hot pants, suits made of ostrich feathers, rhinestones, and bugle beads, and capes customized from 100 white fox skins (75 feet long, $700,000) or 500 Black Glama minks (125 pounds, $750,000). Also on display are the world's largest rhinestone (50 pounds, $50,000) and a grossly ornate rolltop desk from his office. The library building on the other side of Carluccio's Restaurant houses family photos, miniature pianos, silver, china, cut glass, gold records, and historical data. Across the parking lot the piano and car gallery contains several antique pianos, Liberace's 50,000-rhinestone Baldwin, his million-dollar mirror-tiled Rolls, a custom rhinestone car (with matching toolbox), and a 1940s English taxi, among others. A gift shop in the main building sells Liberace tapes, albums, videos, postcards, 8x10 glossies, song books, autobiography ($30), and doll ($300). *1775 East Tropicana just east of Maryland Parkway; (702) 798-5595.*

■ GUINNESS WORLD OF
RECORDS MUSEUM

This museum features photographic, typographic, video, audio, and slide-show exhibits of world records: the tallest, fattest, oldest, and most-married men; longest neck, and smallest bicycle; videos of dominoes; slides of the greatest engineering projects; and an informative display of Las Vegas firsts and foremosts. *2780Las Vegas Boulevard South at Sahara Avenue, behind Circus Circus; (702) 792-3766.*

■ HEADING OUT OF TOWN

■ ETHEL M'S DESSERT
AND DESERT

That's Ethel *Mars,* as in Mars Bars (and Milky Ways, 3 Musketeers, and M&Ms). If you feel like taking a ride after lunch or dinner, the free tour takes you past big picture windows overlooking the bright factory, with workers and machines turning and churning, then out into the tasting room. Sample a nut cluster, caramel, butter cream, or liqueur candy, so rich that one piece is a whole dessert. Outside is an enjoyable two-acre cactus garden, with indigenous desert flora. *Cactus Garden Drive: head out of town on East Tropicana, turn right on Mountain Vista, then left on Sunset Way and quick left onto Cactus Garden Drive in Henderson; (702) 458-8864.*

■ CLARK COUNTY
HERITAGE MUSEUM

On the way to Hoover Dam, your first stop out of the city should be this extensive and interesting complex. The main museum houses an incredible collection of history, tracing Indian cultures from the prehistoric to the contemporary, and chronicling exploration, settlement, and industry. Step outside and into the rail cars for a full course on Nevada's railroads, then stroll down to historical Heritage Street, with its four original houses and print shop. Finally, wander out to haunt the ghost town, little more than ruins in the desert. You'll leave with a complete lesson in the background of the Las Vegas area, especially your next stops—Boulder City and Hoover Dam. *1830 South Boulder Highway in Henderson; (702) 455-7955.*

■ RED ROCK CANYON

West of Las Vegas, stretching across the sun-setting horizon and hemming in the valley, are the mighty and rugged Spring Mountains. Smack in the center of this range is Red Rock Canyon, a multicolored sandstone palisade only 15 miles from downtown Las Vegas. Here you'll find 62,000 acres of outdoor splendor—as dramatic a contrast to the electrified cityscape as might be imaginable. The transition from city to suburb, exurb, and then wilderness, is unforgettable. A mere 18 miles from downtown Las Vegas on West Charleston Boulevard (Highway 159), you're on open road through the outback Mojave; the view—thick stands of Joshua trees, backdropped by the precipitous Spring Mountain walls, with the sandstone Calico Hills standing sentinel— has been known to leave even *National Geographic* photographers speechless. In 20 to 30 minutes, you take a right into the Bureau of Land Management's southern Nevada showcase.

Start with the enormity of the semicircular scenery, swallowing crowds and dwarfing climbers. Then superimpose the gorgeous colors of the sandstone—yellow, orange, pink, red, purple—all overlaid by the stalwart and tempered gray of older limestone. Then add the narrow and steep-walled canyons, moist, cool, lush gashes between the cliffs for wonderland hiking, and the contoured, inviting

boulders that have turned Red Rock Canyon into an international climbing destination. Finally, tack on the cooperative year-round climate, the proximity to the city, and the excellent visitor center, and it's safe to say that the nearly 30 million yearly tourists who don't make it to Red Rock Canyon simply don't see Las Vegas.

Red Rock Canyon clearly reveals the limestone, formed when most of Nevada lay under a warm shallow sea, and the massive sand dunes which later covered this desert. Chemical and thermal reactions "petrified" the dunes into polychrome sandstone; erosion sculpted it into strange and wondrous shapes. When the land began faulting and shifting roughly 100 million years ago, the limestone was thrust up and over the younger sandstone, forming a protective layer which inhibited further erosion. Known as the Keystone Thrust, the contact between the limestone and sandstone is as precise as a textbook illustration, and accounts for the bands of contrasting colors in the cliffs. Except for the spectacular canyons carved from runoff over the past 60 million years, the 15-mile-long, 3,000-foot-high sandstone escarpment today remains relatively untouched by the march of time.

The BLM Visitor Center is nestled in the Calico Hills at the lower end of the wide oval that encompasses all this glowing Aztec sandstone. Take a while and orient yourself to the area at the center's excellent 3-D exhibits of geology, flora and fauna, and recreational opportunities, then walk along the short nature trail out back. A 13-mile loop road is open 7 a.m. to dusk and features half a dozen overlooks, picnic sites, and trails leading to springs, canyons, quarries, and *tinajas* (tanks). There is a small per-vehicle entry fee to the loop road. Gas and food are *not* available either at the Visitor Center *or* on the road, so be prepared. With any luck, you will see hikers and climbers dotted along the rock, demonstrating the amazing scale of the fiery walls.

You can easily spend an entire day exploring the edges of the loop road. Be sure to stop at both Calico Vista points, with humongous 6,323-foot Turtle Head Mountain leaning high and limy over the Calico Hills. A short trail from the second vista gets you into the territory. Another trail enters Sandstone Quarry, where red and white sandstone for Southwestern buildings was mined from 1905 to 1912. Absorb the view of the Madre Mountains, a dramatic limestone ridge line of the Spring Range, then swing around south past the White Rock Hills, Bridge and Rainbow mountains, and Mt. Wilson. Hikes enter Lost Creek, Icebox, and Pine Creek canyons. You could then spend another six days hiking around the 16- by 10-mile park, or devote a lifetime to climbing the 1,500 known routes up

(opposite) Hikers and climbers dot Red Rock Canyon.

the red rock. *To reach Red Rock Canyon from Las Vegas, take Interstate 15/US 93 south to Highway 160 (Blue Diamond); take Highway 160 west to Highway 159 (West Charleston Blvd.).* BLM *Visitor Center, Red Rock Canyon; (702) 363-1921.*

■ SPRING MOUNTAIN RANCH STATE PARK

Watch for wild burros along the stretch between Red Rock Canyon and the state park; it's easy to tell the males from the females. Pay at the gate to enter the ranch, nestled at the base of the Wilson Cliffs, sheer buff-colored sandstone bluffs. The area's cooler temperatures, plentiful water, bountiful land, and gorgeous setting have attracted travelers since the 1830s. By 1869, a ranch had been established with a stone cabin and blacksmith shop (both still standing). Three generations of Wilsons owned the land from 1876 till 1948, after which it was sold several times, once to Vera Krupp and once to Howard Hughes. The State Parks Division finally acquired the 528-acre ranch in 1974; by then, it was worth more than $3 million.

The long green lawns, bright white picket fences, and red ranch house make an idyllic setting for picnics, football or frisbee tossing, daydreaming, and snoozing, as well as for concerts, musicals, and kids' events put on in summer. Stroll around

The red house and white picket fence at Spring Mountain Ranch seem light years from Las Vegas.

the grounds and up to the reservoir, which waters the ranch via gravity-fed pipes. Try to stay late enough for an incomparable sunset. You can take the guided tour or pick up a self-guiding tour brochure at the main Ranch House, which doubles as the visitor center; hours vary, so call first. *Highway 159 (West Charleston Blvd.), five miles past the Red Rock Canyon scenic-route turn-off; (702) 875-4141.*

A half mile south of the state park are two commercial establishments. **Bonnie Springs,** originally a cattle ranch, now includes a motel, cocktail bar and restaurant, petting zoo, and stables. Next door is **Old Nevada,** a Western theme park with a mini-train ride from the parking lot to the entrance, two museums, a beer hall, mine, saloon, opera house, and shops, plus an 1800s melodrama and hangings. *Bonnie Springs/ Old Nevada, Highway 159; (702) 875-4191.*

■ BOULDER CITY

In 1930, when Congress finally appropriated the first funds for the Boulder Canyon Project, the Great Depression was in full swing, and the country was embarking on its most massive reclamation effort to date. The dam would be one of the largest single engineering and construction tasks ever undertaken. Urbanologists across the country were exploring large-scale community planning. Boulder City was born of these unique factors. Today, generations later, it remains the most unusual town in Nevada.

Construction of Boulder City began in March 1931, only a month before work commenced at the dam site. Boulder City became the first "model town" in the country, a prettified all-American oasis of security and order in the midst of a great desert and a Great Depression. The U.S. Bureau of Reclamation controlled the town down to the smallest detail. A city manager, who answered directly to the Commissioner of Reclamation, oversaw operations, and his authority was nearly total.

After the dam was completed in 1935, many thought Boulder City would become a ghost town, but visitors to the dam and Lake Mead began to turn it into a service center for the new tourist attraction and recreation area. For 30 years, the government owned the town and all its buildings, but in early 1960, an act of Congress established Boulder City as an independent municipality. A city charter was drawn up, the feds began to sell property to the long-term residents, and alcohol was no longer prohibited. Gambling, however, was, and remains, proscribed.

Coming into Boulder City is like entering a town in Arizona or New Mexico, with Indian and Mexican gift shops and a number of galleries, as well as crafts, jewelry, antique, and collectibles stores, along the downtown streets. And no casinos. Continue into town and head straight for the Boulder Dam Hotel. (Stop in at the Boulder City Chamber of Commerce, housed in the hotel, where you can collect the requisite pound of brochures and fliers.) The hotel was built in 1933 and still in its original condition. Check out the 65-year-old lobby and the subterranean bar in the basement. *To reach Boulder City from Las Vegas, take US 93/95 South (a.k.a. Boulder Highway) about 23 miles. Boulder City Chamber of Commerce; (702) 293-2034. Boulder Dam Hotel, 1305 Arizona Street; (702) 293-3510.*

Across the street is the Boulder City/Hoover Dam Museum. Watch a stunning 30-minute movie on the dam's construction. Make sure to use your walking-tour brochures and stroll up Arizona Street, then down Nevada Highway, to get a feel for this Depression-era model city. *Boulder City/Hoover Dam Museum, 444 Hotel Plaza; (702) 294-1988.*

(left) View of Black Canyon, looking upstream, on December 1, 1932, after the Colorado River was diverted. (right) Same vantage point downstream of Hoover Dam, on March 26, 1935.

(opposite) Giant electrical turbines inside Hoover Dam.

■ HOOVER DAM

The 1,400-mile Colorado River has been gouging great canyons and valleys with red *(colorado)* sediment-laden waters for nearly 10 million years. For the past 10,000 years, Indian, Spanish, and Mormon settlers coexisted with the fitful river, which often overflowed with spring floods, then tapered off to a muddy trickle in the fall. But in 1905, a wet winter and abnormally severe spring rains combined to wreak havoc: flash floods actually changed the course of the river to flow through California's low-lying Imperial Valley, greatly enlarging the Salton Sea. For nearly two years, engineers and farmers fought the water back into place. But the message was clear. The Rio Colorado must be tamed.

Enter the U.S. Bureau of Reclamation, established only three years earlier. Over the next 15 years, the Bureau narrowed the list of possible dam sites from 70 to two: Boulder and Black canyons in southern Nevada. It took another three years to negotiate an equitable water distribution among the affected states and Mexico, and another six for Congress to pass the Boulder Canyon Project Act, authorizing funds for "Boulder Dam" to be constructed in Black Canyon (it was finally named after Herbert Hoover, then Secretary of Commerce).

The immensity of the undertaking still boggles the brain. The closest civilization was at the sleepy railroad town of Las Vegas, 40 miles west. Two hundred miles of poles and wire had to be run from the nearest large power plant, in San Bernardino, California. Tracks had to be laid, a town built, men hired, equipment shipped in—just to prepare for construction. And then! The mighty Colorado had to be diverted. Four tunnels, each 56 feet across, were hacked out of the canyon walls. Thousands of tons of rock were loosened, carried off, and dumped, every day for 16 months. Finally, in November 1932, the river water was routed around the dam site. Then came the concrete.

For two years, eight-cubic-yard buckets full of cement were lowered into the canyon, five *million* of them, till the dam—660 feet thick at the base, 45 feet thick at the crest, 1,244 feet across, and 726 feet high—had swallowed 40 million cubic yards, or seven million tons, of the hard stuff. The top of the dam was built wide enough to accommodate a two-lane highway. Inside this Pantagruelian wedge were placed 17 gargantuan electrical turbines. The cost of the dam exceeded $175 million. At the peak of construction, more than 5,000 workers toiled day and night to complete the project, braving the most extreme conditions of heat, dust, and danger from heavy equipment, explosions, falling rock, and heights. An average of 50

HOOVER DAM HYPERBOLE

- Nine million tons of rock excavated—roughly enough to build the Great Wall of China

- One million cubic yards of river bottom removed—the equivalent of digging a trench 100 feet long, 60 feet wide, and a mile deep

- 165,000 railroad cars' worth of sand and gravel for cement—enough to stretch a single train from Boulder City to Kansas City

- Nearly seven million tons of concrete poured—enough to pave a two-lane road from Miami to Los Angeles

- 18 million pounds (eight million kilograms) of steel—enough to build the Empire State Building

- A thousand miles of steel pipe

- Nearly 50 trillion pounds of water retained in Lake Mead

- No predictions have been calculated for the dam's life span; it was built in 1935.

injuries per day and a total of 94 deaths were recorded over the 46 months of construction.

The largest construction equipment yet known to the world had to be invented, designed, fabricated, and installed on the spot. Yet miraculously, the dam was completed nearly two years ahead of schedule. In February 1935, the diversion tunnels were closed, and Lake Mead began to fill. The dam was dedicated eight months later by President Franklin D. Roosevelt. A month after that, the first turbine was turned, and electricity started flowing as the Colorado River water finally came under control. Today, Hoover Dam cranks out enough kilowatt-hours of electricity annually for half a million houses, but only four percent of the total goes to Las Vegas.

The new Hoover Dam visitor center has finally opened. It took 12 years, cost $120 million to complete, and is as representative of federal government inefficiency as the dam itself is an example of the competence of an earlier era. Find a parking space in the new five-story parking structure fit snugly into a ravine and buy tickets for the 35-minute dam tour. A 75-second elevator ride whisks you to the bottom of the dam (like descending from the 53rd floor of a skyscraper). Tunnels lead to a truly monumental room housing the monolithic turbines. Next you step outside, where a hundred necks crane to view the top of the dam—looking very much like a daredevil skateboarder's wet dream. Next you walk through one of the diversion tunnels to view a 30-foot-diameter water pipe. The guide packs hours of statistics and stories into the short tour ($5). Also, during the hot

GRAND CANYON FLIGHTSEEING

Las Vegas is the gateway to the Grand Canyon—one of the world's greatest natural wonders—and a number of flightseeing companies offer excursions from McCarran Airport that fly over the city, Boulder City, Hoover Dam, Lake Mead, and the western edge and South Rim on the way to the canyon airport. From there, ground transportation covers the 12 miles to the South Rim services where, depending on the tour, you have from two to four hours for sightseeing, photography, hiking, lunch, the museum, or an IMAX movie.

To say that the Grand Canyon is a mile deep, four to 18 miles wide, and 277 miles long would be to deny this vast chasm its poetry and timelessness. Ever since García Lopez de Cárdenas laid eyes on the Canyon in 1540, great authors have struggled to find words that adequately describe the mindboggling formation. Said naturalist John Muir, "It is impossible to conceive what the canyon is, or what impression it makes, from description or pictures, however good. . . . The prudent keep silence." President

months, the dam's interior temperature of 55-60° F provides exquisite relief. Across the dam is Arizona. (Set your watch ahead if necessary.) *To reach the Hoover Dam from Las Vegas, take US 93/95 South about 23 miles to Boulder City, then US 93 East about 11 miles to reach the dam. Call the visitor center at (702) 293-8906.*

Theodore Roosevelt, who declared the canyon a national monument in 1909, cautioned, "Leave it as it is. You cannot improve it; not a bit. What you can do is keep it for your children, your children's children, and all who come after you, as one of the sights every American, if he can travel at all, should see."

The Hoover and Glen Canyon dams have reduced the once-mighty Colorado River to a mere trickle of its former self; it once carried an estimated 500,000 tons of sediment daily through the canyon. Aside from the river, its tributaries, and the flooding of side gullies, the canyon has also been etched by snow, rain, air, water from melted glaciers, volcanism, and faults. Geologists believe that parts of the canyon are one-third as old as planet Earth itself, having been formed roughly two billion years ago, in the Precambrian Era.

Viewing the canyon's multicolored peaks, buttes, pinnacles, and ravines and pondering its ancient history make for an inspiring side trip and thought-provoking diversion from the glitter and gambling of Las Vegas. Slightly expensive, but worth its weight in philosophical musing. Four companies can take you there:

Scenic Airlines offers a 90-minute flight to the west rim and back for $100; a two-hour flight by the South Rim and back (doesn't land) for $149; and an eight-hour round-trip excursion with two hours at the South Rim for $199. *Call (702) 739-1900.* **Air Nevada** does a three-and-a-half hour, air-only west rim tour for $89; a five-hour air-only tour for $139; a seven-hour air-ground trip for $149; and an eight-hour trip with a bus tour, buffet lunch, and IMAX movie, for $189. *Call (702) 736-8900.* **Las Vegas Airlines** has a seven-hour air-ground excursion at $195. They also do a three-hour air-only trip (an hour and 45 minutes flying time) for $145. *Call (702) 647-3056.* You can also climb aboard a **Sundance Tours** chopper for a thrilling two-and-a-half-hour ride over the city, Hoover Dam, and Lake Mead, then halfway down into the canyon to land on a private plateau, where cheese and champagne are served. Then you're whisked back to the Quail Air Center (behind the Tropicana) by way of the Strip, and shuttled back to your hotel. The whole package is $299. Their two-hour trip (without the landing and bubbly) is $249, their 90-minute tour $199. *Call (702) 597-5505.*

Check with the companies, as they may change their packages, drop some tours, or add new ones. Also, the prices listed do not include taxes, which are substantial.

■ LAKE MEAD NATIONAL RECREATION AREA

Hoover Dam began detaining Colorado, Virgin, and Muddy river water in 1935. By 1938, Lake Mead was full: three years' worth of river water braced by the Brobdingnagian buttress at Black Canyon. Largest man-made lake in the West, Lake Mead measures 110 miles long and 500 feet deep, has 822 miles of shoreline, and contains 28.5 million acre-feet of water (or just over nine trillion gallons). The reservoir irrigates two-and-a-quarter million acres of land in the U.S. and Mexico and supplies water for more than 14 million people. Millions of people each year use Lake Mead as a recreational resource. For all this, Lake Mead is only a sidelight to the dam's primary purpose: flood and drought control. In addition, Lake Mead is only the centerpiece of the 1.5-million-acre Lake Mead National Recreation Area, which includes Lake Mojave and the surrounding desert from Davis Dam to the south and Grand Canyon National Park to the east, all the way north to Overton—making it the largest Department of Interior recreational acreage in the country.

And recreation it certainly provides. Swimming is the most accessibleactivity, and requires the least equipment: a bathing suit. Boulder Beach, only 30 miles from Las Vegas and just down the road from the Alan Bible Visitor Center, is the most popular swimming site. (Bring your zoris: they don't call it Boulder Beach for nothing.) And the water, which can reach 85 degrees in July, is so inviting that even divers can wear just bathing suits (down to 30 feet; in winter, it's time for wet suits). Also for divers, visibility averages 30 feet, the water is stable, and sights of the deep abound. The yacht *Tortuga*, doomed and possibly haunted, rests at 50 feet near the Boulder Islands, and Hoover Dam's asphalt factory sits on the canyon floor nearby. The boat *Cold Duck*, in 35 feet, is an excellent training dive. The old Mormon town of St. Thomas, inundated by the lake in 1938, has many a watery story to tell. The clamming is worthwhile near Saddle Island. Wishing Well Cove has steep canyon walls and drop-offs, caves, and clear water. Ringbolt Rapids, an exhilarating drift dive, is for the advanced only, and the Tennis Shoe Graveyard, near Las Vegas Wash, is one of many footholds of hidden treasure.

Boating on the vast lake is even more varied. Power boats skip across the surface—racing, pulling water-skiers, or just speeding hellbent for nowhere. Houseboats putter toward hidden coves for days of sunbathing, fishing, partying, relaxing, and staying wet. Sailing is a year-round thrill, with conditions described as "between paradise and panic." Spring is fine but fall is king: the blistering heat's

(previous pages) "The prudent keep silence."—John Muir. (photo by Richard Lee Kaylin)

gone, the wind's steady, and the water's warm. Winter winds are fluky, characteristic of large inland bodies of water, and ferocious summer storms can roar across the canyon with little mercy and less warning, only to disappear without a trace 30 minutes later. Likewise, windsurfing is exciting and unpredictable, with strong thermals in summer, good conditions and solitude (not to mention polypropylene underwear and dry suits) in winter.

Fishing is eventful and changeable, too. Largemouth bass, catfish, black crappie, and rainbow, brown, and cutthroat trout, have been the mainstays for decades. These days, though, striped bass provide the sport, especially since tens of thousands of gallons of phosphorous fertilizer were added to the lake to replenish nutrients depleted by the Glen Canyon Dam (topped off in 1963). Phosphorus nourishes algae, which feed plankton, which is consumed by threadfin shad, which is dinner for the striped bass. Striper popularity has also allowed the largemouth bass, fished out in years past, to regenerate.

Recreation is also abundant at Lake Mojave, created downstream by Davis Dam in 1953. This lake backs up almost all the way to Hoover Dam, like an extension of Lake Mead. The two lakes are similar in their climate, desert scenery, vertical-walled canyon enclosures, and a shoreline digitated with numerous private coves. Lake Mojave, however, is much smaller, and thus not nearly as susceptible to Lake Mead's mongrel monsoons—and narrower, so the protection of shore is never too far away. Still, it offers excellent trout fishing at Willow Beach on the Arizona side, where the water is perfect for serious angling. Marinas are found at Cottonwood Cove just north of the widest part of the lake and at Katherine Landing just north of Davis Dam. For all that, it's a much better-kept secret than exalted Lake Mead.

Finally, the desert enclosing all this incongruous water furnishes a sharp contrast worthy of the proximity to its other anomaly—Las Vegas. From the mammoth granite outcroppings in the wild and surreal shapes of Christmas Tree Pass just uphill from Laughlin, to the 1,500-year-old white petroglyphs chiseled into the psychedelic scarlet sandstone of Valley of Fire 100 miles north of Laughlin, you can get as high and dry (and awry) as in any wilderness area in the country. The only way to place Las Vegas in its proper perspective, to truly recognize that the city and the dam embody one of the world's greatest efforts to spruce up a desert, is to get away and look back. Climb a mountain and survey the city, the valley, the dam, the lakes, the desert—all in the indivisible panorama. Experience

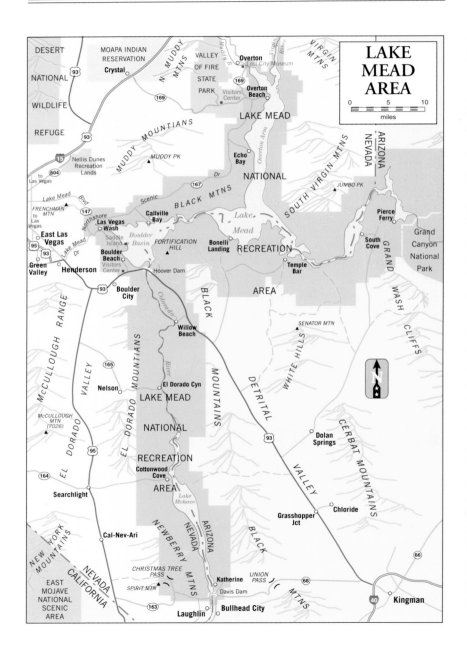

Over seven million people visit Lake Mead National Recreation Area each year.
(photo by Kerrick James)

the contrast. That's what traveling is all about. *The Alan Bible Visitor Center lies at the intersection of Lakeshore Drive and US 93, about 6 miles west of Boulder City and 28 miles southeast of Las Vegas. For more Lake Mead information, call the visitor center at (702) 293-8906.*

■ VALLEY OF FIRE STATE PARK

At this stunning piece of Olympian sculpture, the gods had miles of fire-red rock to carve—and 150 million years to fill in the details. Like Red Rock Canyon, this valley, six miles long and three to four miles wide, is another spectacular ancestral hall of the Navajo Formation, a continuum of Mesozoic sandstone that stretches from southern Colorado through New Mexico, Arizona, Utah, and Nevada. Taken together, the monuments, arches, protruding jagged walls, divine engravings, and human etchings—all in brilliant vermilion, scarlet, mauve, burgundy, magenta, orange, and gold—are an unforgettable archetype of the great American Southwest landscape.

The highest and youngest formations in the park are mountains of sand deposited by desert winds 140 million years ago—the familiar Aztec sandstone. These dunes were petrified, oxidized, and chiseled by time, sun, water, and chemical reactions into their magnificent shapes and colors. Underneath the Aztec is a 5,000-foot-deep layer of brown mud, dating back 200 million years, when uplift displaced the inland sea. The gray limestone below represents another 100 million years of deposits, from the Paleozoic marine environment.

Unlike Red Rock Canyon, where uplift slipped older limestone over the sandstone, here it all remains exactly as it was stratified, and the red rock provides an incomparable lesson in erosion. One of the best and most photographed examples is along the road just beyond the eastern entrance, at Elephant Rock. Continue west to the Cabins, built for travelers out of sandstone bricks by the Civilian Conservation Corps in 1935, when the valley became the first state park in Nevada. The visitor center has a truly spectacular setting, nestled at the foot of a mountain of fire. Inside is a good place to pick up a map of the park and trail guides, books of local interest, slides, and postcards. From here, take the spur road to Petroglyph Canyon Trail, and dig your feet into some red sand. A trail guide introduces you to the local flora. Mouse's Tank is a basin that fills up with water after a rain; a fugitive Indian named Mouse hid here in the late 1890s. The spur road continues through the towering canyon and peaks at aptly named Rainbow Vista. The road used to dead-end here, but in the summer of 1994, the state opened a new four-mile extension all the way to Silica Dome. The route and views are truly spectacular.

Heading west again on the through-road, you come to a quarter-mile loop trail to fenced-in petrified wood, the most common local fossil. On the other side of the highway, another spur road goes past the high staircase up to petroglyphed and sheer Atlatl Rock and into A and B campgrounds. There's a walk-in section to the rear of A Campground, but the back of B Campground has some of the most spectacular campsites in Nevada. The Beehives, a little farther west along the park road, are worth a look. From there, continue west 25 miles to Interstate 15 and back to Las Vegas, or turn around and go back through the park, continuing to the town of Overton. *To reach the park from Las Vegas, take Interstate 15/US 93 north about 35 miles to Highway 169 (Exit 75); take Highway 169 south about 18 miles to the park visitor center. From Lake Mead, drive to Overton Beach on the lake's northern arm. About one mile north of the beach, take the turnoff for the park, and head west about six miles. Visitor Center, Valley of Fire State Park; (702) 397-2088.*

PETROGLYPHS

Petroglyphs are prehistoric rock carvings representative of the culture and religion of ancient Indians. Though some of the shapes and figures of the artwork are recognizable today, their significance has mostly been lost with the ages. Scientists speculate that rock incision was one of the rituals performed by shamans before a hunt, special event, or life passage, or that the renderings served as graffiti, or a sort of community bulletin board.

The petroglyphs in Valley of Fire are particularly numerous and noticeable. The sandstone is coated with a layer of oxidized iron and magnesium which, when carved, becomes white, so the artistic possibilities were propitious. It's not hard to imagine how a smooth, flat, and high-hanging face such as Atlatl Rock would have been irresistible to the graffiti artists of the day, though one does wonder how the ancients *reached* it. The petrogylph of a ladder might shed some light on the question, and would point to a more recent Anasazi carver. But the incised *atlatl* above it returns the aura of mystery; this "spear-launcher" long predates the bow and arrow, which arrived here around A.D. 500.

Experts recognize certain "totems," or clan signs, in the petroglyphs; in fact, some Hopi clan symbols appear in Valley of Fire, supporting the theory that the Anasazi who migrated into Arizona and New Mexico intermingled their culture with that of their eastern cousins.

Some of the artwork's symbolism seems obvious: suns, snakes, animals, people. But you'll also see hieroglyphs that could represent mushrooms and cacti (with renderings reminiscent of the psychedelic peyote cultures farther south), butterflies, octopi and starfish, Greek letters, menorahs, tic-tac-toe games, spermatozoa, treble clefs, even the Great Prophet foretelling the arrival of 747s, roller coasters, and basketball. Road maps? Advertising? Headlines? Interpretations are limited only by imagination.

■ LOST CITY MUSEUM

Over a rise beyond the eastern entrance to Valley of Fire awaits the Muddy River Wash, at the mouth of Moapa Valley. Lake Mead terminates here, and a thin strip of rich agricultural green escorts the road up the river valley. The Anasazi Indians were farming successfully here a thousand years ago and built the Pueblo Grande de Nevada, or Lost City, on the fertile delta between the Muddy and Virgin rivers.

The Mormons began to colonize the valley in 1864, and today this well-tended plot is their legacy.

A glimpse of the Anasazi ("Enemy Ancestors") legacy is found at the Lost City Museum, just south of the small farming town of Overton, 60 miles northeast of Las Vegas. The museum houses an immense collection of Pueblo artifacts, including an actual pueblo foundation, and a fascinating series of black-and-white photos covering the site's excavation in 1924. In an interesting article (*Nevada* magazine, November 1976), David Moore makes the point that the "Lost City" wasn't so much lost as simply overlooked: Jedediah Smith sighted and cited the site during his travels through southern Nevada in the 1820s, and another expedition reported these "ruins of an ancient city" in the *New York Tribune* in 1867. But it was Nevada Governor James G. Scrugham, a mining engineer who, in 1924, initiated the official dig. Some of the Anasazi ruins were drowned by Lake Mead, but even today, the Overton-Logandale area of the delta remains one of the country's "finest bottomless treasure chests of ancient history," according to Moore. Residents who rototill their yards or replace septic tanks uncover scads of shards: in 1975, an entire ancient village was revealed by workmen digging a new leach line.

Famous Elephant Rock at Valley of Fire.

(opposite) The sandstone Cabins provided accommodation for travelers to the state park in the 1930s.

The exterior of the museum, reminiscent of an adobe pueblo, was constructed by the Civilian Conservation Corps in 1935; climb down the log ladder into the authentic pit house in front. Stroll around back for petroglyphs, more pueblos, picnic tables, and a pioneer monument. *To reach Overton from Las Vegas, take Interstate 15/US 93 north about 60 miles to Exit 93; head south about 13 miles. Lost City Museum, Overton; (702) 397-2193.*

■ MT. CHARLESTON

Twenty miles north of Las Vegas on US 95 along the Mojave Desert floor is a turnoff west into Kyle Canyon, one of many short, narrow, and sheer cuts into the northern Spring Mountain Range, which hems in the Las Vegas Valley on the west. The range's highest point is Mt. Charleston, named after Charleston, South Carolina, by Dixie crew members of the Army survey team that mapped this mountain's forest reserve in 1906. Eighth highest point in Nevada, Mt. Charleston's propensity for capturing precipitation from the westerlies gave rise to the name Spring Mountains. The rain, snowmelt, and runoff percolate through the porous limestone, spurtle to the surface in numerous springs, and finally gurgle through the natural aquifers into the deep artesian system below Las Vegas Valley. Being high and wet, and surrounded by low and dry, the Spring Mountains approximate a garden island poking out of a sea of desert. In fact, the local flora and fauna have become biologically isolated: 30 species of plants are endemic. Additionally, these mountains support a system of five distinct life zones; ascending from Las Vegas to Charleston Peak in terms of altitude is the equivalent of traveling from Mexico to Alaska in terms of latitude.

Most of this range is administered by the Bureau of Land Management, though the elevations above 7,000 feet are managed by the Las Vegas Ranger District of the Toiyabe National Forest. And like the Park Service's Lake Mead Recreation Area, Mt. Charleston offers year-round outdoor activities—from cool alpine hikes in the blistering summers to fine snow sports in the mild winters.

A little more than 10 miles from US 95, the Kyle Canyon Road (Highway 157) climbs steeply into the sparse forest of Joshua trees and juniper. First stop is Mt. Charleston Hotel, which has a large lodge-like lobby complete with roaring fireplace, bar and big dance floor, and spacious restaurant. Built in 1984, this is one of the most romantic spots in southern Nevada, a perfect place to propose (and then return to Las Vegas to get married an hour or two later). Up the road is the village of Mt. Charleston, with a few residences and a U.S. Forest Service district office. The road ends at Mt. Charleston Lodge restaurant and cabins; from there the half-mile Little Falls Trail is easygoing, the three-quarter-mile Cathedral Rock Trail is moderately steep, with sheer drops but great views, and the North Loop Trail covers nine hard miles to the peak.

Backtracking on Highway 157 to just before the hotel, Highway 158 heads off to the left and connects in 6 miles with Highway 156, the Lee Canyon Road. Robbers Roost is a short easy hike to a large rock grotto which once sheltered local horse thieves. The South Loop Trail starts just past Hilltop Campground (13 hard miles to the peak).

At the top of Lee Canyon is the Las Vegas Ski and Snowboard Resort, or "Ski Lee." Operated since 1962 by the Highfield family, the base altitude is 8,500 feet and the top of the chairlift is another 1,000 feet higher. Thin air. But cliff walls towering above the slope protect skiers from biting westerlies. A beginner chairlift and ski school feed the bunny slope; a T-bar ferries bodies to the intermediate Strip; and the double chairlift delivers Las Vegans (80 percent of skiers are locals; another 10 percent are their guests) to runs called Keno, Blackjack, and Slot Alley.

Down the mountain a bit from the ski area are plentiful places for tubing, sledding, snowmobiling, and cross-country skiing. Best nordic skiing is on north-facing slopes, in open meadows above 8,000 feet. Scott Canyon, Mack's Canyon, and the Bristlecone Pine Trail are popular. Next nearest skiing to Las Vegas is Brian Head, Utah, four hours away. Where else in the world can you scuba-dive a drowned asphalt factory at sea level in the morning, slalom an advanced ski slope at 9,000 feet in the afternoon, propose and get married in the evening, and then shoot craps all night long? *To reach Mt. Charleston from Las Vegas, take Interstate 95 north about 30 miles to Highway 156; head up the mountain 17 miles to the resort. Las Vegas Ski and Snowboard Resort; (702) 878-5465.*

■ LAUGHLIN

The Colorado River flows out of Mojave Desert country into Sonoran Desert country, where the southern wedge of Nevada splits the Arizona–California border. This is the lowest point in Nevada—450 feet above sea level—and the hottest. The country's highest temperatures are recorded here more than 20 days a year. Other than Tristate City, a minor mining town that lived and died in the 1920s, the wedge remained untouched by human hands until the early 1950s, when Davis Dam was built. A prominent rock shaped like a bull's head was buried beneath Lake Mojave, but not before it gave a name to the dam workers' base of operations: Bullhead City, Arizona. After the dam was topped off, Bullhead City clung to the banks of the Colorado, as it clung to life, a tiny retirement community and fishing service center. Across the river in Nevada, a bait shack squatted on Sandy Point beach, frying to a crisp in the fierce Sonoran sun.

Enter Don Laughlin. Like many an optimistic prospector before him, Laughlin saw a gold mine where everyone else, even the ravens, saw a lunar wasteland. Thirty-

(opposite, and above) The Colorado Belle, a riverboat casino actually on a river!

three years old, in his pocket cash and a gaming license from a dozen good years in the heady Las Vegas of the 1950s, he purchased six acres of land at the end of a sandy road for $250,000, putting down $35,000. On it sat the bait shop, an eight-room motel (half of which was occupied by his family), and a six-seat bar. But it was his gaming license that put Laughlin in the black, and he slowly began to expand his Riverside resort. (An Irish postal official put "Laughlin" on the map. According to legend, the inspector, O'Reilly, listened to Laughlin's suggestions of Riverside and Casino for the name of the town, but settled on Laughlin instead, liking the Irish ring of it. (Today Don Laughlin jokes that the town was named after his mother.)

Both Laughlins struggled for the first decade or so. Banks laughed at his loan applications. But Southern California Edison built a coal-fired power plant just up the hill from the river, expanding the population base. And slowly, people from Needles, Kingman, Lake Havasu, and even as far away as San Bernardino and Flagstaff began frequenting the friendly little river resort-casino as an alternative to Las Vegas. By 1976, the Riverside Hotel had expanded to 100 rooms and 300 slots.

The growth of Bullhead City, Arizona, right across the Colorado River, kept pace. Its population increased from 600 in 1966 to more than 6,000 by 1976, as employees, retirees, and snowbirds moved in, attracted by the weather, the water, and the wagering. By 1984, Laughlin's Riverside was a 14-story, 350-room hotel, and a half-dozen other casinos lined the river. But little else existed there. The same year, Laughlin boasted a grand total of 95 residents—the temperature still higher than the population, and one casino for every 16 people! The rest of Laughlin's 3,000 employees lived on the Arizona side (by then Bullhead City had surpassed the 15,000 mark), commuting across the river by way of the Davis Dam Bridge or the casino ferries.

But the mid-1980s was just the beginning of the boom. Don Laughlin proceeded to spend more than a million of his own dollars in road improvements and more than three million to build the new bridge from Bullhead City to his hotel. He then finally convinced Nevada to take over the bridge. He also spent $6 million to expand the airport across the river. Meanwhile, developers like Bob Bilbray (whose 1978 investment of a couple million dollars in 430 town-site acres has increased exponentially) have been building condos, apartments, shopping centers, a

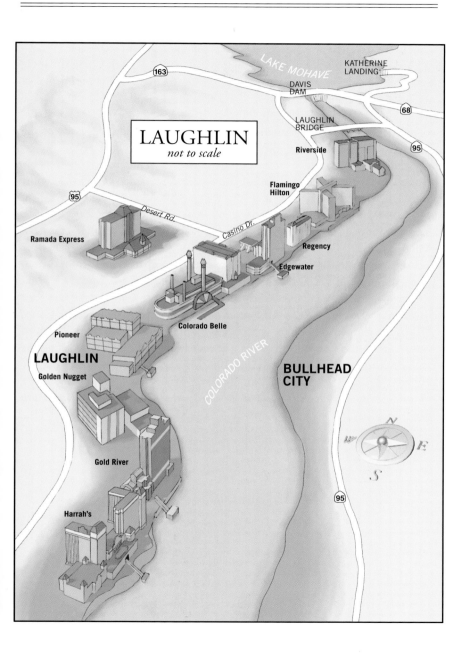

LAUGHLIN
not to scale

LAUGHLIN

BULLHEAD
CITY

LAKE MOHAVE

KATHERINE
LANDING

DAVIS
DAM

163

68

95

LAUGHLIN
BRIDGE

Riverside

Flamingo
Hilton

95

Desert Rd.

Casino Dr.

Ramada Express

Regency

Edgewater

Colorado Belle

Pioneer

Golden Nugget

COLORADO RIVER

Gold River

Harrah's

95

N
W   E
S

school, and a library. And the casinos keep coming: Circus Circus's 1,238-room Colorado Belle opened in July 1987, right next door to its Circus Circus sister, the 600-room Edgewater. The gorgeous 1,000-room Harrah's Laughlin opened in mid-1988. Also on Casino Drive are the 2,000-room Flamingo Hilton, the 300-room Golden Nugget, 1,501-room Ramada Express, 1,003-room Gold River, and the 414-room Pioneer. A river walk extends from the Riverside all the way to the Pioneer, with cold-drink stands, T-shirt and suntan lotion concessions, jet-ski rental kiosks, and back doors to the casinos. Inside, you'll immediately notice how airy and bright the casinos are, thanks to the big picture windows overlooking the river. Their more comfortable and less claustrophobic atmosphere makes you wonder what Las Vegas has against natural light. Also, inside the Riverside and Harrah's casinos, you can snap pictures to your heart's content. And Harrah's has a public beach.

The hotel rooms can be 50 percent cheaper than comparable ones in Las Vegas, which accounts for vacancy rates that you need a micrometer to measure. And food here, like the cheap hotel rooms, expansive casinos, cooperative weather, and playful river, is user-friendly. All nine major hotels have 24-hour coffee shops, restaurants, inexpensive buffets, and casinos. Fishing in Lake Mojave (*big* striped bass), cruising the Colorado in ferries and tour boats and on jet skis, taking the self-guided tour of Davis Dam, swimming, camping, and hiking round out the activities. *To reach Laughlin from Las Vegas, take US 93 (Boulder Highway) to US 95; take US 95 south to Highway 163; head east on Highway 163. The total trip is about 92 miles.*

HOTELS & CASINOS

WITH 70 MAJOR HOTELS AND 250 MOTELS, Las Vegas boasts a grand total of nearly 100,000 places to sleep. With so many to choose from, it seems like easy money to find that one perfect room with your name on it. But think again. More than 30 million visitors visit Las Vegas yearly; that's roughly 82,000 a day. Weekend occupancy rates average over 90 percent (midweek rates average about 80 percent). In addition, each year Las Vegas hosts over 1,000 conventions, with a total attendance of nearly 4 million. Often—usually twice a month—these gatherings land between 10,000 and 130,000 delegates on the town in one fell swoop. And many people, especially in winter, stay for weeks and months at a time in motels.

In short, this town fills up fast—especially the top hotels and best-value motels. But even if you show up on New Year's Eve or during the 230,000-participant Comdex computer trade show the week before Thanksgiving, some kind of room, somewhere, should be available. Besides, your hotel or motel room is where you'll spend the *least* time during your wild Las Vegas weekend or vacation. One way to look at accommodations in Las Vegas is to remember the old traveler's axiom: eat sweet, pay for play, but sleep cheap. Otherwise, as always, it's best to make your reservations far in advance to ensure the appropriate kind, price, and location of your room.

■ HOTELS AND PACKAGES

The cheapest hotel rooms are found weekdays, downtown. Rates rise rapidly on the Strip, and ascend again, both places, on the weekends. Occupancy rates, however, are consistently higher downtown than on the Strip. If you don't have to ask the price of a room or can qualify for a $1,000,000 line of casino credit, the 10,000-square-foot penthouses atop the Hilton or the ultimate bungalows at the Mirage will do you nicely. If you want to splash out in ultra luxury, or if you just received a large insurance settlement or hit a progressive slot jackpot, try a four-bedroom suite with a complete bar, sunken marble tub, swimming pool, and Kuala Lumpur theme at the Desert Inn ($850); or a 23rd-floor corner suite in the Island Tower at the Trop, complete with rock-façade Jacuzzi, eight-person steam room, sauna, and cushion-carpeted bedroom ($400); or even a mini-suite at Bally's with round bed, mirrored ceiling, and pink champagne on ice ($100).

If you're staying for the typical three or four nights, and you're on a budget with a limit that you'd prefer to max out in some other way (a hotel room, after all, is a hotel room, even in Las Vegas), get yourself the best package deal you can find. These usually include one or two meals, several comp cocktails, funbook, tickets to the hotel's showroom or revue, free trip to the spa, discount coupons, and bellman's gratuities. Simply call the 800 numbers in "Hotel Addresses" which follow for up-to-date information and reservations, call your local travel agent, or check with a reservations service. (See "Reservation Services," p. 233.)

Otherwise, pick your room for location (downtown? on the Strip? off the Strip?) or price (garden room? tower room? mini-suite?). Parking and traffic are considerations when deciding on location. If you don't mind parking in a garage or using a valet every time you come and go, downtown won't bug you. If you don't mind walking 20 minutes from a parking lot through the casino to the elevators, then down a long hall to your room, then the Strip megajoints are no problem. But if you want to pull the car right up to the front door of your room, then a motel would be best. Does Strip traffic drive you nuts? Either learn the backroad shortcuts or stay in a locals' casino around town.

Most of the older hotels (and some of the newer ones) have two classes of rooms: "garden," which are the original low-rise motel rooms, and "tower," which are the newer high-rise hotel rooms. Garden rooms are almost always less expensive and more available than tower rooms. They're also older, smaller, and occasionally a little rough around the edges. But if you want to be on the Strip and not pay the premium prices, consider the garden rooms. The Frontier, Lady Luck, and Rio have mini-suites that are a little more expensive than regular tower rooms, but worth it for the extra space and comfort.

■ MOTELS

Motels cluster in five general areas of town. The two groups that are consistently least expensive and most available are those north of downtown on North Main, Las Vegas Boulevard North, and the north numbered streets; and those east/southeast of downtown on East Fremont. The north locations are slightly iffy for walking around securely, but are fine for driving to and from; the closer to downtown, the safer. Some charge as little as $25 nightly and $100 weekly. The East Fremont

(opposite) A re-creation of Abu Simbel in the Luxor's atrium. (photo by Kerrick James)

Weekly Motels

motels line up one after another on the wide straight strip toward Boulder City. It's not too far to the Boulder Highway casinos (the venerable Showboat at the west end, Sam's Town at the east, and Boulder Station in between), so it's a good place to cruise if you don't have a reservation and if most No Vacancy signs are lit.

The two groups south of downtown along Las Vegas Boulevard South are good for location, if a bit more expensive. Most convenient (though nothing fancy and a little insecure) are the motels between Charleston Boulevard and Sahara Avenue, right between downtown and the Strip. Another line of motels stretches down the lower Strip between Bally's on Flamingo Avenue and the south edge of the city just beyond the Hacienda Hotel.

Finally, a good group of motels surrounds the Convention Center along Paradise Road and Convention Center Drive. (See map "Greater Las Vegas," p. 195.)

■ WEEKLY MOTELS

The most affordable way to get your fill of Las Vegas is to take a motel room by the week. Most motels give sizable discounts for these rates; many contain refrigerators or entire kitchenettes. This can save you a lot of money in both lodging and food costs, allowing you to spend it on other pleasures of the senses. The only challenge is *finding* one. Several factors conspire to make the search discouraging. First, not all the motels have weeklies. And those that do often allot a limited number of their total rooms for the discounted rate. Secondly, every winter a flock of snowbirds migrates to Las Vegas, some of whom squat in these weeklies till it gets too hot. These snowbirds reserve their same rooms for the following November right when they depart in spring. Third, with about a thousand people moving to Las Vegas every week to start a new life, and with apartment occupancy rates hovering just below 100 percent, these wanna-be Las Vegans often wind up monopolizing any vacant weeklies.

Where there's life, though, there's hope (in fact, hope is quite a profitable product in this town). If you plan to eat all your meals in restaurants and don't need a refrigerator or stove, you can get weeklies for as low as $100, and you'll have a much easier time locating one. You can also bring your own hotplate and cooler (don't forget an extension cord or two) for your coffee, tea, hot cereal, and sandwiches. The more prepared you are the better—bring all the kitchen stuff you'll need: pots, plates, cups, silverware, spices, toaster oven, sponge, can opener.

Once you land a room, there are several variables which you'll need to understand and make clear with the management. Be sure their week is as long as yours! Some Las Vegas motels have redefined "week" into *six* nights. It's true. Something having to do with Saturday rates. Try not to leave any deposit; in Las Vegas, once the money is gone, it rarely comes back (though toward the end of your stay, a deposit might be as much a security for *you* as the motel!). The telephone situation can also be tricky. Some motels don't have direct-dial phones at all. Some charge 25 cents for local calls; some have free local calls but don't offer long distance; where available, long distance might need to go through the front desk. Find out if the room is cleaned every day, or every week, or at all; sometimes linen is extra. Always look at the room first! Make sure the heat or air conditioning works; it's never a bad idea to have a small space heater or fan just in case. Make sure the windows lock and there's at least a chain on the door; a deadbolt is even better. If there's a kitchenette, test the stove/oven, and see that the refrigerator is cold. You might have to take the room regardless of its flaws, but if you point them out to the front desk, you could try bargaining down the price a little. Or a better room might mysteriously appear.

Use the "Weekly Motels" list on page 244 to call around for availability and reservations. Most motels with weeklies operate on a first come, first served basis. Ask about the price and amenities, and whether a weekly room is available *today*. Management doesn't really know if people are going to leave, except from day to day after it happens. Some, however, will hold a room for you, such as Fun City, King Albert, and the Crest. Another possibility is to take your chances and breeze into Las Vegas, grab a room for one night, then get on the phone the next day. (Best time to call is around noon.) In this case, it's wise to arrive on a weekday, when single-night rooms are readily available, and rates are 20 to 50 percent lower than on a Friday or Saturday. With diligence and luck you'll find a weekly and by the weekend wind up saving a substantial amount of dough, which you can then blow in some other way.

■ CASINO CAMPING AND RV PARKING

RV spaces in Las Vegas are limited, especially between October and April, when snowbirds migrate in their motorhomes from the East Coast, the Midwest, and points north. In July 1995, the *Las Vegas Advisor* calculated that if the ratio of

Camping and RVs

hotel rooms to total visitors equaled motorhome spaces to RVers, Las Vegas would have only 45,000 rooms. In other words, Las Vegas would have to try and handle its 30 million annual visitors with half the number of available hotel rooms.

Four casinos have RV parks nearby: Circus Circus on the Strip, Boomtown south of town, and the Showboat and Sam's Town, both out on Boulder Highway. (The RV park at the Hacienda is a members-only set-up.) Combined, they have a total of around 1,700 spaces. These are the top parks for temporary RVers; KOA and Boulder Lakes (out on Boulder Highway) are the nicest of the dozen trailer parks around Las Vegas that have spaces for transient RVers.

Boomtown is the newest and best RV park in Las Vegas. The 460 spaces are ample, providing room for two RVs where most other parks would squeeze four (260 pull-throughs). There's a laundry, groceries, rec room, two-acre grassy picnic area, and two pools, one for adults and the other for children, complete with a play apparatus and fountains. And it's a bona fide Las Vegas-style bargain ($16–20 per vehicle). Boomtown is located five miles south of Las Vegas Boulevard on Interstate 15 at the Blue Diamond exit; call (702) 263-7777 or (800) 588-7711.

Circusland, next to Circus Circus at 500 Circus Circus Drive, is a prime spot for RVers, especially those with kids, who want to be right in the thick of things but also want to take advantage of very good facilities. There's a laundry, groceries, game room, fenced playground, heated swimming pool, children's pool, spa, and sauna. The convenience store is open 24 hours. There are 370 spaces for motor homes, all with full hookups, and 280 pull-throughs; the fee is $17-20. Ten minutes spent learning the Industrial Road back entrance will save hours of sitting in traffic on the Strip. Call (702) 734-0410 or (800) 634-3450.

The **Showboat** has 83 spaces—wide, with grassy areas and young trees. They're all back-in (no pull-throughs). Full hook-ups, along with cable and phone service, come with every site. The Showboat RV Park is one of the least expensive in town, with rates starting at $14 a night (14-night maximum stay). The Showboat is located at 2800 East Fremont; call (800) 826-2800.

Sam's Town has two RV parks, one connected to the east parking lot and the other across the street on Nellis Boulevard. The Nellis park (200 spaces) is a snowbird set-up that is closed in June, July, and August. Sam's Town, though, has 300 year-round spaces. Both parks have a laundry, heated pools, and spa. The fee is

$16. Sam's Town is on Boulder Highway near Flamingo Avenue; (702) 456-7777 or (800) 634-6371.

Up the street from Sam's Town (toward downtown) is the venerable Las Vegas **KOA**. A little less than half the spaces are taken up by residential units, but the rest are reserved for transients; all are pull-throughs. Tenters are welcome here, the closest place to downtown and the Strip to pitch a little A-frame or dome (60 tent spaces). A laundry, groceries, game room, playground, two heated swimming pools, wading pool, spa, RV wash, and shuttle are available. The fee is $24 for tenters and $26 for RVers, $28 for a full hook-up. The park is at 4315 Boulder Highway; (702) 451-5527.

Boulder Lakes offers 417 RV sites (all back-ins), 4 pools, 4 Jacuzzis, a laundry, and a bare-bones convenience store. The fee is $19 (no tenters). The park is located at 6201 Boulder Highway; (702) 435-1157.

■ RESERVATION SERVICES

These services reserve blocks of rooms at large hotels downtown and on the Strip. If they don't sell them before a certain cut-off date (from two to 20 days in advance), the hotels cancel the service's reservations and sell the rooms themselves. Depending on the cutoff date, you can book a room with a service at an otherwise "sold-out" hotel. The services also book two, three, and four-night packages. Some handle tours and shows. Others book air and hotel combination packages as well. Some offer rooms at a lower rate due to the block discount (the hotel pays the service's commission). Often the services (and the hotels themselves) require a two-night minimum over the weekend at the premium price; the hotels are reluctant to sell for Saturday night only, and hold out till the last minute before they release any one-night weekend rooms. Also, weekends often require reservations far in advance, especially during holidays and high season. You confirm your room with a credit card number, so make sure that you understand the cancellation policy; usually you can get all your money back with 48-hours' notice, but at some places you forfeit your first night's deposit. The commercial reservation services come and go with the wind; the most stable service is provided by the **Las Vegas Convention and Visitors Authority**; (702) 386-0770.

Reservation Services

Las Vegas Hotel Addresses

Las Vegas Hotels

Aladdin. 3667 Las Vegas Blvd. South; (702) 736-0111/(800) 634-3424
The 1,100 rooms here are fairly standard, but the hotel does offer the 10,000-seat Aladdin Theatre (which has hosted some hotshot performers), pools, tennis courts, shopping arcade. $65–90

BALLY'S

Bally's isn't lying: 3,000 rooms, two large showrooms, half a dozen restaurants (including a very reliable buffet), 10 tennis courts, health spas, and a 40-store shopping arcade. And, of course, an enormous casino. $85–180

ALADDIN HOTEL

Alexis Park. 375 E. Harmon Ave.; (702) 796-3300/(800) 582-2228
This all-suite, elegant hotel—a favorite among conventioneers who don't want the Vegas experience—has no neon and no gambling. The red-tiled, white buildings overlook lawns and rock pools. Some rooms have Jacuzzis and fireplaces. $125–1000

Arizona Charlie's. 740 S. Decatur Blvd.; (702) 258-5200/(800) 342-2695
Westside locals' casino with a Klondike theme. Pool and poolside service; restaurants, bar, casino. $30–45

Bally's. 3645 Las Vegas Blvd. South; (702) 739-4111/(800) 634-3434
Billing itself as "A City Within a City,"

Barbary Coast. 3595 Las Vegas Blvd. South; (702) 737-7111/(800) 634-6755
The San Francisco Gold Rush theme here is played out in the Victorian-style brass and lace decor of the 200 guest rooms. The relatively few rooms here are very good value, so reserve early. $35–500

BARBARY COAST

Binion's Horseshoe. 128 Fremont St.;
(702) 382-1600/(800) 634-6811
Today, Benny's kids run this 300-room
hotel. Many of the better rooms are reserved for big gamblers, but the cheaper
ones are good value. Reserve early. $30–80

Boomtown. 3333 Blue Diamond Hwy.;
(702) 263-7777/(800) 588-7711
Not right in the center of the action,
but there's shuttle service to the Strip.
Restaurant with health-conscious menu,
buffet in casino. $25–85

Boulder Station. 4111 Boulder Hwy.;
(702) 432-7777/(800) 683-7777
A classy spot: wood and brick floors, won-
derful restaurants, and a high-ceiling pit.
While 300 rooms may be small by Vegas
standards, the entertainments here are numerous: 11 restaurants plus buffet, 11
movie theaters, Kids' Quest, swimming
pool, and two lounges. $30–90

BOULDER STATION

Caesars Palace. 3570 Las Vegas Blvd.
South; (702) 731-7110/(800) 634-6661
This massive, spectacular hotel, with its
dramatic entrance, toga'd handmaidens and
helmeted centurions, expensive restaurants,
and upscale shopping mall with 70 shops

and animated statues, is quintessential Las
Vegas splash. Tennis and squash courts,
pools, spas, Omnimax theater, big-name
showroom, and 9 restaurants. *See photo pp.
70-71.* $95–300

CALIFORNIA HOTEL

California Hotel. 12 E. Ogden Ave.; (702)
385-1222/ (800) 634-6255
This hotel's low rates and "aloha"-style
decor have made it a favorite among
Hawaiian tourists. Casino, 600 rooms, 3
restaurants, cocktail lounge. $40–60

Circus Circus. 2880 Las Vegas Blvd.
South; (702) 734-0410/(800) 634-3450
Truly a colossal circus in many ways: ri-
otous pink-and-blue striped circus tent fab-
rics decorate hallways and rooms; kids run
between the video midway and the ongoing circus acts; and inside, disoriented
crowds of guests search for their rooms
among the hotel's 2,800. *See photo p. 153.*
$35–85

Debbie Reynolds. 305 Convention Ctr.;
(702) 734-0711/(800) 633-1777
Home to the Hollywood Movie Museum,
with Ms. Reynolds's very impressive collection of movie memorabilia. The 200-room
hotel is smallish by Vegas standards; there's

DEBBIE REYNOLDS HOTEL

one small casino, a restaurant, pool, Jacuzzi, and showroom. $65–275

Desert Inn. 3145 Las Vegas Blvd. South; (702) 733-4444/(800) 634-6906
The DI is geared to upscale gamblers who play golf: its PGA championship golf course hosts three major events a year. The South-western-style rooms are elegant; some even have private swimming pools. In addition to the gourmet restaurants are 10 tennis courts, spa, pool, and showroom, where top headliners perform. $75–1500

El Cortez. 600 Fremont St.; (702) 385-5200/ (800) 634-6703
Small rooms with narrow beds for cheap in this convenient, clean hotel downtown. And it's historic, by Las Vegas standards. (See essay, "El Cortez Hotel" p. 80.) $25–40

Excalibur. 3850 Las Vegas Blvd. South; (702) 597-7777/(800) 937-7777
Live the legend of Camelot—or at least, eat like a Medieval peasant in the "King Au-thur's Tournament" showroom while watching "knights" joust. In addition to pools, restaurants, shops, theaters, and Merlin's Magic Motion Machine thrill ride,

the 4,000 rooms in this cartoony castle are good value. *See photo pp. 122-23.* $55–175

Fiesta. 2400 Rancho Dr., North Las Vegas; (702) 631-7000/(800) 731-7333
This 100-room "Rancho Strip" hotel draws a crowd for its trendy restaurants, endless buffet, and great video poker. $50–130

FITZGERALDS

Fitzgeralds. 301 Fremont St.; (702) 388-2400/(800) 274-5825
The Luck of the Irish theme in this 34-story hotel means green, green, everywhere. Perhaps to make up for the green you'll lose in the Fremont Street casinos? $25–80

FLAMINGO HILTON

Flamingo Hilton. 3555 Las Vegas Blvd. South; (702) 733-3111/(800) 732-2111

The Flamingo is as pink as Fitzgeralds is green, but in more glamorous fashion. Five towers of over 3,500 rooms overlook a spectacular 15-acre pool park; there are also 8 restaurants, tennis courts, a showroom, and multi-language services. $65–150

Four Queens. 202 Fremont St.;
(702) 385-4011/(800) 634-6045
This hotel is meant to recall New Orleans, with its turn-of-the-century decor (vintage lamps and four-posters) and live jazz playing in the French Quarter lounge. $45–60

Fremont. 200 Fremont St.;
(702) 385-3232/(800) 634-6182
A basic hotel (450 rooms) with casino, restaurants, bar. $25–60

Frontier. 3120 Las Vegas Blvd. South;
(702) 794-8200/(800) 634-6966
This hotel, with its tower of reasonably priced mini-suites, markets itself to a young and hip clientele. And the great, cheap buffet and low table minimums draw the crowds in. $35–85

Gold Coast. 4000 W. Flamingo Rd.; (702) 367-7111/(800) 331-5334
Well-suited for families, this 700-room hotel offers movie theaters, bowling, pool, and day care, in addition to the casino, restaurants, and bar. $40–150

Gold Spike. 400 E. Ogden Ave.; (702) 384-8444/(800) 634-6703
This hotel and casino bills itself as "Las Vegas as it Used to Be," and with its penny slots, $1 blackjack tables, and breakfast included in all room rates, that may be right. $20–30

Golden Gate. 111 S. Main St.;
(702) 385-1906/(800) 426-1906
Over 100 rooms; restaurant and deli. Low rates in the thick of Glitter Gulch. $35–50

GOLDEN GATE

Golden Nugget. 129 Fremont St.; (702) 385-7111/(800) 634-3454
Spacious Victorian-style rooms (1,900 of them), formal lobbies with marble and red carpet, and gold detailing everywhere are the hallmarks of this hotel and casino downtown. Pool, health spa, 5 restaurants, and showroom. *See photo p. 109.* $50–150

Hard Rock. 4455 Paradise Rd.; (702) 693-5000/(800) 473-7625.
The world's only rock 'n' roll hotel-casino, with memorabilia throughout the casino, G-clef carpeting, music piped underwater in the pool, and 340 classy, oversized, and hard-to-get rooms. $85–300

Harrah's. 3475 Las Vegas Blvd. South;
(702) 369-5000/(800) 634-6765
The big old Ship on the Strip—that's Harrah's. In contrast to the flashy exterior and casino, the 1,600 rooms are subdued and quiet. Pool, 5 restaurants, showroom, spa, and shopping center outside. $70–350

Hotel Addresses

Holiday Inn Boardwalk. 3750 Las Vegas Blvd. South; (702) 735-2400/ (800) HOLIDAY
Over 650 rooms, 24-hour restaurant, buffet, and a huge low-roller casino. The hotel's sign includes a gargantuan neon clown face that's downright disturbing. $39–99

Imperial Palace. 3535 Las Vegas Blvd. South; (702) 731-3311/(800) 634-6441
Built on an Asian theme, with carved wood and jade, this hotel has over 2,700 rooms, laid out in a rather maze-like fashion, and is known for its auto collection and superstar impersonator show. With 10 restaurants, pool, shopping arcade, showroom, wedding chapel, and doctor's office. $45–100

IMPERIAL PALACE

Lady Luck. 206 N. Third St.; (702) 477-3000/(800) 523-9582
At this downtown hotel and casino, the 700-or-so rooms—some with whirlpools —are small and bright. Swimming pool, 2 restaurants, bar . . . and the famous free foot-long hot dogs. $40–100

Las Vegas Club. 18 Fremont St.; (702) 385-1664/(800) 634-6532
One of Vegas's old respectable casinos, the Las Vegas Club is now a smallish downtown hotel with a sports theme. It still draws many gamblers with its liberal multi-deck blackjack game. $35–125

LAS VEGAS HILTON

Las Vegas Hilton. 3000 Paradise Rd.; (702) 732-5111/(800) 732-7117
Adjacent to the Convention Center, this 3,000-or-so-room hotel offers over a dozen restaurants, 6 tennis courts, swimming pool, and a putting green. Regular guest rooms are large—or stay in the Elvis Suite, where the King himself slept. $80–250

Luxor. 3900 Las Vegas Blvd. South; (702) 262-4000/(800) 288-1000
Impossible to miss the giant pyramid, with its 13 acres of glass facing and spotlight beam through the apex, right on the Strip. Reproductions of Egyptian artifacts provide contrast to the high-tech video arcade and movie theaters: imagine an ancient city of the future. The "inclinators" are elevators which rise at 39-degree angle. The close to 4,500 rooms are done in a tasteful Egyptian theme; 7 restaurants, large lounge, showroom, resort spa. *See photo pp. 114-15.* $70–250

Main Street Station. 200 N. Main. St.; (702) 387-1896/(800) 465-0711
Possibly the classiest casino in Las Vegas, Main Street is chock full of antiques, stained glass, bronze bas relief, marble, and wood wood wood. It boasts 400 rooms, the largest buffet, and the only microbrewery downtown. $40–85

Maxim. 160 E. Flamingo Rd.; (702) 731-4300/(800) 634-6987
Almost 800 mid-size rooms, done in soft colors, with 2 restaurants, showroom, lounge, swimming pool. Look for their ubiquitous special offers in local papers. $40–125

MGM Grand. 3799 Las Vegas Blvd. South; (702) 891-1111/(800) 929-1111
Over 5,000 rooms make this the city's biggest hotel; the casino is so big that it's divided into three casinos. Equally impressive is the 33-acre amusement park. $70–250

Mirage. 3400 Las Vegas Blvd. South; (702) 791-7111/(800) 627-6667
Set on 100 acres are this 3,000-room hotel and its more famous fake volcano. In addition to the rainforest and the dolphin and white tiger habitats, the hotel offers an 18-hole golf course, good restaurants, tennis courts, pool, and bright guest rooms. *See photo pp. 36-37.* $90–280

Monte Carlo. 3770 Las Vegas Blvd. South; (702) 730-7777/(800) 311-8999
Opened in June 1996, this new megaresort has a stunning lobby (the front desk overlooks the pool), the Lance Burton Theater, a big bingo hall upstairs, a barn of a microbrewery, and 3,000 standard-megaresort rooms that are surprisingly inexpensive, given the location. $69–99

MONTE CARLO

New York–New York. 3790 Las Vegas Blvd. South; (702) 740-6969/(800) 693-6763
Just like its namesake, this joint is small (area-wise) and crowded (people-wise). Finding (and dodging) your way from the front desk to your hotel room can be an adventure. The rooms themselves are standard, but beware: the roller coaster noise, especially in the front lower rooms, is overwhelming. *See picture pp. 130-31.* $99–129

Orleans. 4500 W. Tropicana; (702) 365-7111/(800) 675-3267
Opened in December 1996, this is a nice enough locals casino—for a barn. It has a rocking lounge, lots of bars, and a big bowling alley upstairs. The rooms are bigger than standard, and there's often a bargain play here; the east-facing rooms have a nice view of the whole Strip. $59–99

Las Vegas Hotel Addresses

Palace Station. 2411 W. Sahara Ave.; (702) 367-2411/(800) 634-3101

This 1,000-room hotel just west of the Strip has a casino, restaurants (including a huge buffet), and 2 pools. $40–350

PLAZA

Plaza. 1 Main St.; (702) 386-2110/(800) 634-6575

At the top of Fremont Street, the Plaza has 1,000 rooms, 3 restaurants, tennis courts, swimming pool, and showroom. $20–120

Rio Suite. 3700 W. Flamingo Rd.; (702) 252-7777/(800) 888-1808

The first all-suite hotel with a casino, this red and blue Brazilian-theme hotel has 6 restaurants, a fitness center, and a swimming pool with its own sandy beach(!).

THE RIO

The continuously expanding Rio also boasts the highest-tech theater in town, with video screens that curve around the room, as well as a massive casino and a great buffet. $85–130

Riviera. 2901 Las Vegas Blvd. South; (702) 734-5110/(800) 634-6753

A somewhat confusing assortment of towers contain the 2,300 rooms here. There are also 4 showrooms, pool, health spa, and 4 restaurants. $60–150

Sahara. 2535 Las Vegas Blvd. South; (702) 737-2111/(800) 634-6666

Have a drink poolside at one of the little huts in the Sahara's courtyard, then try to find the tower with your room! The hotel's still pretty intimate despite its 2,000 rooms. Health club, 2 pools, 5 restaurants, lounge, and showroom. $45–225

SAM'S TOWN

Sam's Town. 5111 Boulder Hwy.; (702) 456-7777/(800) 634-6371

This popular locals' hotel on Boulder Highway has a lush atrium, 650 rooms, a stunning laser and dancing waters show, and the best sports bar in town. There's also a bowling alley, swimming pool, casino, RV park, and 5 good restaurants. $40–245

San Remo. 115 E. Tropicana Ave.; (702) 739-9000/(800) 522-7366
Over 700 rooms, some with balconies; pool with poolside service; 24-hour restaurant. $60–155

Santa Fe. 4949 N. Rancho Rd.; (702) 658-4900/(800) 872-6823
Good for families, this 200-room hotel lets kids under 13 stay for free, and offers supervised children's activities. There are also bowling lanes and an ice rink. Casino, 24-hour restaurant, bar. $40–50

Showboat. 2800 E. Fremont St.; (702) 385-9123/(800) 826-2800
Although most of the original paddlewheel design is gone, the bowling alley, large bingo parlor, and low rollers keep it steaming full speed ahead. Close to 500 rooms, swimming pool, free transport to airport, trains, and buses. $30–85

Stardust. 3000 Las Vegas Blvd. South; (702) 732-6111/(800) 634-6757
With close to 2,300 rooms, the Stardust is known for its gorgeous race and sports

STARDUST

book and its "Handicappers Library," popular low-limit poker room, and sizzling extravaganza, "Enter the Night." $25–300

STRATOSPHERE

Stratosphere. 2000 Las Vegas Blvd. South; (702) 380-7777/(800) 998-6937
Thanks to its marginal location and its 1,500 rooms, staying here can be a surprisingly inexpensive. And with the good gambling, tower, rides, and Top of the World restaurant and lounge, shopping, and fast food, there's plenty to keep you occupied when you do. $49-89

Texas Station. 2101 Texas Star Ln., North Las Vegas; (702) 631-1000/(800) 634-4000
This sprawling, Texas-themed hotel-casino on the Rancho Strip offers a vast buffet and a 12-screen movie complex. $40–180

Treasure Island. 3300 Las Vegas Blvd. South; (702) 894-7111/(800) 944-7444
Connected by monorail to the Mirage, the TI continues the South Seas theme with a swashbuckling twist. In addition to the

(top) A "day" lasts three hours inside the Forum Shops at Caesars, while the members of Cirque du Soleil (bottom) create their own surreal world in the showroom at Treasure Island. (both photos by Kerrick James)

outrageous pirate show in "Buccaneer Bay" and Cirque du Soleil in the showroom, the TI boasts almost 3,000 rooms, highly trained personnel, 5 restaurants, generous comps, and a casino a la Captain Hook. *See picture p. 95.* $50–100

Tropicana. 3801 Las Vegas Blvd. South; (702) 739-2222/(800) 468-9494
At the self-proclaimed "Island of Las Vegas," you can swim from the waterslide straight to the blackjack table or to the bar.

The lovely landscaping (bridges, Polynesian totems) and rattan furniture carry out the tropical theme. *See photo p. 104.* $25–300

Westward Ho. 2900 Las Vegas Blvd. South; (702) 731-2900/(800) 634-6803
A *motel?* With 1,000 rooms, 7 pools,and a casino? Well, it's the largest in the world. The location—between the Stardust and Circus Circus—is extremely convenient (do learn the Industrial Road shortcut for getting in and out). $40–50

Laughlin Hotels

Colorado Belle. 2100 S. Casino Dr.; (702) 298-4000/(800) 47-RIVER
Along with its signature replica paddle-wheeler, the Belle has 2 pools, a casino, and a 24-hour coffee shop. *See photos pp. 222-23.* $20–120

Edgewater. 2020 S. Casino Dr.; (702) 298-2453/(800) 257-0300
Next to the Colorado Belle, this hotel and casino has pool and whirlpool, 24-hour restaurant, and entertainment. $25–70

EDGEWATER

Flamingo Hilton. 1900 S. Casino Dr.; (702) 298-5111/(800) 352-6464

Sharing the pink flamingo theme with its Vegas parent, this hotel offers a shopping arcade, pool, lighted tennis, and 24-hour restaurant. Most of the 2,000 guest rooms and the casino (thanks to floor-to-ceiling windows) have river views. $30–90

Golden Nugget. 2300 S. Casino Dr.; (702) 298-7111/(800) 237-1739
This 300-room, tropical themed hotel on the river features a rainforest atrium, pool with poolside service, 24-hour restaurant, and shopping arcade. $20–70

Gold River. 2700 S. Casino Dr.; (702) 298-2242/(800) 835-7903
Pool, shopping arcade, restaurant, bar, and nightclub round out the facilities at this 1,000-room riverside hotel. $20–85

Harrah's. 2900 S. Casino Dr.; (702) 298-4600/(800) 427-7247
With over 1,600 rooms, this riverfront hotel has 2 casinos (1 that's non-smoking!), 5 restaurants, 2 pools, a spa, and a beach on the river. *See photo p. 244.* $25–100

Weekly Motels

HARRAH'S

RAMADA EXPRESS

Pioneer. 2200 S. Casino Dr.;
(702) 298-2442/(800) 634-3469
This motor hotel and casino offers over 400 rooms, some with river views. Pool, two 24-hour restaurants, bar. $30–100

Ramada Express. 2121 Casino Dr.;
(702) 298-4200/(800) 2-RAMADA
With its turn-of-the-century railroad motif,

this 1,500-room hotel is a block from the river. Casino, 3 restaurants, bar, buffet, pool, and whirlpool. $20-200

Riverside. 1650 Casino Dr.; (702) 298-2535/(800) 227-3849
Boat dockage, movie theaters, and a bus depot onsite; plus 2 pools, casino, 24-hour restaurant, bar, and lounge shows. $20-250

Weekly Motels

Crest. 207 N. Sixth St.; (702) 382-5642
Kitchen, television, VCR, cable, breakfast. $160

Downtowner. 129 N. Eighth St.; (702) 384-1441 With kitchen. $165

Fun City. 2233 Las Vegas Blvd. South; (702) 731-3155 With kitchen. $145

Glass Pool. 4613 Las Vegas Blvd. South; (702) 739-6636 With kitchen. $219

Holiday Royale. 4505 Paradise Rd.; (702) 733-7676 With kitchen. $125–225

Hops. 3412 Paradise Rd.; (702) 732-2494 With kitchen, sitting room. $190

King Albert. Albert and Koval; (702) 732-1555 With kitchen. $150–190

Sun Harbor Budget Suites. *5 locations*
1500 Stardust; (702) 732-1500/
4205 W. Tropicana; (702) 889-1700/
3684 Paradise Rd.; (702) 699-7000/
4625 Boulder Hwy.; (702) 454-4625/
4855 Boulder Hwy.; (702) 433-3644/
With kitchen, sitting room. $225-285

Tod. 1508 Las Vegas Blvd. South; (702) 477-0022 With kitchen. $126
(Without kitchen available. $98)

PRACTICAL INFORMATION

■ AREA CODE

The area code for Las Vegas and environs (and all of Nevada) is **702**.

■ RESTAURANTS

Las Vegas is both a gourmet's kingdom come and a gourmand's hog heaven. You can max out the lines on two of your credit cards at some of the finest dining west of New York City and east of Paris, or you can stuff yourself silly for under $5, shoveling home sheer tasteless volume at any one of two dozen buffets around town. Most major hotels have a gourmet room with four dollar signs next to the name, as well as a $5 steak or prime rib in the coffee shop, some combination of Italian, Japanese, Chinese, Mexican, and steakhouse restaurants under the same roof, plus snack bars, fast food, and ice cream parlors. A handful of restaurants around town have survived 30, 40, even 50 years (described in the listings as "Old Las Vegas"), while trendy Southwestern, American regional, and California cuisine meals are served fresh from the latest high-tech kitchens. Coyote Cafe of Santa Fe, Emeril's of New Orleans, Spago of Los Angeles: these and other well-known restaurants have been opening branches in Las Vegas over the past few years with a vengeance—30 million visitors annually are hard to resist. Likewise, familiar chains and fast food take-outs are around every corner, as are plenty of exotic ethnic eateries. Following are brief descriptions of Las Vegas restaurant styles.

Restaurants

Restaurants

■ GOURMET ROOMS

"Gourmet room" is a restaurant category specific to Las Vegas, and in general the term refers to expensive hotel restaurants that cater particularly to high rollers. In these restaurants, service is formal, prices are high, and the cuisine is elaborate—if not necessarily sophisticated. For while the dinners served at the very top rooms in town might compete with those served in New York's or San Francisco's best restaurants, in most cases the dishes offered in gourmet rooms tend to be traditional. Menus commonly list "continental" entrees like veal medallions, shrimp Scampi, and beef Wellington, and desserts like baked Alaska and bananas Foster.

■ VALUE GOURMET ROOMS AND STEAKHOUSES

Another type of restaurant is known as "value gourmet." Restaurants in this category would probably be called steakhouses elsewhere (as might some of the gourmet rooms proper). Still, "value gourmet" rooms serve good food at great prices. Of course, many popular eateries *do* call themselves steakhouses, and offer every cut in every size. Clearly, beef is popular in this town (perhaps there aren't many vegan Las Vegans?), especially along the Strip and downtown. A non-carnivore might fare better in a Chinese or Thai restaurant than in a hotel dining room.

■ BUFFETS

Buffets are one small step up from fast food, and—bite for bite—one giant leap down in price. For the cost of satisfying a Big Mac attack, you can shovel home, on average, 23 choices of chow. Breakfast presents the usual fruits, juices, toast, steam-table scrambled eggs, sausage, potatoes, and pastries. Lunch consists of salads and cold cuts. Dinner buffets offer salads, steam-table mook, vegetables, potatoes, and usually either a baron of beef, shoulder of pork, leg of lamb, saddle of mutton, or breast of turkey. Unless you're really starving and must have food!—now!—check out the buffet first by asking the cashier if you can sneak a peek. For more on buffets, see the essay "Eating Cheap" on p. 256.

■ SPECTACLE AND SCENERY

There are some restaurants in Las Vegas that are worth visiting just for the experience. A few pull you far from the everyday: at Bacchanal, for instance, you're served a gluttonous feast by toga-wearing "wine goddesses." Others offer a stunning view of the city, or an unusual setting. While the actual food prepared in these establishments ranges from fair to fantastic, the restaurant's real hope is that the time you spend there is unforgettable.

Restaurants

> ### *Restaurant Prices*
> $ = under $10; $$ = $10-20; $$$ = $20-30; $$$$ = over $30
> *(per person, excluding tax, tip, and drinks)*
> *Dress is casual and reservations are not necessary, unless otherwise noted.*

All-American Bar and Grille. *Steakhouse* Rio Suite, 3700 W. Flamingo Rd.; (702) 252-7777

The large mesquite grill area here faces the downstairs dining room; upstairs are more tables, along with an unusual collection of antique slot machines. Order your meat—top sirloin, New York steak, filet mignon—and then choose your sauce —bearnaise, dijon, peppercorn, mushroom, horseradish. Dinner daily. $$

Andiamo's. *Italian* Las Vegas Hilton, 3000 Paradise Rd.; (702) 732-5801 before 5 P.M./732-5111 after 5 P.M.

Beautiful, bright, and comfortable, with the big kitchen facing the room. Roast duck and noodles, pasta with cream sauce, veal scallopine marsala are all good deals for the quality. Dinner daily. Reservations advised; casual, but shorts not allowed. $$

Andre's. *French* 401 S. Sixth St.; (702) 385-5016

This expensive restaurant in a converted house downtown boasts an impressive wine list and comfortable French decor. The kitchen specializes in innovative, fresh fish preparations. Dinner daily. Jacket required. $$$$

Bacchanal. *Spectacle/Roman* Caesars Palace, 3570 Las Vegas Blvd. South; (702) 731-7731

Walk past the stone lions guarding the door for Caesar and down to the sunken room with a lighted pool and statue at center stage. The set 7-course Roman feast is accented by toga-clad wine goddesses who serve all the juice of the vine your heart desires and your liver can stand, then massage your shoulders just before dessert. At $70 per person, it's one of the most expensive meals in town, but men especially may find it worth it for the experience, if not for the banquet-style food. Two dinner seatings Tuesday through Saturday. Reservations, jacket required. $$$$

Bagelmania. *Deli* 855 E. Twain Ave.; (702) 369-3322

Thanks to Northeastern sunbirds (and the Jewish Mafia), Vegas is a great town for lox, bagels, matzoh brie. This is one of the best sources. Breakfast through late lunch daily. $

Bagels 'n' More. *Deli* 2405 E. Tropicana Ave.; (702) 435-8100

Jewish deli with the best homemade corned beef hash this side of the Hudson River, and fancy-schmancy omelettes. Breakfast through lunch daily. $ - $$

Restaurants

Battista's Hole In The Wall. *Italian* 4041 Audrie St.; (702) 732-1424

Family-style meals (antipasto, garlic bread, minestrone, all-you-can-eat pasta on the side, and all-you-can-drink red wine) start at around $10 for spaghetti and meatballs and go up to the mid-$20s for cioppino. Classic Italian restaurant decor. Just across the street from Bally's. Dinner daily. $$

Battista's Pizzeria. *Pizza* 4041 Audrie St.; (702) 733-3950

Voted Las Vegas's best pizza. Lunch through dinner daily. $

Benihana. *Japanese/Spectacle* Las Vegas Hilton. 3000 Paradise Rd.; (702) 732-5801

This spectacle of a restaurant consists of a cocktail lounge out front with musical waters (fountains synchronized to splash to the beat—a classic Las Vegas motif) and an animated bird show. Hibachi tableside and robata barbecue rooms feature similar menus, with dinners of meat, fish, and veggies. For just the show, though, sit in the lounge and sip some steaming sake. Performances on the hour starting at 5 P.M.). Dinner daily. Reservations advised. $$ - $$$

Billy Bob's. *Steakhouse* Sam's Town, 5111 Boulder Hwy.; (702) 456-7777

A reliably good steakhouse. Dinner daily. Reservations advised. $$

Bootlegger. *Italian* 5025 S. Eastern Ave.; (702) 736-4939

Cozy, family-run, great service, reasonable and tasty food. All the old-time Italians eat here. Lunch and dinner Tuesday through Saturday, dinner only on Sunday. Reservations advised. $ - $$

Boston Pizza. *Pizza* 1507 Las Vegas Blvd. South; (702) 385-2595

The crispy crust and secret sauce on the pizza in this place will transport all Yankees right back to the famous Greek-style Houses of Pizza from Lowell to Provincetown. Lunch and dinner daily. $

Burgundy Room. *Steakhouse/Value Gourmet* Lady Luck, 206 N. Third St.; (702) 477-3000

Entrees such as beef Wellington, salmon, veal, and porterhouse. Dinner daily. Reservations advised. $$

Cafe Michelle. *Eclectic* 1350 E. Flamingo Rd. in Mission Center; (702) 735-8686

Very popular with Las Vegans for its patio dining (overlooking the shopping center parking lot), eclectic American and European dishes (crepes to spanikopita), and extremely reasonable prices. Crowded at lunchtime; a bar next door has live music at night. Lunch and dinner daily. $ - $$

Camelot. *Steakhouse/Value Gourmet* Excalibur, 3850 Las Vegas Blvd. South; (702) 597-7777

Chicken, lamb, veal, beef. Dinner daily. Reservations advised. $$

Carluccio's Tivoli Gardens. *Italian* 1775 E. Tropicana Ave. in the Liberace Plaza; (702) 795-3236

The decor is straight out of Liberace—with good reason: Liberace opened this joint next door to his museum. Check out the grand piano bar and the twinkling overhead lights. The food is good workmanlike Italian in the $7–15 range. Can't go wrong here. Early to late dinner Tuesday through Sunday. $ - $$

Carnival World. *Buffet* Rio Suite, 3700 W. Flamingo Rd.; (702) 252-7777
The best buffet in Las Vegas: you've got your choice of American (ribs, burgers), Chinese, fried fish, Italian, Mexican, Mongolian (the "Amazon Grill," where your choice of meats and vegetables are barbecued to order), salad bar, steaks, sushi, and a big dessert bar (with the best selection of sugar-free sweets in town). $

Cathay House. *Chinese* 5300 Spring Mountain Rd.; (702) 876-3838
One of the best Chinese restaurants in town, with a great view from big picture windows overlooking the Strip. Chinese patrons pack this place for the dim sum lunch. Lunch and dinner daily. $ - $$

Circus Circus Buffet *Buffet* Circus Circus, 2880 Las Vegas Blvd. South; (702) 734-0410
The busiest buffet on the Strip, and probably the cheapest, too. Expect kid-oriented, colorful plates, but not the highest quality. $

Coyote Cafe. *Southwestern* MGM Grand, 3805 Las Vegas Blvd. South; (702) 891-7349
An outpost of the famous Sante Fe restaurant, the Coyote offers sophisticated Southwestern cuisine. There's a casual cafe in the front, too. $$$ - $$$$

Dona Maria's. *Mexican* 910 Las Vegas Blvd. South; (702) 382-6538
Pretty low key, with good and inexpensive food. The tamale with green enchilada sauce ($3) is a lip-smacker. You'll forget you're in Las Vegas inside Dona Maria's, serving the city faithfully since 1977. Open daily for breakfast, lunch, dinner. $

El Sombrero. *Mexican/Old Vegas* 807 S. Main St.; (702) 382-9234
In the same location since 1951, when it was opened by Clemente Greigo, El Sombrero is today run by Greigo's nephews Jose and Zeke Aragon. The best thing about El Sombrero is that this stucco cantina, with 6 booths, 6 tables, and an all-Mexican-hit jukebox, looks its age and has certainly seen it all, but retains its baby-boomer vitality and devotion to service and quality. Dinners are cheap, the service no-nonsense. Lunch and dinner; closed Sunday. $

Embers. *Steakhouse/Gourmet* Imperial Palace, 3535 Las Vegas Blvd. South; (702) 731-3311
Open for dinner Wednesday through Sunday; make reservations. $$

Emeril's New Orleans. *Creole* MGM Grand, 3799 Las Vegas Blvd. South
Another Vegas offshoot of a famous restaurant, Emeril's serves excellent New Orleans fare. Try the etouffee. $$$ - $$$$

Empress Court. *Chinese* Caesars Palace, 3570 Las Vegas Blvd. South; (702) 731-7731
Probably the fanciest and most expensive Chinese restaurant you'll ever eat in, this spot consistently ranks among the top Cantonese restaurants in the country. Dinner daily. Reservations required; jacket. $$ - $$$$

Fiesta Buffet. *Buffet* Fiesta, 2400 N. Rancho Dr.; (702) 631-7000
In addition to adopting Rio's "action" concept, where items are cooked to order, Fiesta has the largest open-pit barbecue this side of San Anton, along with a Mongolian grill and coffee bar. $

Restaurants

Fong's Garden. *Chinese/Old Vegas* 2021 E. Charleston Blvd.; (702) 382-1644

In 1933, J. S. Fong, a cook at the Rainbow Club downtown, opened the Silver Café at 106 North First, next to the Silver Club. He advertised 25-cent American breakfasts and 35-cent dinners, but he also served Chinese food by request. (Fong was the only Las Vegas restaurateur to do so before 1941.) The Silver Café changed its name to Fong's in 1955, when it relocated to the present site on East Charleston. You can't miss it: big neon pagoda-roof signs grace the entrance. Inside are red booths and a rock shrine, along with the same American and Chinese dishes this family has been serving for years. Lunch and dinner daily. $

Ginza. *Japanese* 1000 E. Sahara Ave.; (702) 732-3080

This Japanese restaurant is always occupied by at least several tourists from Tokyo. Ten a la carte dishes, in true Japanese style, will run $40. Dinner Monday through Saturday. $$$

Golden Wok. *Chinese* 4670 S. Eastern Ave.; (702) 456-1868

Many Chinese locals frequent the Golden Wok. It has a typically varied menu, with spicy Szechuan dishes and fresh Cantonese-style vegetables, from $7–12. Lunch buffet for $6. Lunch and dinner on weekdays, closed on weekends. $ - $$

Green Shack. *Southern/Old Vegas* 2504 E. Fremont St.; (702) 383-0007

Not only is this the oldest continuously operating restaurant in Las Vegas, but it's also in the same location, even in the same building! Green Shack opened, as the Colorado, in 1929, when Jimmie Jones sold fried chicken from the window of her two-room house. In 1932, she purchased a barracks from Union Pacific, hauled it to her house, and called it the Green Shack. This barracks-turned-dining room has been hosting chicken dinners, birthdays, weddings, divorces, wakes, and hearty parties for nearly 60 years—ancient history for Las Vegas! Today the Shack is run by Jimmie Jones's great grandnephew. There is simply nowhere else in this town to go for chicken —white meat, dark meat, fried, roasted, gizzards, livers—all close to 10 bucks. They also serve fish, steak, and tasty bread pudding. The Green Shack has it all—informality, friendliness, great food, and best of all, a long history. Dinner Tuesday through Sunday. $ - $$

Hugo's Cellar. *French/Gourmet Room* Four Queens, 202 Fremont St.; (702) 385-4011

Dinner daily. Reservations required; jacket and tie. $$$$

Kokomo's. *Continental/Spectacle* Mirage; 3400 Las Vegas Blvd. South; (702) 791-7111

It's a gas to sit under hut-like canopies within the rainforest of the Mirage's domed atrium. Though the room's slightly noisy from the casino and the waterfalls, the hubbub quickly becomes part of the unusual atmosphere. Continental-style dishes include Dungeness crabcakes, salmon, filet mignon, prime rib, or lobster tail. Lunch and dinner daily. $$ - $$$

Le Montrachet. *French/Gourmet Room*
 Las Vegas Hilton. 3000 Paradise Rd.;
 (702) 732-5755
Formal atmosphere, French-based seasonal cuisine, and elaborate service: sorbets are served between courses. Dinner Wednesday through Monday. Reservations, jacket required. $$$$

Lilly Langtry's. *Chinese* Golden Nugget,
 129 Fremont St.; (702) 385-7111
Cantonese specialties—almond duck, lemon chicken, ginger beef—served in an 1890s' San Francisco atmosphere. Western desserts. Dinner daily. Reservations. $$

Lindo Michoacan. *Mexican* 2655 E. Desert
 Inn Rd.; (702) 735-6828
One of the most popular Mexican eateries in Las Vegas—don't let the humble exterior fool you. Huge menu, big choice of combinations, with interesting cactus dishes. Lunch and dinner daily $$

Main Street Station Buffet. *Buffet*
 Main Street Station, 200 N. Main. St.;
 (702) 387-1896
The best buffet downtown: this one's got a good selection and offers the "action buffet," where your food is cooked to order. $

Michael's. *French/Eclectic/Gourmet Room*
 Barbary Coast, 3595 Las Vegas Blvd.
 South; (702) 737-7111
Long one of the best kept secrets in town is this restaurant in the hotel at the corner of Flamingo and the Strip. *Esquire* once called it the best restaurant in the country. It's tough to get reservations here, because the room is small and most of the tables are reserved for the hotel's high rollers. The restaurant office opens at 3:30 P.M. Tuesday through Thursday, so call for a reservation then. Everything is a la carte; plan to spend $200 for two, without drinks. The service is unforgettable. Two seatings per evening. Reservations required; jacket and tie. $$$$+

Monte Carlo. *French/Gourmet Room*
 Desert Inn, 3145 Las Vegas Blvd. South;
 (702) 733-4444
Classic continental cuisine—roast duck, veal chops—are served in this formal room. Dinner Thursday through Monday. Reservations, jacket required. $$$$

Moongate. *Chinese/Spectacle* Mirage,
 3400 Las Vegas Blvd. South;
 (702) 791-7111
This restaurant, next to Kokomo's, is meant to replicate a Chinese village square, with a big lilac tree in the middle, pagoda roofs, scalloped walls, and great curves. The food is as pleasing as the environment, and the prices are reasonable. Try satay beef, moo shu pork, tea-smoked duck, strawberry chicken, or scallops. Dinner daily. $$ - $$$

Osaka. *Japanese* 4205 W. Sahara Ave.;
 (702) 876-4988
A close second to Ginza. Lunch and dinner weekdays, dinner only on weekends. $$$

Palace Court. *French/Gourmet Room*
 Caesars Palace, 3570 Las Vegas Blvd.
 South; (702) 731-7731
Often rated by travel guides as the city's best, this very formal restaurant offers classic French cuisine—beef tournedos, duck breast with pink peppercorn sauce—in an elegantly appointed room topped with a stained-glass skylight. Dinner daily. Reservations, jacket required. $$$$

Restaurants

Pamplemousse. *French* 400 E. Sahara Ave.;
(702) 733-2066
This spot, like Andre's, is in a converted house. There's no menu; the waiters recite the handful of available entrees of the day. This is the place to sit back, have them bring you the works, and savor each bite. Nothing will be anything but superb here. Dinner Tuesday through Sunday. $$$

Pasta Palace. *Italian* Palace Station, 2411 W. Sahara Ave.; (702) 367-2411
These folks almost always have a special deal going on, such as two-for-one pasta dinners, early-bird specials, or $5 large pizza and beer. While you're there, start with a 99-cent margarita from the Guadalajara Bar. Dinner daily. Make reservations. $

Pasta Pirate. *Italian* The California, 12 E. Ogden Ave.; (702) 385-1222
One of the best-value Italian restaurants in a Las Vegas hotel. The decor is industrial lite—vents, pipes, beams, neon. The pasta is plentiful and inexpensive (especially the kids' plates); the $10 filet mignon dinner could be the best in town. Dinner daily. $

Pegasus. *French/Gourmet Room* Alexis Park, 375 E. Harmon Ave.; (702) 796-3300
The strains of classical guitar float through this elegant room, which features an Italian crystal chandelier and arched windows overlooking a waterfall and garden. Order a la carte from the fabulous French menu; try the lobster Princess or veal medallions. Dinner daily. Reservations, jacket required. $$$ - $$$$

Poppa Gar's. *Diner* 1624 W. Oakey Blvd.;
(702) 384-4513
"Poppa" Garland Miner goes about as far back as anybody in the Las Vegas restaurant business—50 years! He started out at the Round-Up Drive-In on the Strip in the early 1940s, then took over the food service at the El Cortez in 1945. After a few years he moved up Fremont Street to Bob Baskin's, where he and Bob put out the victuals till 1965, when he moved to his present location. The historical black-and-white photographs alone are worth the visit, and the quail and eggs, served with fresh country sausage, are legendary. Open all day on weekdays, mornings on Saturdays, and closed Sundays. $$

Primavera. *Italian* Caesars Palace, 3570 Las Vegas Blvd. South; (702) 731-7731
Overlooking the Garden of the Gods swimming pool. Poolside dining, too. The thing to have here, naturally, is the Caesars salad, but also try anything from eggs for breakfast and hamburgers for lunch to Maine lobster for dinner. Breakfast, lunch, dinner daily. Reservations required for dinner; casual but no shorts. $$ - $$$$

Ranch House. *Steakhouse/Spectacle* Binion's Horseshoe; 128 Fremont St.;
(702) 382-1600
Located on the hotel's 24th floor, this steakhouse restaurant has great views in all directions. The food is only fair: steaks, a few seafood entrees, chicken. Or just have a cocktail. Dinner daily, bar open until 1:00 A.M. $$ - $$$

Redwood Bar & Grille. *Steakhouse/Value Gourmet* California Hotel, 12 E. Ogden Ave.; (702) 385-1222
Try the bargain porterhouse. Dinner daily. Make reservations. $$

Saigon Restaurant. *Vietnamese* 4251 W. Sahara Ave.; (702) 362-9978
With its classic plain Vietnamese interior, this spot could be right out of San Francisco. The incomparable Imperial rolls are $3, and try the long-simmered beef-noodle soup *(phö)* and satay in Sahara West Village just beyond the Statue of Liberty. Opens early for lunch and dinner. $

Seasons. *Continental/Gourmet Room* Bally's, 3645 Las Vegas Blvd. South; (702) 739-4111
A true continental gourmet room. The wide-ranging menu changes seasonally; nightly specials take advantage of the freshest ingredients the chefs can find. Dinner Tuesday through Saturday. Reservations, jacket required. $$ - $$$$

Spago. *California/Eclectic* Forum Shops at Caesars, 3500 Las Vegas Blvd. South; (702) 369-6300
This counterpart to Wolfgang Puck's L.A. restaurant specializes in classic California cuisine—unusual pizzas and salads, stylish presentation. Jazz piano adds to the lively atmosphere. Lunch and dinner daily; reservations advised. $$ - $$$$

The Steak House. *Steakhouse* Circus Circus, 2880 Las Vegas Blvd. South; (702) 734-0410

This place captures the essence of the Las Vegas steakhouse. Wend your way through the permanent crowds of grinds and kids to the Steak House. The split-level dining area surrounds the grill, which lends an authentic, slightly smoky air to the room. Chicken,filet mignon, surf and turf all $20 or less. Dinner daily. $$

Texas Station Buffet. *Buffet* Texas Station, 2101 Texas Star Lane; (702) 631-1000
This reliable buffet offers a Texas chili bar, action fajitas, and a root-beer-float station.

Thai Spice. *Thai* 4433 W. Flamingo Rd.; (702) 362-5308
The best Thai food in Las Vegas by a long shot. Quiet subdued room, traditional Thai cuisine, some with Vegas-y names (blackjack noodles). Try the tom kha kai or tom yum soups. Lunch and dinner, Monday through Saturday. $

Tropicana. *Pizza* (702) 798-6707
Six locations around town deliver this reasonable facsimile of New York–style pizza. Stick with the thick crust and have them cook it well done. $

The Venetian. *Italian/Old Vegas* 3713 W. Sahara Ave.; (702) 876-4190
This award-winning restaurant began in 1955 as the Pizzeria Restaurant, down the block from the Green Shack, and is one of the first pizzerias in Las Vegas. It moved to its present site in 1966 and changed its name to the Venetian Pizzeria ("Pizzeria" was later dropped). Check out the murals of Venice. Daily, 24 hours. $$

Viva Mercado's. *Mexican* 6182 W. Flamingo Rd.; (702) 871-8826
Bobby Mercado has one of the most imaginative Mexican menus around: traditional Tex-Mex dishes are dressed in nouveau duds. Good ceviche (stick with the appetizer, not the salad), great grilled meats. Lunch and dinner daily. $$ - $$$

William B's. *Steakhouse* Stardust, 3000 Las Vegas Blvd. South; (702) 732-6111
Dinner daily. Informal but neat attire required. $$

Yolie's Churrascaria *Brazilian* 3900 Paradise Rd.; (702) 794-0700
The only place in Nevada to get marinated meat, mesquite-broiled, *rodizio* style, which means sliced continuously from a skewer onto your plate by a waiter in the fashion of a true *churrascaria* (Brazilian house of meat). Sausage, turkey, brisket, lamb, pork, along with salad, soup, and sides come for a reasonable set price. The room is soft and inviting, the bar big and comfortable. Or sit outside on the deck. Dinner daily. $$

Restaurant Index:
Restaurants in Hotels

Alexis Park
Pegasus

Bally's
Seasons

Barbary Coast
Michael's

Binion's Horseshoe
Ranch House

Caesars Palace
Bacchanal
Empress Court
Palace Court
Primavera
Spago

California Hotel
Pasta Pirate
Redwood Bar & Grille

Circus Circus
Circus Circus Buffet
The Steak House

Desert Inn
Monte Carlo

Excalibur
Camelot

Fiesta
Fiesta Buffet

Four Queens
Hugo's Cellar

Golden Nugget
Lilly Langtry's

Imperial Palace
Embers

Lady Luck
Burgundy Room

Las Vegas Hilton
Andiamo's
Benihana
Le Montrachet

Main Street Station
Main Street Station
Buffet

MGM Grand
Coyote Cafe
Emeril's New Orleans

Mirage
Kokomo's
Moongate

Palace Station
Pasta Palace

Rio Suite Hotel
All-American Bar and Grille
Carnival World Buffet

Sam's Town
Billy Bob's

Stardust
William B's

Texas Station
Texas Station Buffet

Restaurant Index:
Restaurants by Cuisine/Special Feature

Brazilian
Yolie's Churrascaria

Buffets
Circus Circus
Carnival World
Main Street Station
Texas Station
Fiesta

Chinese
Cathay House
Empress Court
Fong's Gardens
Golden Wok
Lilly Langtry's
Moongate

Creole
Emeril's New Orleans

Deli/Diner
Bagelmania
Bagels 'n' More
Poppa Gar's

Eclectic
Cafe Michelle
Michael's
Spago

French/Continental
Andre's
Hugo's Cellar
Kokomo's
Le Montrachet
Michael's

Monte Carlo
Palace Court
Pamplemousse
Pegasus
Seasons

Gourmet Rooms
Hugo's Cellar
Le Montrachet
Michael's
Monte Carlo
Palace Court
Pegasus
Seasons

Italian
Andiamo's
Battista's
Bootlegger
Carluccio's
Pasta Palace
Pasta Pirate
Primavera
The Venetian

Japanese
Benihana
Ginza
Osaka

Mexican
Dona Maria's
El Sombrero
Lindo Michoacan
Viva Mercado's

Old Vegas
El Sombrero
Fong's Garden
Green Shack
The Venetian

Pizza
Battista's Pizzeria
Boston Pizza
Tropicana

Southwestern
Coyote Cafe

Spectacle/Views
Bacchanal
Benihana
Kokomo's
Moongate
Ranch House

**Steakhouses/
Value Gourmet**
All-American Bar/Grille
Billy Bob's
Burgundy Room
Camelot
Embers
Redwood Bar & Grille
The Steak House
William B's

Thai
Thai Spice

Vietnamese
Saigon Restaurant

Eating Cheap

EATING CHEAP: BUFFETS, STEAKS, AND FREEBIES

■ BUFFETS

Las Vegas is a great city for a cheap meal. Casino owners know they can draw in customers if they use food and drink deals—steak bargains, 99-cent drinks—as bait.

If you're looking for variety, volume, and value, a hotel buffet is your best bet. Most cost $3–4 for breakfast, $5–6 for lunch, and $8–13 for dinner. Buffet times and prices are listed in most of the free visitors guides, and in the Friday *Review-Journal*. Generally, breakfast is served 7–10 A.M., lunch 11 A.M.–3 P.M., and dinner 4–10 P.M. —give or take an hour. (For more information on what's served, see "Buffets," p. 246, as well as restaurant listings for the following top four hotel buffets). Best on or near the Strip is **Carnival World at Rio,** best downtown is at **Main Street Station.** In North Las Vegas, try either the **Fiesta** or the **Texas Station Buffet.** Other good buffets are found at the **Aladdin, Bally's,** the **Golden Nugget,** and the **Fremont** (Paradise Buffet). *Rio Suite, 3700 W. Flamingo Rd.; (702) 252-7777. Main Street Station, 200 N. Main. St.; (702) 387-1896. Fiesta, 2400 N. Rancho Dr.; (702) 631-7000. Texas Station, 2101 Texas Star Lane; (702) 631-1000. Aladdin, 3667 Las Vegas Blvd. South, (702) 736-0111. Bally's, 3645 Las Vegas Blvd. South, (702) 739-4111. Golden Nugget, 129 Fremont St., (702) 385-7111. The Fremont, 200 Fremont St., (702) 385-3232.*

■ STEAK AND PRIME RIB SPECIALS

Nearly all the fabled meat bargains are served in the hotel coffeeshops. If none is listed on the marquee or menu, ask. The $3 late-night steak dinner at **Binion's Horseshoe** is an institution: it's been around for so long that it's the standard for every other meal deal in town. Other good steak specials ($7–11) can be found at the **Gold Coast,** the Fremont's **Second Street Grille;** the **Frontier,** and the California's **Redwood Bar & Grill.** Steak and eggs can be had for under $4 at the **Frontier** and **San Remo,.** Prime rib specials are served all over town for $5–7. Try the **Aladdin, Bally's,** and the **California.** *Binion's Horseshoe, 128 Fremont, (702) 382-1600. Gold Coast, 4000 W. Flamingo Rd.; (702) 367-7111. The Frontier, 3120 Las Vegas Blvd. South; (702) 794-8200. The California, 12 E. Ogden Ave., (702) 385-1222. San Remo, 115 E. Tropicana Ave.; (702) 739-9000.*

■ FREEBIES (AND ALMOST FREEBIES)

The **Lady Luck** at 206 North Third gives out free foot-long hot dogs with a coupon from its funbook. You need non-Nevada ID to get one and there's a limit of one per week. The **Golden Gate,** at 111 South Main, serves the best shrimp cocktail, 24 hours, 99 cents. **Roberta's at the El Cortez** at 600 Fremont Street, has the best inexpensive king crab leg dinner, around $10. You can get free popcorn at **Silver City** and **Slots-A-Fun,** and the bar at the front of the **Golden Nugget,** 129 Fremont, serves a choice of 40 bottled beers for a buck and a few bits.

■ ENTERTAINMENT

With half a dozen arenas and concert halls hosting everything from headliners to prize fights and rock 'n' roll to rodeos, plus two dozen Las Vegas–style revues, more than 50 lounges with Las Vegas–style combos performing every night of the week and some afternoons, a score of discos, nightclubs, and country-western saloons, a dozen topless or bottomless bump-and-grind joints and regiments of private exotic dancers, comedy clubs, plus light shows, people-watching, bargain movies, amusement parks, and local theater, dance, music, and art exhibitions—the only way to arrive in Las Vegas and not be entertained is in a coffin.

■ H E A D L I N E R S

The Thomas & Mack Center, MGM Grand Arena, Aladdin Theatre for the Performing Arts, Hard Rock Hotel, Bally's, Caesars, and the Desert Inn all have venues where Las Vegas performers earn Las Vegas wages in front of Las Vegas crowds. A recent lineup included Jerry Seinfeld, Bernadette Peters, David Copperfield, Penn & Teller, Tom Jones, Julio Iglesias, and Bill Cosby. Unless the performer is a perennial sell-out, you should be able to get into any show that's in

Siegfried & Roy

Entertainment

town when you are. Check out the stars and revues as soon as you settle in, and make reservations immediately at the particular box office.

■ S H O W S

This is the classic Las Vegas entertainment. These days there are still a handful of major extravaganzas: "Folies Bergere" at the Tropicana, "Jubilee" at Bally's, "Enter the Night" at the Stardust, "Siegfried and Roy" at the Mirage, "EFX" at the MGM Grand, and "Splash II" at the Riviera. Most include elaborate song-and-dance production numbers with performers costumed in anything from the skimpiest five-ounce G-string to the most outrageous 20-pound headgear—and often both. Live or taped music accompanies some combination of Broadway show tunes, Geritol oldies, cabaret classics, and dirty-dancin' disco. The sets are lavish, the costumes dazzling, the special effects surprising, and the exposed mammaries curious. Specialty acts are interspersed among the production numbers for variety: magicians and illusionists, often with large animals, jugglers, comics, daredevils, acrobats and aquabats, musclemen and musclewomen, marionetteers, and indescribable gimmicksters. The emphasis is on spectacle, and there's a distinct emptiness where theme, meaning, or redeeming social commentary might be found.

Then there are the smaller revues. "Legends in Concert" at the Imperial Palace and "American Superstars" currently at the Stratosphere present superstar impersonators (classic Vegas performers like Liberace, Elvis, Sammy, and the Temptations at "Legends;" more risque stars like Madonna, Blues Brothers, Little Richard, and Michael Jackson at "Superstars"). Female impersonators are found in "La Cage" at the Riviera. Danny Gans, the super-talented "Man of Many Voices" at the Rio, does impressions of 80 celebrities, from Dean Martin to Kermit the Frog.

"Country Fever" at the Golden Nugget and "Country Tonite" at the Aladdin attract the C&W crowds. "Lance Burton" at the Monte Carlo and "Spellbound" at Harrah's work the illusion theme, though nowhere near the scale and scope of "Siegfried and Roy" or "EFX" (and nowhere near the price, either). "Starlight Express" at the Hilton is an Andrew Lloyd Webber Broadway show; Cirque du Soleil's show at Treasure Island is a chic, New Age circus unlike anything you've ever seen; and "King Arthur's Tournament" at Excalibur is a dinner show with a knights-in-shining-armor theme.

Ticket prices can range from $22 for "American Superstars" all the way up to $90 for "Siegfried & Roy." The price often, but not always, includes two cocktails.

■ SHOWROOM DARWINISM

In the past six years, upwards of half the shows have converted their ticket procedure to reserved seating. This makes it smooth and easy for showgoers. Simply call ahead, reserve your seats, and show up anytime. The only considerations here are finding out how far in advance you can reserve tickets and what the cancellation policy is. As with buying tickets anywhere else, the earlier you reserve, the better your seats will be.

The old system remains in place in the other half of the shows. Here, you make reservations for general seating, which is first come, first served. Seating begins 90 minutes to two hours before showtime. The night of the performance, you show up at the door and enter into a Darwinian domain: "survival of the tippest." A few hints are in order for the old system. To begin with, it's not really necessary to tip at all; no seats are in Siberia. At worst you'll be sandwiched into a banquet table on the floor right in front of the stage with the other low rollers. Preferable, though, is to get a booth on the first or second tier near the center. At the revues, a party of two, a $10 toke to the maitre d', and an early arrival might do the trick. If it doesn't, and the captain (seater) starts to usher you to a corner, you might flash some cash and ask him for a better placement. If that doesn't work, you'll have to go back to the maitre d' and bargain some more. Worst is to tip everybody and still get an unsatisfactory seat. Best is to save your money, show up early, and be satisfied wherever you're seated.

Some hotels on the old system accept reservations a few days ahead, others only on the day of the show. Some hotels on either system prioritize reservations for their own guests, so you might pick your hotel by the show you'd like to see—especially if it's included in a package deal. Otherwise, be persistent. If you can't get reservations, you could show up at show time and hope for a no-show. Or, consult your bell captain or motel manager, who might have the necessary juice, or at least a suggestion. At shows on the old system, the waiters and waitresses collect for admission and refreshments. Two drinks per person are generally included in the price; both will be brought at the same time.

■ LOUNGE ACTS

Another Las Vegas institution: several dozen of the major hotels have live entertainment in bars usually located right off the casino. These acts are listed in the tabloids and magazines, and if you look hard enough, you can usually find one

Entertainment

KIDS IN LAS VEGAS

Las Vegas has traditionally had little to offer impressionable youngsters, since strictly enforced state laws prohibit minors from gambling in casinos. Young children can pass through casinos on the way to shows, restaurants, and rooms, but they have to be with adults and they have to keep moving; the fastest way to summon a security guard is to linger with children in a casino.

In recent years, however, a number of facilities catering to kids have opened, including Circus Circus's Grand Slam Canyon, the MGM Grand amusement park, all of Luxor, and the pirate show at Treasure Island. But don't forget the slightly older attractions, such as the dolphins and the white tigers at the Mirage, the Renaissance midway and motion simulators at Excalibur, or even "oldies" like Wet 'n' Wild, Circus Circus, the Lied Discovery and the Natural History museums, and Ethel M's chocolate factory.

■ AMUSEMENT PARKS

MGM Grand Adventures has seven rides (roller coaster, flume, rapids, haunted mine, motion simulator, river tour, and bumper cars), four theater presentations (shows featuring pirates, acrobats, and the Three Stooges, and a fourth called "You're in the Movies"), good fast food, and a few retail shops. The rides are totally tame, so kids between 5 and 12 years old love it, and teenagers find their own level. *MGM Grand Adventures, 3799 Las Vegas Blvd. South; (800) 929-1111.*

Grand Slam Canyon, on the other hand, has the world's largest indoor roller coaster, and it is a thrill, with two 360-degree loops and a corkscrew, even if it lasts all of 90 seconds. The other attractions—a flume and some kiddie rides—aren't quite worth the price of admission. *Grand Slam Canyon, 2880 Las Vegas Blvd. South; (800) 634-3450/info hotline (702) 794-3912.*

Wet 'n' Wild is a huge water park where the thrills and spills and chills are non-stop and never-ending. The Blue Niagara is a six-story, 300-foot-long slide of "blue innerspace;" the 75-foot-long Der Stuka gives you the sensation of free fall; the Wave Pool has four-foot-high surf. HydraManiac, Banzai Boggan, Raging Rapids, Bubble Up, Lazy River, and the Flumes will keep you, your kids, and your granny wet and wild all day long. *2601 Las Vegas Blvd. South; (702) 737-3819.*

Scandia Family Fun Center is a bit drier 'n' tamer than Wet 'n' Wild, but it offers some variety for the kids, such as a creative 18-hole miniature golf course, race cars and bumperboats, automated pitching machines, video arcade, and snack bar. *Scandia Family Fun Center, 2900 Sirius Ave.; (702) 364-0070.*

■ HIGH- AND LOW-TECH

Luxor's trio of futuristic entertainment attractions on the second floor are great for anyone over seven or eight years old. The Nile River ride is boring for kids, but interesting for adults. The **Sega arcade at Luxor** is the best in town. It's interactive video-oriented, but has a good selection of games for the younger set. The **MGM Grand arcades** are more like a midway. **Mutineer Bay at Treasure Island** combines the better features of Luxor's and MGM's arcades. The **midways at Circus Circus and Excalibur** are low-tech: rubber balls, water pistols, and sledgehammers in lieu of joysticks and software. Better prizes too, if you don't mind lugging stuffed animals around. *All the above are located on Las Vegas Blvd. South: Luxor, at 3900; Treasure Island, at 3300; Circus Circus, at 2880; Excalibur, at 3850.*

■ LIED DISCOVERY
CHILDREN'S MUSEUM

Located in the Central Las Vegas Library building, this museum features 130 thought-provoking *and* entertaining exhibits. Highlights include an athletic ability

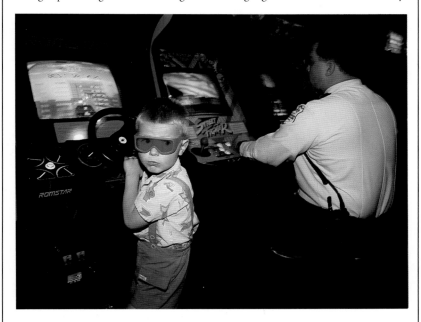

Kids in Las Vegas

testing area with ski, baseball, and football machines to challenge your sports skills; a money display to teach about savings accounts, writing checks, and using ATMs. Telescopes await atop the eight-story science tower; at the "What Can I Be?" exhibit, kids can look at and play with career ideas. A radio and TV station, newspaper office, bubble machine, space shuttle display, 120 other attractions, and a museum store and restaurant are also contained in the 40,000-square-foot facility. *Lied Discovery Children's Museum, 833 Las Vegas Blvd. North; (702) 382-3445.*

■ **L A S   V E G A S   N A T U R A L   H I S T O R Y   M U S E U M**

Across the street from the Lied is this wildlife museum, with a large collection of taxidermied animals from around the world. There are also dinosaur dioramas, live sharks in big tanks, and an educational gift shop. *Las Vegas Natural History Museum, 900 Las Vegas Blvd. North; (702) 384-3466.*

■ **O T H E R   A C T I V I T I E S**

You can also take the youngsters bowling. **Gold Coast, Sam's Town,** and the **Showboat** all have lanes. You might also go horseback riding (at **Bonnie Springs**), or roller-skating (**Crystal Palace** rinks in three locations). *Gold Coast, 400 W. Flamingo Rd.; (702) 367-7111. Sam's Town, 5111 Boulder Hwy.; (702) 456-7777. Showboat, 2800 E. Fremont St.; (702) 385-9153. Bonnie Springs Ranch, 1 Gun Fighter Ln.; (702) 875-4191. Crystal Palace, 4680 Boulder Hwy.; (702) 58-7107 (locations also on S. Decatur and N. Rancho).*

Don't forget the **Guinness Museum, the zoo,** and **Ethel M's chocolate factory** (go on a weekday morning: that's when chocolate is made). *Guinness World of Records Museum, 2780 Las Vegas Blvd. South; (702) 792-3766. Southern Nevada Zoological Park, 1775 N. Rancho Dr.; (702) 648-5955. Ethel M's, Cactus Garden Dr. (head out E. Tropicana, right on Mountain Vista, left on Sunset Way, quick left onto Cactus Garden Dr.); (702) 433-2500.*

Day trips should definitely include **Red Rock Canyon, Spring Mountain Ranch,** and the **Bonnie Springs** and **Old Nevada** loop, as well as **Hoover Dam** and **Lake Mead**. *Red Rock Canyon BLM Visitor Center, (702) 363-1921. Spring Mountain Ranch State Park, Hwy. 159; (702) 875-4141. Old Nevada, Hwy. 59; (702) 875-4191. Hoover Dam, Hwy. 93 east of Boulder City; (702) 293-8367 for museum. Lake Mead National Recreation Area, (702) 293-8906.*

or two that manage to be entertaining. Mostly, though, these groups (boy-girl duos, techno-trios, classic foursomes) absorb more energy than they supply.

In fact, the "good old days," when up-and-coming stars earned $10,000 a week to hone their acts in the lounges on their climb to the showrooms, are over. Gone are the comedians doing a fourth show at three in the morning; gone are the singers sitting in with their friends in other lounges; gone is the Rat Pack, any one to six of whom could invade a performance and proceed to treat the crowd to a night they'd never forget. The stars and singers all work the headliner rooms, comedians appear at the clubs, and the novelty acts are incorporated into the extravaganzas. The show lounges of yesterday have been turned into the keno lounges of today. The show lounges of today are mostly meant to be Muzak to the slots.

■ COMEDY

Comedy clubs are now a staple of the city's entertainment scene. The clubs occasionally hotel-hop or change their names. The latest configuration of comedy is: **Catch A Rising Star** at MGM Grand; the **Comedy Club** at the Riviera; **Comedy Stop** at the Tropicana; **Improv** at Harrah's; and **Comedy Max** at the Maxim. Most venues have two shows on weeknights and three on weekends; tickets run $10-15.

■ DISCO

As you might expect, disco is alive and kicking in Las Vegas. Half a dozen clubs around town roar every night of the week, and not one of them has a cover charge. This is extremely cheap entertainment, if you can live with the crowds, the drunks, and the often deadening beat. One caveat, however. Make sure to call up first—not only to find out what's happening but to ascertain that a club still exists at all. These places open and close faster than you can deal and draw a bum hand from a quarter poker slot, and even the *weekly* visitors guides and newspaper listings often fall way behind in keeping track of this pack.

■ CULTURAL LAS VEGAS

Allied Arts Council is the local arts agency that glues together the music, dance, theater, and visual arts of this rapidly expanding city. Before visiting, send for a complimentary copy of their classy black-and-white magazine, *Arts Alive,* if you want to get beyond the "Strip tease" and into the entertainment that many of the enormously talented locals present to each other. Write 3135 Industrial Rd., Suite 204, Las Vegas, NV 89109, or call (702) 731-5419 to see what's going on.

Entertainment

Showgirls—A Reality Check

SHOWGIRLS: A REALITY CHECK

It would have been hard to miss the '77 Toyota amid all the gleaming rentals in the Luxor parking lot, even if Lissa hadn't jumped from her car and clomped toward me in her well-worn clogs. Lissa had on the clothes I always think of her wearing in dance class back in San Francisco: baggy and faded gray knit pants, gray T-shirt, and an oversized plaid shirt for extra coverage—even though it must have been 85 degrees.

"Oh my God! Oh my God! How are you?" she said as we hugged.

"I'm fine, I'm fine! Oh my God, how great to see you!" I returned, falling immediately into uptempo dancer-speak—patter which, with down-to-earth performers like Lissa, flows with an undercurrent of self-parody. Up close, I could see that although she was wearing her day-off, slacker clothes, her eyebrows were perfectly plucked and shaped, her hair flawlessly highlighted and cut, her nails—if bitten a little short —painted a stylish flat brown. I understood that being a dancer in Las Vegas must require an awful lot of maintenance.

"Could it be any hotter?" Lissa said as she yanked off the flannel shirt, tied it around her waist, and headed for the car. Inside her car, the temperature must have been 120 degrees. As I perched on the edge of the near molten, brown vinyl passenger seat, she pulled a copy of the *Dirt Alert*—the Las Vegas entertainers' rag—from the back. "Want to audition? There's one at Bally's for 'Jubilee.' But we've only got about 5 minutes to decide." Yikes. I realized that although I'd brought my fishnets, T-straps, even lashes, I hadn't brought an appropriate G-string. I could easily have borrowed one, but I wasn't, well, properly groomed for such a high-cut outfit. Again, showgirl maintenance. And I had to admit to myself that I wasn't mentally prepared for the moment, after the first cut, when you're asked to lift your shirt—though it's only a quick check for the director to make sure you're "easy on the eyes" (Lissa's words) and silicone-free. It's true: implants are a no-no in Vegas.

So we blew off the audition (Lissa didn't meet the 5-foot, 8-inch requirement anyway), and headed to the dance studio to take class. While stuck in traffic on Tropicana, we talked about Lissa's current job as a dancer in "Siegfried & Roy." It was certainly a steady gig, and an easy one, but she felt she was ready to move on. First problem? Steel stage. The stage in this high-tech show is a massive, illusion-making, special-effects-generating machine, but the huge heap of metal doesn't give much under the feet of a barely shod dancer. Instant tendinitis.

What frustrated her more, it seemed, was the dancers' role in the show: she described her role as "backdrop." In "Siegfried & Roy," the cast has to run for miles to cover the vast stage, and the actual choreography is limited at best. Lissa, meanwhile, is what I'd call a dancer's dancer: she grabs movement, makes it her own, and works it with every fiber in her body. While other Vegas shows might well feature some pretty lame choreography, she acknowledged, at least the dancers get to *dance*. "Let's just say I'm open to auditioning," she said, chuckling and firing up a Marlboro Light.

"So, I guess 'backdrop' doesn't get to wear anything too fabulous," I commented.

"Oh my God. We wear white unitards. White." I was horrified. Any dancer can tell you that nobody—nobody—looks good in a white unitard. "No, wait. It's even better: they're *hooded* unitards. I wear a hood. And flat shoes. Like, ballet slippers. Just *kind* of hideous!"At that point, my heart went out to her. No doubt she felt like a shrink-wrapped Barbie doll—confined in Lycra, as well as made anonymous by a far-from-flattering uniform. But I knew, too, that having a consistent, well-paid dance job in Vegas was nothing to sniff at. Besides, there were definitely some plusses in working for "Siegfried & Roy" that Lissa appreciated. For one, the backstage and tech crew (100 strong) made everything run like clockwork: one woman seemed to appear— you might say magically—whenever a dancer needed her unitard zipped up.

Equally helpful were the other dancers in the show when she started. Because Lissa was a replacement dancer, the cast stayed after the second show for a rehearsal *at 2 A.M.* so Lissa could be "blocked in"—that is, staged and set with the other dancers. "I kept saying, 'I'm so sorry! I'm so sorry! I won't mess up!' But they never pressured me." For her first week in the show, the women next to Lissa would remind her of her cues, or lead her by the hand when her group went onstage in the black. Hardly a scene out of *Showgirls*. Besides, she added, the show itself is damn impressive.

Overall, Lissa said she was happy with her daily routine. She gets up around 11 A.M., has coffee and fruit, takes class or works out, writes a letter or reads, heads for the Mirage at 5 P.M., does two shows, gets home around 1 A.M., steams vegetables for dinner, finishes the letter or chapter along with a handful of M&Ms, and calls it quits around 3. Her roommate, a dancer in another show, manages to fit in more work on weekends: after her second show Andi runs across the street to another hotel, where she performs in a high-energy nightclub act. It made me tired just thinking about it.

After dance class, we headed back to Lissa's apartment, where we showered and went through photo albums documenting her four years of professional work—in Tahoe, in Japan, on cruise ships. They, along with her box of well-worn classics and historical biographies, seemed to help anchor her in a city which for me still seemed pretty bizarre. I had less than an hour to get to the airport, but I can't deny that I did feel a pull to stay, to go through with an audition. I hugged Lissa goodbye, and gave her my best showgirl pose (bend the right knee in, hands on hips, smile) before running to the taxi.

—Julia Dillon

Showgirls—A Reality Check

Getting There

■ METRIC CONVERSIONS

meters = .305 (feet)
kilometers = 1.6 (miles)
degrees C = $\dfrac{\text{degrees F} - 32}{1.8}$

■ GETTING THERE

■ BY AIR

More than 1,400 daily scheduled flights on 18 major airlines and 19 charter companies service more than 27 million people a year at Las Vegas's stunning McCarran International Airport. The wide-eyed, rubber-necking amazement that this town is famous for kicks in the moment you step into the terminal, with its slots, palm sculptures, billboards, and large video displays. In 1994, McCarran ranked as the eighth busiest airport in the world (based on total number of flights) and fourteenth worldwide (based on total number of passengers). Based on the number of residents in the city, it supposedly handles a greater percentage of passengers per capita than any other airport in the world.

Las Vegas is one of the easiest cities in the world to fly to. And although flying to and from Las Vegas isn't the cheap junket it once was, the number of airlines keeps fares competitive. Package deals can be an especially good value, if you're only staying the usual three or four days; any good travel agent should be up on the latest. Or contact the Convention and Visitors Bureau, which can pinpoint packagers or wholesalers in your area. Also try reservations services which handle hotel packages, often including airfare. The travel supplements of the Sunday dailies frequently list the latest special deals and fares and packages to Las Vegas.

Las Vegas Transit buses don't serve the airport. You can take a Gray Line airport shuttle van to your Strip (about $4 one way) or downtown (about $5 one way) destination; (702) 384-1234 for reservations. A classier, regularly scheduled, more Las Vegas way is to catch a Bell Trans limo, for about the same fares as Gray Line, but with regular pick-ups at most hotels every half-hour (on the half-hour and hour), and always available outside the baggage claim at the airport; (702) 385-LIMO. Taxis are also available, running about $10 to $18, with south Strip hotels at the low end and downtown ones in the costlier range.

■ BY ROAD

Las Vegas crowds around the intersection of Interstate 15, US 95, and US 93. The Interstate runs from Los Angeles, 272 miles, four to five hours at 65 mph to Salt Lake City, 419 miles, six to eight hours. US 95 comes into Las Vegas from the north (Reno is 440 miles). US 93 starts in Phoenix and hits Las Vegas 285 miles later, then merges with I-15 for a while, only to fork off and shoot straight up the east side of Nevada, exiting the state at Jackpot, 500 miles away.

The Greyhound depot is right next door to the Plaza Hotel on the south side, at 200 South Main; (800) 231-2222. These buses arrive and depart frequently throughout the day and night from and to all points in North America, and are a reasonable alternative to driving or flying. Advance purchase fares are extremely inexpensive, and with extended travel passes you can really put the miles on.

■ GETTING AROUND

■ BY BUS AND TROLLEY

Citizens Area Transit (CAT features 128 buses on 21 routes all over town, with discounted fares for kids 5-17 and senior citizens over 65. Monthly passes are available. They operate from 5:30 A.M. to 1:30 A.M., except for the Strip service (24 hours). Transfers are good for an hour. All buses depart from and return to the Downtown Transportation Center (DTC), at Stewart St. and Casino Center behind the post office. From downtown to the Strip, take either bus 301 or 303, which leave the DTC every 15 minutes. The Strip buses cost $1.50 (exact change) —watch for pickpockets on these buses, especially when they're crowded; fare on the residential buses is $1. For further info, call (702) 228-7433.

Trolleys also serve the Strip. They're operated privately, and follow the same route as the Strip shuttle buses, but they pull right up to the front door of all the major Strip hotels. Four trolleys run at any given time, passing your stop roughly every 30 minutes, from 9:30 A.M. to 2 A.M., $1 exact change. Trolleys are a good alternative to public buses, especially from Friday afternoon to Sunday night. Call 382-1404 for more information.

Getting Around

Casino Comps

CASINO COMPS

The term "comps" is short for "complimentaries", otherwise known as freebies. These are hotel amenities which the casino uses to reward to people already gambling and to entice other people through the door. Comps come in many varieties—drinks, room, food, shows, limo rides, golf—but they have two things in common: they're either free or highly discounted, and the value of the comp increases in direct proportion to the value of the bet.

The two easiest comps to come by in Las Vegas are parking and funbooks. Parking is free everywhere. Downtown, it's mostly in high-rise parking garages. You're entitled to three or fours free hours, but you must have your parking ticket validated in the casino. Simply go to the main casino cashier; some have validating machines, while at others you have to hand it over for validation by hand. On the Strip, you park in lots and garages, and you won't have to take a ticket. Funbooks are little bound booklets full of coupons. They usually contain some "lucky bucks," which pay a bonus on certain wagers, as well as coupons for free drinks, meal discounts, and souvenirs. For parking and funbooks, you don't have to play; you only need to walk into the casino to get them.

The lowest level comp for gamblers is the free drink. Complimentary soft drinks, wine, beer, or cocktails are standard operating procedure for every casino in Nevada. Nickel slot machine players are just as entitled to free drinks as $500-a-hand blackjack bettors. (Of course, the blackjack high roller will probably get a lot more attention from the cocktail waitresses than the nickel grind.)

Five- and ten-dollar bettors can qualify for buffet and coffee shop comps. Quarter ($25) players can get preferred-customer status, casino rate on a room (an average 50 percent discount), limited food and beverage (coffee shop and maybe a gourmet meal), and line passes to the hotel's show. Players who bet $100 a hand generally qualify for full "RFB" (room, food, and beverage) at some of the downtown and smaller Strip joints, but it takes bets averaging $150 to $250 to rate full RFB at the high-class Strip properties.

The highest rollers (those few thousand players who bet $500 a hand and have $100,000 lines of casino credit) enter the fabled realm of huge suites with butlers and personal chefs, unlimited gourmet meals and room service, Lear jets and limos, private parties for 20, 50-yard-line box seats at the Super Bowl, and the like—all arranged with the utmost efficiency, courtesy, and discretion by a personal casino host.

How do casinos determine who gets what comps? The standard equation is based on the size of the average bet, the number of hours played, the house advantage of the game played, and the percentage of the casino's expected win that it's willing to return to the player in comps. Let's take an example. Say you make $25 bets at blackjack and play for eight hours. The casino estimates 60 hands an hour, so in the eight hours of play, you'll provide the casino with $12,000 worth of action. The casino figures its edge over the player at 2 percent, meaning it expects to win $240 of the $12,000. Of that, it's willing to return 40 percent in comps. Thus, you're entitled to $96 in comps (maybe a couple of coffee shop comps for two).

How does the casino evaluate your average bet and hours played? That's where the pit personnel come into the comp system. The floormen and pit bosses observe your play and record the data on "rating slips." The information goes into the casino's marketing database, which can be accessed by pit bosses, hosts, and accounting department staff, who decide what comps will be extended to you.

For at least a decade or so, the complimentary system was the casinos' most closely guarded secret. Why? Because it's particularly vulnerable to attack by casino exploiters. But since *Comp City—A Guide to Free Casino Vacations* by Max Rubin was published in 1994, the secret's been out of the bag. For anyone interested in comps, *Comp City* is a must-read. It's a fun read, too.

■ BY TAXI AND LIMO

Except for peak periods, taxis are numerous and quite readily available, and the drivers are great sources of information, and often entertainment. They cost $2.20 for the flag drop, $3.70 for the first mile, and $1.50 for each additional mile.

With a local fleet of over 200 limousines, Bell Trans can handle anything you might dream up. Their rates are most reasonable too: $33 an hour for a standard limo, and $45 for a stretch with a one-hour minimum. They also do the airport limo transfers (702) 385-LIMO. Presidential Limousine charges $42 an hour for a six-seater, and $65 an hour for an eight-seater; (702) 731-5577. Both include TV/VCR, mobile telephones, champagne, and roses for the ladies.

■ BY RENTAL CAR

Renting a car allows you to experience some real thrills while you travel around town. If you're visiting Las Vegas for the first time on a package deal at a Strip

Getting Married in Vegas

GETTING MARRIED
IN VEGAS

More than 100,000 marriages are performed in Las Vegas every year, nearly 300 every day of the year. In Nevada, there's no waiting period, no blood test, and the minimum age is 18 (16 and 17 need a notarized affidavit of parental consent; under 16, a court order). All that's required is a license. Simply appear at the Marriage License Bureau office, 200 South Third Street downtown (455-3156 in the day, 455-4415 after business hours) with your money ($35), your ID, and your fiancé. It's open 8 A.M. to midnight Monday through Thursday, and 24 hours Friday, Saturday, and holidays. Then, if you want a no-frills, justice-of-the-peace nuptial, walk a block over to 309 South Third, to the office of the Commissioner of

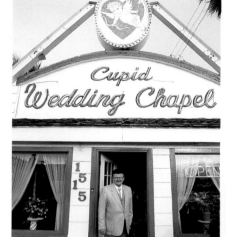

Minister administers nuptials.

Civil Marriages, open same hours as above, where a surrogate-J.P. deputy commissioner will unite you in holy matrimony for another $35. No appointments, no waiting, just "I now pronounce you . . ." and it's done.

But a more traditional setting, with flowers, organ music, photographs, and a minister, awaits at the renowned wedding chapels of Las Vegas. Some are found in hotels: Bally's, Excalibur, Flamingo Hilton, Harrah's, MGM Grand, Plaza, Riviera, Treasure Island. Others are grouped around the courthouse, or on Las Vegas Boulevard South between downtown and Sahara Avenue. Within a 10-block stretch are a dozen or so; wander in, talk to the receptionist, tour the facilities, and if you're lucky you might be able to observe a ceremony or two in progress. Within an hour you'll have a good impression of the Las Vegas wedding industry: the concept lovely, the execution a matter of taste.

You have your choice of ceremonies: "civil" means no mention of God, "non-denominational" uses the word. You can also supply your own text—much depends on the minister. The basic chapel fee is $40-60, and $35 is the recommended donation to the minister. Spring for a $5 silk boutonniere and $45 bouquet, and throw in $50 worth of snapshots, plus the limo ride to the courthouse for a license or back to your hotel ($25 toke to the driver—worth it for the stories alone!). You can really build up a tab by arranging to have live organ music and a video taping of the wedding, by renting tux and gown, and by buying rings, cake, garter, and wedding certificate holder, right there on the spot.

The spring wedding season starts in February, around Valentine's Day, and continues through June, the monster month. New Year's Eve is the biggest wedding night of the year. Weekends are always busiest. Most chapels like to book weddings at half-hour intervals, so even without reservations, you can probably squeeze "a beautiful ceremony" into an available slot.

Perhaps the most famous of all the wedding chapels is the **Little Church of the West**, 4617 Las Vegas Boulevard South. This historic chapel opened in 1942 at the Last Frontier Village, the western theme park next to the Last Frontier Hotel. It was designed by the Last Frontier's architect and manager Bill Moore, as an exact, half-size replica of a famous church built in Columbia, California, in 1849, with redwood walls and gas lamps. The Las Vegas chapel remained in place for almost 40 years. It was moved to its present grassy and shady location, next to the Hacienda Hotel, in the early 1980s.

The **Little White Chapel**, 1301 Las Vegas Boulevard South, has been in the same location since 1954; Joan Collins and Michael Jordan were married here (not to each other). The Little White is also famous for its drive-up wedding window. That's right—you don't

even have to get out of the car (convertibles work best). The **Candlelight**, 2855 Las Vegas Boulevard South, right in the heart of the Strip, is probably the most popular chapel, with a 24-hour-a-day conveyor belt of ceremonies. **L'Amour Chapel**, 1903 Las Vegas Boulevard South, has red velvet love seats in the chapel, a store full of wedding gowns for rent or purchase, and a 36-foot RV —Weddings on Wheels—for getting married outside the Mirage, for example, just as the volcano blows. **Graceland Wedding Chapel**, 619 Las Vegas Boulevard South, features an Elvis-impersonator minister. Contact the Las Vegas Convention and Visitors Bureau, 3150 Paradise Road, Las Vegas, NV 89109; (702) 733-2323, for their list of three dozen marriage parlors.

Candlelight Chapel.

Getting Around

hotel and don't plan on going off the beaten track, you probably don't need a car; just ride the Strip shuttles or trolleys, or grab a cab. But if you've been here before and want to peel out a little, or see more of stunning southern Nevada, why not do it in the style to which you've always wanted to become accustomed? You can rent everything from a Corvette to a Cadillac, from a Camaro to a 4WD Bronco, from a Subaru station wagon to a 16-passenger van. Most rentals give you unlimited mileage; you have to pay extra for mileage on the exotics. If you're going to be in town for four or even three days, ask about weekly rates; with the extra mileage and discounted charges, it might save you money off the cumulative daily cost. Check with your insurance agent at home about coverage on rental cars; often your insurance covers rental cars (minus your deductible) and you won't need the rental company's. Also, American Express and Visa Gold credit cards will pay the deductible if you use the cards to rent the car and have a wreck.

Be aware that morning and evening **rush hours** are brutal all over Las Vegas, and the Strip can turn into a sweltering and tense parking lot, especially at the traffic lights in front of Circus Circus, the Fashion Show Mall, Flamingo, and Tropicana. In fact, the Strip is an absolute zoo from Friday afternoon till Monday morning. Pick up a map and learn the Paradise Road, Industrial Road, and backstreet shortcuts.

■ TOURS

The ubiquitous **Gray Line**, as always, is representative of the ground sightseeing available in the area. They offer tours of the city and Laughlin; they also make trips to Hoover Dam with connections to Lake Mead cruises; (702) 384-1234.

Ray and Ross Transport covers the same general territory, with city, nightclub, Hoover Dam, Colorado River, and Laughlin tours.

A few local companies have also started doing trips to Stateline, where Buffalo Bill's has the world's tallest and fastest roller coaster, and to Mesquite, with its new Player's International Hotel-Casino. Call (702) 646-4661/(800) 338-8111.

■ VISITOR MAGAZINES AND MAPS

No less than nine free publications for visitors are available in various places around town; motel lobbies are the best bet. They all cover basically the same territory—showrooms, lounges, dining, dancing, buffets, gambling, sports, events, coming attractions—and most have numerous ads that will transport coupon clippers to discount heaven.

The best source of up-to-the-minute information on the visitor experience in Las Vegas is available in the *Las Vegas Advisor*. This monthly newsletter is a must for serious and curious tourists (and locals). Monthly columns include "Couponomy" (how to take advantage of the best casino deals and promotions), "Top Ten Values" (alone worth the $5 for a single issue before your vacation), plus accomodations, dining, entertainment, gambling, slot clubs, and much more. With a subscription you also get a package of coupons for free gambling money, free rooms, food and show discounts; your subscription price is immediately recouped if you use just one of the free room coupons. For subscription or single copy, contact Huntington Press, 3687 S. Procyon Ave., Las Vegas, NV 89103; (702) 252-0655/ (800) 244-2224.

Today in Las Vegas is an 80-page weekly mini-mag bursting its staples with listings, coupons, 20 pages of restaurants, and a good column on free casino lessons. For a free copy, write or call Lycoria Publishing, 3626 Pecos McLeod, Suite 14, Las Vegas, NV 89121; (702) 385-2737.

Just as good for listings, though with very few coupons, is the 48-page weekly *Tourguide of Las Vegas*. Available Fridays from Desert Media Group, 4440 S. Arville, Suite 12, Las Vegas, NV 89103; (702) 221-5000.

"What's On" in *Las Vegas Magazine* provides comprehensive information, plus articles, calendars, phone numbers, and lots of ads—recommended. For an issue of the magazine with a good map of Las Vegas, send $4.95 to Las Vegas Magazine, 4425 S. Industrial, Las Vegas, NV 89103; (702) 891-8811.

Front Boy sells state-by-state Rand McNally maps and United States Geological Survey topographical maps in different scales ($5). They also sell a street-map book of the city (about $20), and poster-size maps of Las Vegas, the United States, and other places. Front Boy, 1149 Maryland Pkwy. South; (702) 384-7220.

Visitor Magazines and Maps

■ INFORMATION BUREAUS

The **Chamber of Commerce** (711 E. Desert Inn Rd.; 735-1616) has a large rack of commercial brochures and general fact sheets. They also sell maps, satellite images, a dining guide, and Las Vegas Perspective, a yearly statistical overview of the community (demographics, retail, business, tourism, construction, and trends), one of the best sources of local information on Las Vegas. Call the above number for good information on their computerized phone line.

The **Las Vegas Convention and Visitors Authority** has a Visitor Information Center full of brochures and handouts just inside the main entrance of the Convention Center at 3150 Paradise Rd., (702) 892-0711. One of the services that the LVCVA provides is filling up hotel rooms; call their reservations line at (702) 892-0777. The marketing department, also inside the Convention Center, has a ton of visitor statistics and trends, plus information on convention dates and attendance, hotel-room construction, and free videotapes.

■ LIBRARIES

The **Clark County Library** main branch is at 1401 E. Flamingo Rd., roughly two miles east of the Strip, (702) 733-7810. This is an attractive and modern library.

The **Las Vegas Library** (833 Las Vegas Blvd. North; 382-3493) shares its space with the Lied Children's Discovery Museum, which is why its award-winning architecture resembles a kids' playground: wedges, cylinders, cones. Be sure to explore all the nooks and crannies inside. Upstairs is a long stretch of connecting rooms with children's books, computers, and activities; the far end has windows overlooking the Lied Museum.

The **James Dickinson Library at** UNLV (4505 Maryland Pkwy.; 895-3531) is an odd and initially confusing structure, and very red. Study the two buildings, one rectangular and the other circular, with tunnels connecting them, then wander around inside a bit to get your bearings. The rectangular building houses the circulation desk (first floor); periodicals, video, audio, and computer labs (second floor); and Special Collections (fourth floor). Go through the tunnels on the second and third floors to the round building for reference and the stacks.

Special Collections, on the fourth floor of the library (895-3252), has hundreds of computer entries under Las Vegas—everything from Last Frontier Hotel promotional material (circa 1949) and mobster biographies to screenplays for locally filmed movies and the latest travel videotapes. And that's just what's catalogued. Ask the supremely solicitous staff to help you find photographs, manuscripts, theses, records, archives, phone books, diaries, private collections— all on Las Vegas and environs. If this place had a kitchen and shower, I could live here.

Also in Special Collections is the **Gaming Research Center,** largest and most comprehensive gambling research collection in the world. It covers business, economics, history, psychology, sociology, mathematics, criminology, and biography, all contained in books, periodicals, reports, promo material, photographs, posters, memorabilia, and tape.

■ MUSEUMS AND PLACES OF INTEREST

Clark County Heritage Museum. 1830 S. Boulder Hwy.; 455-7955.

Ethel M's. Cactus Garden Dr. (head out E. Tropicana, right on Mountain Vista, left on Sunset Way, quick left onto Cactus Garden Drive); (702) 458-8864. They make chocolate weekday mornings.

Guinness World of Records Museum. Las Vegas Blvd. South near Circus Circus; (702) 792-3766.

Imperial Palace Auto Collection. Imperial Palace Hotel. 3535 Las Vegas Blvd. South, fifth floor of parking structure; (702) 731-3311.

Las Vegas Natural History Museum. 900 Las Vegas Blvd. North; (702) 384-3466.

Liberace Museum. 1775 E. Tropicana just east of Maryland Pkwy.; (702) 798-5595.

Lied Discovery Children's Museum. 833 Las Vegas Blvd. North; (702) 382-3445.

Lost City Museum. 721 S. Moapa Valley Blvd.; (702) 397-2193.

Marjorie Barrick Museum of Natural History. UNLV campus—head east on Harmon Ave., which dead-ends at the arena parking lot just beyond the museum; (702) 895-3381.

Nevada State Museum and Historical Society. 700 Twin Lakes Dr. (in back of Lorenzi Park); (702) 486-5205.

Old Mormon Historic Fort. Las Vegas Blvd. North and Washington (in northwest corner of the Cashman Field parking lot); (702) 486-3511.

Red Rock Canyon BLM Visitor Center. (702) 363-1921.

Valley of Fire State Park. Visitors Center, Box 515, Overton, NV 89040; (702) 397-2088.

Emergency Money

■ EMERGENCY MONEY

Anybody reading this section is either 1) a victim of lost or stolen cash, 2) a degenerate gambler, or 3) a die-hard guidebook finisher. It wouldn't have been inappropriate, perhaps, to place this section at the end of the gambling chapter. But for one thing, while all degenerate gamblers are victims of lost or stolen cash, all theft victims aren't necessarily degenerate gamblers. For another, there's something somewhat inevitable about the closing statement of a Las Vegas guidebook addressing the eventuality of being broke and wondering what to do. After all, Las Vegas is the ultimate magnet for currency. Its attraction is directly proportionate to the action. The more money you bring to Las Vegas, the stronger its pull. As the money departs your possession, Las Vegas loosens its grip. To a weaker-willed minority of visitors, this place can become the ultimate con. It's like the devil, instigating—with every seduction of the flesh, every temptation of the mind—the ultimate agony, or ecstasy (thin line there): the final surrender of the will. It's a palpable moment, when the house insinuates its nimble fingers into the wallets of potential and removes, without guilt, the last remaining currency of hope. It instantly pinpoints all suckers and losers.

Luckily, only a small minority of visitors arrive already weak enough for their little remaining will to disappear. Most abide by limits and enjoy themselves. But this section is not for the recreational players who can live with the slings and arrows of winnings and losses. It's for the suddenly broke, the newly fleeced, the first-time bust-out from Anywhereville who mounted a fearsome bucking bummer and rode it out till the bitter end, and now finds himself suckered and plucked. Even after his wife, hovering nervously, pleaded, "Please don't, honey . . . That's the gas money." Even as he watched, from a ringside seat, that manicured, jeweled, and hypnotic hand slowly, inexorably, like fate itself, pick him completely clean. Immediately, he's no longer of any use to the house, and he stumbles out into the darkness of midnight or noon—either. And as his will gradually returns on the wings of instinct, he repeats the wayworn words of the first question ever asked, "Well, what now?"

Carrying any personal checks? It's not difficult to cash personal, out-of-state checks in Las Vegas. Simply go to the cage (main cashier) in any casino and present your driver's license, major credit card, and a check for up to the house limit (usually $100–200). The hard part, if you're in this situation, is walking through the casino into the clear without succumbing to the foolhardy notion that your luck has turned and now's the time to get even.

Got any credit left? There are instant cash-advance machines in nearly every casino nowadays, but the fees are steep, from $9.75 for $50 to $50 for $1,000. It's better to take a cash advance off a credit card at a local bank. The service fee isn't quite so high, and you're not faced with carrying cash through the casino.

No checks or credit cards? You can try hitting up a casino manager for "walking money"—a few bucks for gas or bus fare, especially if you've dropped a good portion of your bankroll there.

If that doesn't work, a number of pawn shops will hock your possessions for cash. On South First Avenue and East Carson downtown, directly across the street from the side of the Golden Nugget, is **Stoney's Loan & Jewelry**. Stoney's is one of the biggest, busiest, and oldest pawnbrokers in Las Vegas. **Pioneer Loans** is just down First Street across Fremont. **Super Pawn** has 11 locations around town. And for dire emergencies, look in the Yellow Pages for the places that will hock your car or RV.

As an absolute last resort, you'll simply have to telephone your parents, children, siblings, or friends and have them wire you money through Western Union, one of the busiest telegraph offices in the world. Pick up your cash at Barbary Coast Casino or one of 50 outlets around town—then go home, lick your wounds, think it over, and be better prepared, with both will power and bill power, when you find you're back in Las Vegas, with cards, dice, or a handle in your hand.

RECOMMENDED READING

■ BIBLIOGRAPHY

Gardner, Jack. *Gambling Bibliography*. Gale Research Company, 1980. The definitive bibliography on books about gambling—games, systems, bookmaking, probability, history, ethics, cheating—compiled by an administrator for the Clark County libraries.

Paher, Stanley. *Nevada—An Annotated Bibliography*. Nevada Publications, 1980. One of, if not *the*, most useful books for any researcher into Nevadana, with over 2,000 listings and descriptions of books about the state. Hundreds of entries about Las Vegas alone.

■ BIOGRAPHY

Berman, Susan. *Easy Street*. The Dial Press, 1981. The incredibly poignant story of a young girl growing up in Las Vegas in the late 1940s and early 1950s as the only child of Davie Berman, boss gambler from Milwaukee, front man for the eastern mob, and colleague of Bugsy Siegel, Gus Greenbaum, etc. In this book, Susan Berman, as good as orphaned at 12, reclaims her father from mob mythology, and imbues the difficult transition made by the illegal gamblers to Las Vegas legitimacy with humanity and sensitivity.

Garrison, Omar. *Howard Hughes in Las Vegas*. Lyle Stuart, 1970. Everything about this troubled, mysterious billionaire is gripping. But this book, centered around the four years Hughes spent sequestered on the ninth floor of the Desert Inn, is especially eye-opening, shedding light on the public events and private life of the recluse, as he set about to buy and redesign the city that may well have been "his true spiritual home."

Glass, Mary Ellen. *Lester Benny Binion*. Oral History Project, University of Nevada, 1973. One of many outstanding personal remembrances recorded by researchers and historians for the U. of Nevada collection. Highly informed questions and uninhibited answers make for an entertaining read about this legendary gambler and hotel owner.

Hoffa, James and Oscar Findlay. *Jimmy Hoffa—The Real Story.* Stein and Day, 1975. Told by the Teamster leader himself, this chronicles his blood feud with Robert F. Kennedy, who spent 10 years putting Hoffa in prison and whom Hoffa describes as a vicious, vindictive, immature, and incompetent.

Linn, Edward. *Big Julie of Las Vegas.* Fawcett, 1974. The fast-paced and fascinating story of high-roller junkets, as conceived, organized, and chaperoned by Jules Weintraub, an irrepressible promoter who achieved legendary status as Junket King of Las Vegas.

Smith, John L. *No Limit—The Rise and Fall of Bob Stupak and the Stratosphere Tower.* Huntington Press, 1997. This is the fascinating story of the most flamboyant modern casino operator, Bob Stupak, owner of the infamous Vegas World and the man who started, but couldn't finish, the Stratosphere Tower. The whole colorful tale is told with style by John Smith, the lead columnist for the *Las Vegas Review-Journal.*

Torgenson, Dial. *Kirk Kerkorian—An American Success Story.* The Dial Press, 1974. A beautifully written, rags-to-riches biography of one of Las Vegas's biggest names—and biggest hotel builders. Among the myriad fascinating stories herein are how Kerkorian was forced to sell out the International and Flamingo hotels to Hilton, primarily due to Meyer Lansky's 20-year hidden ownership in the Flamingo, and Howard Hughes's strange competition with Kerkorian when they were both commandeering Las Vegas in the late 1960s.

■ FICTION

Anderson, Ian. *The Big Night.* Simon and Schuster, 1979. About a notorious gambler who assembles a team of five women to beat Las Vegas out of a million bucks in one night. A quick page-turner, enjoyable as long as you suspend most of your disbelief. Also see *Turning the Tables on Las Vegas,* in which "Anderson," a pseudonym for R. Kent London, describes one of his dreams: training a squad of women to stick it to macho Las Vegas. The September 1987 *Blackjack Forum* reported that London was convicted in New York in the Wedtech fiasco.

Branon, Bill. *Devil's Hole.* HarperCollins, 1995. Branon, a Las Vegas writer, hit the big time with his first novel, *Let Us Prey,* which he self-published and then managed to sell to New York. This second novel is a about a professional killer who accepts jobs based on a personal morality that revolves around true justice. He's hired by a Las Vegas sports book to hit a sports bettor with a wildly successful system. The complications occur when it turns out that the killer and victim share a girlfriend—and the victim isn't the monster the sports book makes him out to be. Expertly described life on the edge of death—rugged, bloody, edgy.

Brown, Harry. *The Wild Hunt.* Harcourt, Brace, Jovanovich, 1973. This wild and rollicking tale, written in a style that seems to combine Pynchon, Fariña, and Joyce, follows PFC Beaudin P. Black as he kills the prized geese of his CO colonel, who chases him across the country—including a short stop in Las Vegas.

Chandler, David. *Father O'Brien and His Girls.* Appleton-Century, 1963. Based on the true story of Father Crowley, who responded to Las Vegas's unique challenges by, for one, holding Mass in a showroom at 4 A.M. The priest and his nuns battle the forces of evil for lost Las Vegas souls.

Demaris, Ovid. *The Vegas Legacy.* Dell, 1983. By a co-author of the *Green Felt Jungle,* this story is very loosely based on Nevada history, about a presidential convention taking place in Las Vegas at which the Nevada powers-that-be attempt to install their corrupt favorite son as the candidate.

Dunne, John Gregory. *Vegas—Memoir of a Dark Season.* Random House, 1974. Quirky first-person narrative about a troubled writer who gravitates to Las Vegas to weather a mild breakdown, and becomes involved with an assortment of characters: hooker, private eye, lounge comic, apartment manager.

Haase, John. *Big Red.* Pinnacle Books, 1980. Towering novel about the building of Boulder-Hoover Dam, from the point of view of Frank Crowe, the dam's chief engineer. As monumental and epic a book as the dam itself.

Kantor, Hal. *The Vegas Trap.* Beeline Books, 1970. One of a *legion* of pulp novels centered around "the Great Las Vegas heist." Here, a casino enforcer, the nephew of an underworld owner, runs a counterfeit-chip scam, fronted by an old Army buddy. Characters have some dimension; a couple of good plot twists; fair writing.

McMurtry, Larry. *The Desert Rose*. Simon and Schuster, 1983. An affectionate and poignant character study of an aging showgirl and her ties to Las Vegas—men, daughter, neighbors, co-workers—that McMurtry penned during a three-week lull in the writing of his epic *Lonesome Dove*.

Powers, Tim. *Last Call*. William Morrow, 1992. A strange, suspenseful, violent tale in which chaos and randomness, the patron saints of Las Vegas, manifest themselves from certain combinations of cards in poker hands. A particular poker game called Assumption is played once every 21 years on a houseboat on Lake Mead, using the most contraband tarot deck in existence, by players unaware that the stakes are life and death. The driving force of the book is magic; supernatural forces are invoked and manipulated by the characters. Five hundred pages of chilling fantasy.

Puzo, Mario. *Fool's Die*. Putnam, 1978. A sprawling, semi-autobiographical novel about a writer who starts out as an orphan, gets married and raises a family in New York, makes a pilgrimage to Las Vegas, and publishes a blockbuster novel which is turned into a box-office smash. Contains some of the best writing in fiction about a Las Vegas hotel owner and his right-hand assistant, scams on both sides of the gaming table, and casino color.

Ross, Sam. *Fortune Machine*. Delacorte Press, 1970. Hair-raising roller-coaster ride taken by a novice card-counter, hitting Las Vegas for $200,000 to "buy" his girlfriend from her rich and rough father. Gripping style: first person, short tight sentences, terse dialogue; you really *feel* the action. Good characters, affirming conclusion.

Silberstang, Edwin. *Snake Eyes*. Thomas Congdon Books, 1977. Attention-holding and spare story of a card-counter, a chip hustler, a compulsive and suicidal gambler, a cheating blackjack dealer and his dope-running confederate, a hotel owner, his underworld backers, and a has-been household-name entertainer. Money, as is true throughout this genre, is a character of its own, a ping-pong ball bouncing among, and gluing together, the people, then finally settling right back where it comes from and belongs—the house. The protagonists are left with nothing but their affection for each other and their faith.

■ GAMBLING

Anderson, Ian. *Turning The Tables On Las Vegas*. Vintage Books, 1976. "Ian Anderson" was a pseudonym for R. Kent London, a highly successful and anonymous card counter. Goes into extraordinary detail about playing and betting strategies, camouflage, interaction with the pit personnel, and maintaining a winning attitude. Required reading for aspiring counters.

Bass, Thomas. *Eudaemonic Pie*. Houghton Mifflin, 1985. A true hippie adventure story about a group of physicists at UC Santa Cruz who invented a computer that fit in a shoe to beat the casino at roulette.

Eadington, William R. *The Evolution of Corporate Gambling in Nevada*. University of Nevada-Reno, 1980. A brief, incisive survey of the challenges faced since the mid-1950s by the casino industry and the state to achieve popular legitimacy, conventional financing, federal tolerance, and control of undesirables.

Eadington, William R. and James Hattori. *Gambling in Nevada—Legislative History and Economic Trends*. University of Nevada-Reno, 1980. Reports on legislation passed by Nevada lawmakers since gambling was legalized to control the casino industry, on court challenges to determine the constitutionality of the legislation, and on the gradual acceptance of corporate ownership.

Eadington, William R., editor. *Gambling Papers: The Card-Counter Controversy*. University of Nevada-Reno, 1982. A compelling collection of articles and court briefs about the conflict among Atlantic City casinos, the New Jersey Casino Control Commission, and the blackjack card counters, spearheaded by Ken Uston, one of the all-time great blackjack players and writers.

Findlay, John. *People of Chance—Gambling in American Society from Jamestown to Las Vegas*. Written by a Pennsylvania State U. history professor, this incredible book is not only *the* best book on the evolution of American gambling, but also one of the great books on American history itself.

Gambler's Book Club Catalog. This 28-page tabloid lists and describes more than 1,000 titles on every aspect of gambling, from baccarat to video slots. The catalog itself provides enjoyable and highly informative reading, and helps pinpoint exactly what kind of book you're looking for. Write: Box 4115, Las Vegas, NV 89127, or call (800) 634-6243.

Griffin, Peter. *Theory of Blackjack.* Huntington Press, 1988. The bible for serious blackjack players, the classic text on the mathematics of blackjack, providing insight into the development of basic strategy and card counting.

Humble, Lance, and Carl Cooper. *The World's Greatest Blackjack Book.* Doubleday, 1980. A college course covering all aspects of blackjack, from memorization aids for basic strategy and card counting (Hi-Opt I and II systems) to cheating dealers and the best places to play. Has useful comparison charts on the different counting systems.

Miller, Len. *Gambling Times' Guide to Casino Games.* Gambling Times, 1983. One of a slew of how-to books about craps, roulette, keno, blackjack, and the Wheel of Fortune. Covers the usual rules, odds, and etiquette.

Ortiz, Darwin. *On Casino Gambling.* Dodd, Mead & Company, 1986. One of the best-written and most useful how-to books for playing casino games.

Patterson, Jerry, and Eddie Olsen. *Break The Dealer.* Another book for serious blackjack players, which tracks the subtle changes in casino blackjack strategies to maintain, without fanfare, an edge over card counters. Introduces the shuffling aspect.

Regan, Jim. *Winning at Slot Machines.* Citadel Press, 1985. Written by the slot manager at Bally's Reno, this small book dispels some myths about slots, goes into detail about theoretical odds, describes the differences between the many reel machines, and discusses etiquette.

Riddle, Major, and Joe Hyams. *Weekend Gamblers Handbook.* Random House, 1963. Another casino how-to, but with a twist: Riddle was a congenital gambler and a long-time owner of the Dunes. Fascinating perspective about gambling from the percentage side of the pit, and great anecdotes about gamblers, streaks, and the Dunes.

Rubin, Max. *Comp City—A Guide to Free Casino Vacations.* Huntington Press, 1995. More than a half billion dollars worth of comps are given away every year in Las Vegas, and this book contains the whole story on how the system works and how it can be exploited for major hedonistic gain. Required reading for anyone who plays $10-and-up blackjack and eats and sleeps in hotel-casinos.

Scarne, John. *Scarne's Guide to Casino Gambling.* Simon and Schuster, 1978. One of a score of books written by one of the world's great experts on gambling. Scarne lived, breathed, dreamed, and *was* gambling. He invented games and systems. He traveled around the world tracking down obscure stories and history, consulting with casinos, catching cheaters. He calculated odds and percentages and basic strategies long before computers. And he wrote and published prolifically, and encyclopedically.

Skolnik, Jerome. *House of Cards—Legalization and Control of Casino Gambling.* Little, Brown & Co., 1978. The most in-depth look at the sociology of control within the casino industry. Covers everything from chip-transfer and fill-slip procedures in the pit to the potential for corruption of Gaming Commission members. A must-read for anyone looking behind the scenes.

Snyder, Arnold. *Blackbelt in Blackjack—Playing 21 as a Martial Art.* RGE, 1983. Snyder, one of a core group of successful blackjack card counters and writers, has a thorough facility with the game and the language, as well as an active and unusual imagination. He devised the Red Seven unbalanced count, that combines the running count and true count. He established the First Church of Blackjack. He also publishes *Blackjack Forum,* a quarterly full of blackjack articles, issues, editorials, and general ranting and raving.

Soares, John. *Loaded Dice—The Story of a Casino Cheat.* Taylor Publishing, 1985. Incredible story of one of, if not the, greatest crews of "crossroaders" ever to rip off Las Vegas, with elaborate dice and slot scams. Takes a very hard look at all the cheating and stealing from outside *and* inside the casino.

Solkey, Lee. *Dummy Up and Deal.* Gamblers Book Club, 1980. Written by a Las Vegan who earned a degree in urban ethnology and dealt blackjack for seven years as part of her "field study." Talks with great authority about the dealer culture, language, territorial domains, and the dealer relationship with the casino.

Thorp, Edward. *Beat The Dealer.* Vintage Books, 1966. This was the book that launched a thousand brains. Thorp was the first to publicize a card-counting system, and though the years have proved it nearly inoperable, it stimulated the whole idea that casino blackjack could be beaten, and therefore played as a profession, and therefore analyzed to the Nth degree.

Wong, Stanford. *Professional Video Poker.* Pi Yee Press, 1991. Offers insight into basic and sophisticated video poker strategies.

Wykes, Alan. *Complete Illustrated Guide to Gambling.* Doubleday, 1964. Exhaustively researched, beautifully written, and profusely illustrated book on the history (with a little psychology) of gambling.

■ HISTORY

Best, Katherine, and Katherine Hillyer. *Las Vegas—Playtown U.S.A.* David McKay and Co., 1955. This snapshot of Las Vegas, by a travel-writing pair of Virginia City residents, remains the all-time most incisive, insightful, and humorous portrait of the boomtown during its most exciting boom. Could easily inspire a novel about Las Vegas that takes place in the critical year of 1955.

Cahlan, Florence Lee, and John F. Cahlan, *Water—A History of Las Vegas.* Las Vegas Water District, 1975. Written by the long-time publisher of the Las Vegas *Review-Journal* and his reporter-wife, this is a sprawling, two-volume history of Las Vegas which "shows how its evolution as a city closely paralleled the development of its water."

Demaris, Ovid, and Ed Reid. *Green Felt Jungle,* Trident Press, 1963. The classic and ultimate "Diatribe" book—a savage indictment of Las Vegas and its mobsters, payoffs, cheating, and prostitution. Though highly sensational, it was lively, authoritative, and a veritable desk reference for many exposé writers to come.

Ehrlich, Fred. *Chinese Restaurants in Las Vegas.* Term paper, University of Nevada-Las Vegas, 1981. Good effort to record the history of Chinese restaurants in the city, and relate their development to the history of the Chinese people in Nevada.

Kaufman, Perry Bruce. *Best City of Them All—Las Vegas: 1930-1960.* Thesis, UC Santa Barbara, 1979. An exhaustive survey of the 30-year period following legalized gambling, and all of its conditions, controversies, and conclusions.

Kelley, Ralph. *Liberty's Last Stand.* Pioneer Publishing, 1932. An exciting and vivid contemporary account of the Las Vegas underworld around 1929, with marvelous descriptions of Block 16 clubs and Boulder Highway roadhouses.

Meyers, Sid. *The Great Las Vegas Fraud.* Mayflower Press, 1958. This was the first title in a long series of books that came to be called the Diatribe, and is perhaps the most vicious, with several score of examples and comments that project Las Vegas as a greedy, ruthless, and treacherous booby trap.

Moehring, Eugene. *Resort City in the Sunbelt.* University of Nevada Press, 1989. An amazingly dense—comprehensive, academic, heavily footnoted—description of Las Vegas's development since the 1930s as "typical not only of a sunbelt, resort, and casino city, but of all cities in general." Indispensable for Las Vegas researchers.

Moldea, Dan. *Dark Victory—Ronald Reagan, MCA, and the Mob.* Viking, 1986. A highly detailed investigative report on the Reagan-Hollywood-underworld connection, with startling revelations about Las Vegas: the Parvin-Dohrman story, the Chicago mob's preeminence and its connection to the Teamster Pension Fund, and Reagan's intervention to circumvent the FBI and Justice Department's probes of organized crime.

Murphy, Don R. *The Role of Changing External Relations in the Growth of Las Vegas.* Thesis, University of Las Vegas, 1970. A comprehensive overview of the various social, political, economic, and environmental factors, mostly originating outside of Las Vegas, that contributed to the city's great growth.

Paher, Stanley. *Las Vegas: As It Began—As It Grew.* Nevada Publications, 1971. This outstanding history, with hundreds of fascinating black-and-white photographs and half a dozen historical maps, covers in detail the popular history of Las Vegas from the Old Spanish Trail up through the building of Hoover Dam.

Paher, Stanley, ed. *Nevada—Official Bicentennial Book.* Nevada Publications, 1976. A collection of historical stories and vignettes. Clark County articles include a fascinating look at Las Vegas as a "Temperance Town" by Charles "Pop" Squires, a fascinating look *at* Squires, and a visit to the rough-and-tumble town during Christmas in 1905, among others.

Ralli, Paul. *Nevada Lawyer.* Mathis, Van Nort & Co., 1946. Unusual cases, characters, and local color that this Las Vegan since 1933 ran across during his first 10 years. An expanded second edition was published by Murray & Gee in 1949.

Ralli, Paul. *Viva Vegas.* The sequel to *Nevada Lawyer,* with hometowny sketches, events, and short bios of prominent men in the community.

Reid, Ed. *Las Vegas—City Without Clocks.* Prentice Hall, 1961. Written by a reporter for the Las Vegas *Sun.* By comparison, a slightly more affectionate and less sensational look than *The Great Las Vegas Fraud* that preceded it, and *Green Felt Jungle* that followed, of which Reid was a co-author.

Reid, Ed. *Grim Reapers—Anatomy of Organized Crime in America.* Henry Regnery Co., 1969. Reid departed Las Vegas already a top organized-crime reporter. The Las Vegas chapter details the sordid story of how Caesars Palace arose from the desert, federal wire-tap revelations, skimming operations, and the like.

Roske, Ralph. *Las Vegas—A Desert Paradise.* Continental Heritage Press, 1986. A large pictorial history, which covers many aspects of Las Vegas from past to present. The backmatter celebrates roughly 60 local companies instrumental in the growth of Las Vegas.

Sifakis, Carl. *Mafia Encyclopedia.* Facts on File Publications, 1987. Biographies of scores of top underworld personalities and locales, including Las Vegas, Moe Dalitz, Bugsy Siegel, Gus Greenbaum, Virginia Hill, and Johnny Roselli.

Taylor, Dick and Pat Howell. *Las Vegas—City of Sin?* Naylor Company, 1963. Written by two casino executives, this book was another semi-Diatribe-style exposé, like *City Without Clocks,* that combined a wide-eyed view of Las Vegas's glittery surfaces with a peek at its slimy underbelly. It reprinted feature articles about Las Vegas that had appeared in *Reader's Digest, Saturday Evening Post, Life,* and even *Sports Illustrated.*

Turner, Wallace. *Gambler's Money—A New Force in American Life.* Houghton Mifflin, 1965. Written by a reporter for *The New York Times,* this is an insightful, negative interpretation of the Nevada "experiment" in legalized gambling, with a detailed investigation into the business practices of Las Vegas bosses, specifically Moe Dalitz and the Desert Inn group.

■ DESERT ROOTS

Alley, John. *Las Vegas Paiutes—A Short History.* Las Vegas Tribe of Paiute Indians, 1977. A short but extremely informative, well-written, and sensitive story of the southern Nevada Tudinu. The best history of Las Vegas from the Paiute perspective.

Benioh, Travis. *The Paiute Language for Beginners.* Multi-Cultural Center, Southern Utah State College, 1980. Brief guide to the pronunciation and important vocabulary of the local Indian dialect.

Fiero, Bill. *Geology of the Great Basin,* University of Nevada Press, 1986. An attractive, profusely illustrated, and comprehensive title in the University Press's Great Basin series. A highly accessible and readable survey of the forces that shaped the great Nevada desert, from the beginning of time to the present.

Geology and Mineral Deposits of Clark County, Nevada. Nevada Bureau of Mines, Bulletin 62, University of Nevada. A highly specific, technical, though decipherable, report on the geology, mineralogy, stratigraphy, and hydrology of the individual basins and ranges surrounding Las Vegas.

Lillard, Richard G. *Desert Challenge.* University of Nebraska Press, 1942. Interesting interpretive history of Nevada, with a great section on geology, and a look at Las Vegas as a divorce village.

Lyneis, Margaret, et al. *Archaeological Element, Historical Preservation Assessment and Planning Process, City of Las Vegas.* Department of Anthropology, University of Nevada–Las Vegas, 1978. A survey of archaeological and historical sites—remains, springs, cemeteries—in central Las Vegas.

McPhee, John. *Basin and Range.* Farrar, Straus, & Giroux, 1980. Another breathtaking book by this master nonfiction storyteller. Here he manages to relate the entire history of geology in the course of a drive along Interstate 80 in northern Nevada with a geologist who located an old unworked-over mine, and took a million dollars in metals from it.

Rafferty, Kevin A. *Cultural Resources of the Las Vegas Valley.* BLM Environmental Research Center, 1985. An authoritative and incisive description of the geology, ecology, hydrology, topography, and climate of the Las Vegas Valley. Also offers highly detailed coverage of the paleohistory, including fascinating speculation about the disintegration of the Anasazi society in a Mesoamerican context.

Shepperson, William, et al. *Archaeological Element, Historical Preservation Assessment and Planning Process, City of Las Vegas.* Department of Anthropology, University of Nevada-Las Vegas, 1978. A survey of archaeological and historical sites—remains, springs, cemeteries—in central Las Vegas.

■ PROSTITUTION

Frey, James, et al. *Prostitution, Business and Policy: Maintenance of an Illegal Economy.* University of Nevada-Las Vegas, 1980. A report on the social organization of the illicit enterprise of prostitution as an extension of legitimate marketing activities.

Frey, James, et al. *Analysis of a Prostitution Network: Exchange and Illegal Economy.* University of Nevada-Las Vegas, 1980. A fascinating inside look at hotel prostitution operations centered around the bell desk: bell captain, bellmen, "bellgirls," and guest-tricks.

Gallagher, John, and John Cross. *Morals Legislation Without Morality.* Rutgers University Press, 1983. An academic exploration of Nevada's "puzzling criminal statutes" concerning drugs, gambling, prostitution, and divorce, which are based more on money than morality.

Kasindorf, Jeannie. *The Nye County Brothel Wars.* Linden Press, 1985. Spellbinding account of outsider Walter Plankinton, who tried to open a brothel in Pahrump, Nevada, and the harassment, arrest, arson, and attempted murder that he brought upon himself. Also the racketeering and white-slavery involvement of his competition, and the high-level corruption of local law enforcement.

Lane, Bert. *Las Vegas—Shelter, Food, Sex.* Tandem House, 1976. A guidebook from the mid-1970s, its value now is more historical, especially the coverage of sex for sale in Las Vegas at the time that the state outlawed it.

Prince, Diane. *A Psychological Profile of Prostitutes in California and Nevada.* Thesis: United States International University, 1986. An exhaustive study of attitudes of prostitutes: family and sexual histories, self-esteem, motivation, emotional relationships, and character traits.

Schwartz, J. R. *Best Cat Houses in Nevada.* Straight Arrow Publishing, 1989. A guide to 36 brothels in Nevada, including several near Pahrump, just over the Clark County line in Nye County, where brothel prostitution is legal.

Vogliotti, Gabriel R. *The Girls of Nevada.* Citadel Press, 1975. One of the best books written about Nevada, including the complete rundown of prostitution issues, a great bio of Joe Conforte, and a unique history of Las Vegas.

■ STYLE AND LOCAL COLOR

Graham, Jefferson. *Vegas—Live And In Person.* Abbeville Press, 1989. This large format, profusely photographed book lives up to its name. Graham's brief history carries him right up to Las Vegas live— games, high rollers, movers and shakers, entertainers, waitresses, bellmen, maitre d's, wedding chapel owners, and signmakers. Las Vegas has needed such a book for a long time.

Knepp, Don. *Las Vegas—The Entertainment Capital.* Lane Publishing, 1987. This Sunset Pictorial is packed with hundreds of black and whites and color plates that illustrate Las Vegas's long, fascinating, and larger-than-life entertainment heritage—collected and captioned by a writer, photographer, and illustrator extraordinaire who works for the famous Las Vegas News Bureau.

Las Vegas Perspective. Nevada Development Authority and First Interstate Bank, 1990. Chamber of Commerce demographics for the Las Vegas and Clark County metropolitan statistical area.

Murray, Jack. *Las Vegas—Zoom Town, U.S.A.* 1962. Self-published and chatty little book that provides a bit of local color from the early 1960s.

Nevada Magazine. Published continuously (though under several names) since 1936, this bi-monthly contains an extraordinary amount of coverage on the 36th state, with proportionate attention paid to Las Vegas. Great writing, photography, and productio. The "Events" section alone is worth a subscription.

Pearl, Ralph. *Las Vegas Is My Beat.* Lyle Stuart. 1973. Similar to though not as self-indulgent as *Zoom Town,* this book is loaded with descriptions of the mobsters, stars, high rollers, and low-life, among others, with whom the author, a long-time Las Vegas newspaperman and TV personality, came into contact.

Puzo, Mario. *Inside Las Vegas.* Charter Books, 1976. A humorous, sensitive, and insightful glimpse into the gambling life of Las Vegas. This book could only be written by Puzo, an inveterate though not degenerate gambler, and an intimate friend of the city who, in Stan Paher's words, "gently and lovingly pierced through the smut, glitter, and attendant myths to the patient personality waiting within for someone to understand the elusive city."

Thompson, Hunter S. *Fear And Loathing in Las Vegas.* Fawcett Popular Library, 1971. The famous account of a trip by the master of gonzo journalism to Las Vegas to cover the Mint 400 Desert Race for *Sports Illustrated,* with his 300-pound Samoan attorney, a red Cadillac convertible, and enough illegal and exotic drugs to hurtle the whole city toward a psychotic break.

Tronnes, Michael, ed. *Literary Las Vegas.* Henry Holt, 1995. For Vegasphiles, historians, and the literarily minded, this is a collection of two dozen previously published articles, stories, and excerpts from books about Sin City by some of America's top wordsmiths: Tom Wolfe, Hunter S. Thompson, John Gregory Dunne, Albert Goldman, Michael Herr. The excerpts span more than 40 years of writing.

Venturi, Robert et al. *Learning From Las Vegas—The Forgotten Symbolism of Architectural Form.* MIT Press, 1977. A technical, though fairly readable, analysis of the shapes, sizes, and placement of Las Vegas signs, casinos, parking lots, and false fronts in the service of intensified communication of the commercial vernacular along the new American "Strip."

Vinson, Barney. *Las Vegas: Behind The Tables, Parts I and II.* Gollehon, 1986. In the tradition of *Zoom Town* and *Las Vegas Is My Beat,* these books provide an entertaining, informative look at gamblers and gambling, casino management and procedures, amazing stories and statistics, with a little history, helpful hints, and trivia, by an insider of 25 years.

Wolfe, Tom. *The Kandy-Kolored Tangerine-Flaked Streamlined Baby.* Farrar, Straus & Giroux, 1965. The Las Vegas chapter in this big book of essays is perhaps the classic look at the city as the penultimate expression of the new culture—glamour, entertainment, art—style!—that emerged from 1960s America.

I N D E X

COMPASS AMERICAN GUIDES

Critics, Booksellers, and Travelers All Agree You're Lost Without a Compass

Arizona (4th Edition)
0-679-03388-2
$18.95 ($26.50 Can)

Chicago (2nd Edition)
1-878-86780-6
$18.95 ($26.50 Can)

Colorado (3rd Edition)
1-878-86781-4
$18.95 ($26.50 Can)

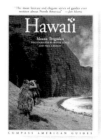

Hawaii (3rd Edition)
1-878-86791-1
$18.95 ($26.50 Can)

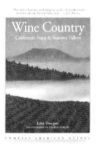

Wine Country (1st Edition)
1-878-86784-9
$18.95 ($26.50 Can)

Montana (3rd Edition)
1-878-86797-0
$18.95 ($26.50 Can)

Oregon (2nd Edition)
1-878-86788-1
$18.95 ($26.50 Can)

New Orleans (2nd Edition)
1-878-86786-5
$18.95 ($26.50 Can)

South Dakota (1st Edition)
1-878-86726-1
$16.95 ($22.95 Can)

Southwest (1st Edition)
1-87866779-2
$18.95 ($26.50 Can)

Texas (2nd Edition)
1-878-86798-9
$18.95 ($26.50 Can)

Utah (3rd Edition)
1-878-86773-3
$17.95 ($25.00 Can)

Idaho (1st Edition)
1-878-86778-4
$18.95 ($26.50 Can)

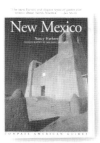

New Mexico (2nd Edition)
1-878-86783-0
$18.95 ($26.50 Can)

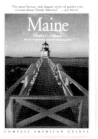

Maine (2nd Edition)
1-878-86796-2
$18.95 ($26.50 Can)

Manhattan (2nd Edition)
1-878-86794-6
$18.95 ($26.50 Can)

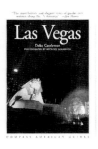

Las Vegas (5th Edition)
0-679-00015-1
$18.95 ($26.50 Can)

San Francisco (4th Edition)
1-878-86792-X
$18.95 ($26.50 Can)

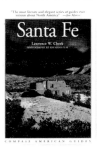

Santa Fe (2nd Edition)
0-679-03389-0
$18.95 ($26.50 Can)

South Carolina (1st Edition)
1-878-86766-0
$18.95 ($26.50 Can)

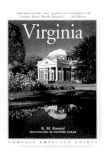

Virginia (2nd Edition)
1-878-86795-4
$18.95 ($26.50 Can)

Washington (1st Edition)
1-878-86758-X
$17.95 ($25.00 Can)

Wisconsin (2nd Edition)
1-878-86749-0
$18.95 ($26.50 Can)

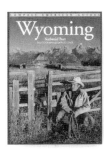

Wyoming (2nd Edition)
1-878-86750-4
$18.95 ($26.50 Can)

■ ABOUT THE AUTHOR

"Las Vegas" is Deke Castleman's middle name. He's been covering the boomtown since 1987, when he researched the first edition of Moon Publications' *Nevada Handbook*. He has also contributed to *Las Vegas Access,* the *Unofficial Guide to Las Vegas,* and several Fodor's guides, including *Las Vegas, Fodor's USA, Great American Vacations,* and *Great American Vacations for Travelers with Disabilities.* He has edited two guides to Las Vegas for Huntington Press, and he is the managing editor of the *Las Vegas Advisor,* a monthly newsletter for Las Vegas visitors and locals. Castleman is also the author of *Las Vegas 2040,* a novel about the future of Las Vegas.

■ ABOUT THE PHOTOGRAPHERS

Michael Yamashita has been shooting pictures for National Geographic books and magazines since 1979. He has participated in five *Day in the Life* projects, and has received awards from the National Press Photographers Association and the New York Art Directors Club, among others. His work has been exhibited at the National Gallery of Art, the Los Angeles County Museum of Art, and Kodak's Professional Photographer's Showcase at EPCOT Center. Mr. Yamashita's images are also featured in Compass *San Francisco* and *Manhattan.*

Kerrick James is well known for his photography of the Southwest. In addition to appearing in Compass *Arizona, San Francisco,* and *The American Southwest,* his work is featured frequently in *Hemispheres* and *National Geographic Traveler,* as well as several Smithsonian guidebooks and school textbooks. He lives in Mesa, Arizona, with his wife and two sons.

Questions, comments, or updated information? Write:
Compass American Guides
5332 College Ave., Suite 201
Oakland, CA 94618
